D1780078

The Hour-Glass

Manuscript Materials

THE CORNELL YEATS

PLAYS

The Death of Cuchulain, edited by Phillip L. Marcus
Purgatory, edited by Sandra F. Siegel
The Herne's Egg, edited by Alison Armstrong
The Hour-Glass, edited by Catherine Phillips

POEMS

The Early Poetry, Volume I: "Mosada" and "The Island of Statues,"
edited by George Bornstein
The Wind Among the Reeds, edited by Carolyn Holdsworth
The Early Poetry, Volume II: "The Wanderings of Oisin" and Other Early Poems to 1895,
edited by George Bornstein
Michael Robartes and the Dancer, edited by Thomas Parkinson, with Anne Brannen

The Hour-Glass

Manuscript Materials

BY W. B. YEATS

EDITED BY

CATHERINE PHILLIPS

Cornell University Press

ITHACA AND LONDON

The preparation of this volume was made possible in part by grants from the National Endowment for the Humanities, an independent federal agency, and from the British Academy.

First published 1994 by Cornell University Press.

Library of Congress Cataloging-in-Publication Data

Yeats, W. B. (William Butler), 1865–1939.
The hour-glass: manuscript materials / by W. B. Yeats ; edited by Catherine Phillips.
p. cm. — (The Cornell Yeats)
ISBN 0–8014–2982–X
1. Yeats, W. B. (William Butler), 1865–1939. Hour glass—Criticism, Textual. 2. Yeats, W. B. (William Butler), 1865–1939—Manuscripts—Facsimiles. 3. Manuscripts, English—Facsimiles. I. Phillips, Catherine. II. Series: Yeats, W. B. (William Butler), 1865–1939. Works. 1982.
PR5904.H6 1994
822'.8—dc20 94–5759

Printeu in the United States of America

♾ The paper in this book meets the minimum requirements of the American National Standard for Information Sciences—Permanence of Paper for Printed Library Materials, ANSI Z39.48-1984.

THE CORNELL YEATS

The volumes in this series will present the manuscripts of W. B. Yeats's poems (all extant versions), plays (complete insofar as possible), and other materials (including selected occult writings) from the rich archives preserved in the collections of Senator Michael B. Yeats, the National Library of Ireland, and elsewhere. The primary goal of the editors is to achieve the greatest possible fidelity in transcription. Photographic facsimiles will be used extensively to supplement the texts.

The series will include some important unpublished works of high literary quality, and individually and as a whole the volumes will help to illuminate Yeats's creative process. They will be essential reference works for scholars who wish to establish authoritative texts of the published works. The emphasis throughout, however, will be on the documents themselves, and critical analysis will be limited to discussion of their significance in relation to the published texts; the editors assume that the publication of the documents will stimulate critical studies as a matter of course.

Contents

Preface

I joined the Yeats editorial project in 1977 through the good offices of Norman H. MacKenzie and of David and Mary Clark. The project has grown considerably since then, not only in the number of editions envisaged but also in the contents of each volume, so that, for example, while my edition initially contained only holographs, typescripts, and one annotated theatre edition, it now consists of some forty manuscript groups and annotated copies, which inevitably together provide a much fuller picture of what this play contributed to Yeats's development than my earlier work could have done. In recent years I have been much indebted to Stephen Parrish, who not only discovered the Quinn manuscripts for me but has advised me editorially and done much to make publication possible. I have also been assisted by the Yeats Editorial Board and in a variety of generous ways by Mrs. E. E. Duncan-Jones, Philip Gaskell, the late Monk and Winefred Gibbon, Warwick Gould, John Handford, Frank Kermode, James Pethica, and John Rathmell, and by my husband. Senator Michael Yeats and Anne Yeats kindly allowed me to examine and reproduce the unpublished material included in the volume. I would also like to thank A. P. Watt Ltd and Professor Roy Foster for permission to quote manuscripts.

I have much appreciated the help given me by the staff at a number of institutions, and gratefully acknowledge permission to include information from manuscripts held in the following collections: the Henry W. and Albert A. Berg Collection, Astor, Lenox and Tilden Foundations and the John Quinn Memorial Collection, Rare Books and Manuscripts Division of the New York Public Library; the Yale Collection of American Literature, Beinecke Rare Book and Manuscript Library at Yale University; the Manuscript Collections of the British Library; Special Collections, Robert W. Woodruff Library of Emory University; the Harry Ransom Humanities Research Library of the University of Texas at Austin; the Kenneth Spencer Research Library of the University of Kansas; and the Library of University College, Dublin. Thanks are also due to the Council of Trustees of the National Library of Ireland and to Oxford University Press. I am grateful to the staffs of the Bibliothèque Nationale and the university libraries of Cambridge and Exeter for their assistance.

Financial support for my research has been provided by the Judith E. Wilson Fund of the University of Cambridge and by the National Endowment for the Humanities.

I wish to thank Warwick Gould, editor of *Yeats Annual*, for permission to include in my introduction material that appeared in an article in his journal, and the Trustees of the National Library of Ireland, the State University of New York at Stony Brook, and the Berg Collection of the New York Public Library for permission to include facsimiles of their manuscripts.

Catherine Phillips

Downing College, Cambridge

Census of Manuscripts

Because Yeats wrote *The Hour-Glass* over so many years, producing two versions sufficiently different that he called the second essentially "a new work," there are extant a large number of typescripts, printed copies with revisions or proof alterations, and manuscript groups. To facilitate identification, each group of texts has been assigned a letter. For manuscripts, typescripts, or printed copies belonging to the prose version of the play, this letter is prefixed by a P; similarly, all groups of the later mixed version into which verse was introduced are indicated by a V. This system of identification is of greatest relevance in the holographs of the mixed version, where it indicates editorial decisions about which leaves belong to the same draft and the sequence in which passages were written. Printed copies with manuscript annotations are identified by the numbers given them in Allan Wade, *A Bibliography of the Writings of W. B. Yeats*, 3rd edition, rev. R. K. Alspach (1968), and Edward O'Shea, *A Descriptive Catalog of W. B. Yeats's Library* (1985).

THE PROSE VERSION

PA Berg (1) Three variant holograph pages, unsigned and undated, from early in the play's development. The writing is in black ink on faded white wove paper torn from a notebook without watermark. The pages measure 20.6 cm (high) x 15.2 cm (wide). Like the other Berg manuscripts, below, this manuscript was part of the Lady Gregory papers acquired by the New York Public Library.

PB Berg (2) A typewritten draft, of which fifteen sheets out of a probable total of seventeen are extant. The pages are numbered by hand 1 to 12, with two versions of page 1 and page 3, and a passage to be interpolated in the second page 1 typed on another sheet. The draft is a ribbon copy, unsigned and undated, on typing paper without watermark. Yeats revised it in black ink and Lady Gregory inserted phrases in pencil. The pages measure 26.2 x 20 cm. The draft, probably dictated to Lady Gregory, includes a page in her hand setting out the "scene."

PCi LCP Add MS. 65635.0 [THE HOUR GLASS. / A MORALITY.] Lord Chamberlain's Plays, London. This is a carbon copy of PCii. It was performed at the Victoria Hall West in order to obtain a license which was granted on 20 October 1902. Some of the typing mistakes were corrected while the carbon was in place; other corrections and the page numbers were inserted by Lady Gregory in black ink, now faded to greyish brown. The page numbers were subsequently cancelled and rewritten in pencil by the staff of the British Library to count the cover sheet as 1. All the numbers in PCii allocating speeches to the Young Men and stating how many there are of them are missing, as are Lady Gregory's interpolated passages and the typed revision on the foot verso of page 15, which has been shortened in this copy. The paper is faded yellowish without a watermark or chain lines. Pages measure 26.2 x 20 cm, except for p. 6, which is 28.5 x 20 cm, and p. 15, which is 18.5 x 20 cm. As with PCii the pages were evidently at one point fastened in the upper left corner. They are now sewn together.

PCii NLI (1) MS. 8763(1) [THE HOUR GLASS. / A MORALITY.] A complete typescript in purple on typing paper measuring 26.2 x 20 cm with no watermark. The draft is sixteen pages long including a title page. The pages, which are numbered 1–15 in ink, were held together in the manner of the Abbey Theatre scripts by a fastener in the upper left corner; the cover sheet has "1st y.[oung] m.[an]" written in faded black ink at the top; p. 6 has a piece pasted onto the foot, making it longer than the others. Alterations and corrections to typing errors were made in black ink and pencil, probably by Lady Gregory, who also numbered the pages in ink and inserted a passage in which the Wise Man explains why he cannot leave the room. On the verso of the last page is a typed revision of the Wise Man's explanation to the Angel of his doubts. The manuscript was given to the National Library of Ireland (NLI) by Mrs. George Yeats in September 1957.

PD Berg (3) [THE HOUR GLAS.S. / A Morality.] A seventeen-page typescript, a carbon of PF. It contains written revisions in blue-black ink by Yeats, and is signed but undated. On the title page Yeats wrote:

Ecstasy—reason
Imagination—argument
Nature—logic
Belief—clerical formulae / [?sermon].

Page 1 has no watermark but the rest are marked SILVER LINEN; all the pages measure 26.2 x 20 cm.

PE NLI (3) MS. 10,950 ["THE HOUR GLASS."] A typed prompt copy from 1903 with typed emendations, and handwritten alterations generally in black ink in several hands including that of Yeats. There are fifteen numbered pages of purple typescript on typing paper measuring 27 x 20 cm with no watermark. Stage directions are underlined in red and supplemented in pencil. The brown cover, sewn like Lady Gregory's play *The Deliverer*, is tattered but not singed. *The Hour Glass* is written on the cover in green ink. A typed cover sheet reads: "'THE HOUR GLASS' / A Morality / By / W. B. Yeats." There is also a printed properties plot, typed on the recto of which in green-blue is: "Dundalk 15 May / Galway Whit Monday and Tuesday 4 & 5 June / Longford / Tuam." The prompt copy was among the Fay papers given by G. Fay to NLI in October 1960.

PF Quinn (1) 72 M 63 Folder 8. [THE HOUR GLAS.S. / A Morality. By W. B. Yeats] In the Manuscript Division of the New York Public Library, like other Quinn MSS. The ribbon copy of PD, signed on p. 17. It is on four different types of paper. The unnumbered cover sheet and pp. 2–17 are on yellowed typing paper measuring 25.4 x 20.3 cm, with the watermark SILVER LINEN and horizontal chain lines 2.7 cm apart. The page numbered 1 is on typing paper that measures 25.4 x 20.3 cm, watermarked W. S. & B. REGENT LINEN without chain lines.

The text of much of this page is cancelled. It is replaced by a holograph page of Lady Gregory's writing on a separate sheet of ruled tablet paper with blue lines 0.8 cm apart. The page is 17.8 cm wide and extended to a length of approximately 27 cm by a strip pasted onto the bottom; this paper was used for strips pasted or pinned to pages 4, 5, 9, 14, and 16. The fourth paper is typing paper with the watermark BRITISH BOND. It was used for a slip so pinned to the back of p. 11 that it faces p. 12. All the annotation is in Lady Gregory's hand with the exception of "stet" on an additional p. 13 and "there" on the slip marked "A" attached to p. 11, which were probably written by Yeats. At the top of the title page Lady Gregory wrote in ink "(Wise Man)."

PF add The typescript of PF has two additional pages numbered 9 and 13. These incorporate some of the handwritten changes made to PF (ll. 184–209 and 269–286) and have been kept in the folder of Quinn (3).

PGi Quinn (3) 72 M 63 Folder 10. [THE HOUR GLASS / A Morality / By / W. B. YEATS] A typescript of 20 pages, numbered [1], 2–20 with few emendations, probably not by Yeats. The folder contains two additional sheets numbered 9 and 13 which do not belong to the typescript (see PF add). There is also a cover sheet on which the title appears as above but with the space omitted between W. and B. All sheets are 26.8 x 20.3 cm and have the watermark EXCHANGE BOND. They are in a blue cardboard wrapper.

PGii Quinn (4) 72 M 63 Folder 17. [THE HOUR GLASS / A Morality / By / W. B. YEATS] A carbon copy of PGi Quinn (3) but with emendations inserted separately. The two manuscripts vary only slightly. The paper is identical to that of Quinn (3) and the sheets are also in a blue wrapper. An archivist's note on the folder suggests that the annotation was by [?Townsend] Walsh.

PH Emory (1) PR5904/H59 [THE HOUR-GLASS. / A MORALITY.] Unbound quarto taken from *The North American Review* (September 1903), probably prepared for a pamphlet printed in 1903 for copyright purposes. The title is signed, and the copy has autograph annotations and a slip of paper on which a new ending is typed. It was in a folder annotated by Lady Gregory with *The Golden Helmet* (later, *Green Helmet*) (similarly prepared) and was bought as part of Lady Gregory's papers by the Robert W. Woodruff Library in December 1979.

PI Quinn (2) 72 M 63 Folder 9. [THE HOUR-GLASS / A MORALITY] An incomplete set of printer's proofs on 17 double pages originally numbered [35], 37–67 and renumbered in pencil 1–33. The text breaks off after the stage direction to l. 306, "[Goes out and shouts". It is stamped "1st Rev." and has occasional holograph typographical corrections, not in WBY's hand. The paper has no watermark and measures 30 x 23.5 cm. This seems to be the first set of proofs for the 1904 edition of *The Hour-Glass and Other Plays.*

PJ ABY (1) [THE HOUR-GLASS / A MORALITY] A copy belonging to Anne Yeats of the American edition of *The Hour-Glass and Other Plays: Being Volume Two of Plays for an Irish Theatre*, published in New York and London by Macmillan & Co. in 1904. It is Wade 52, O'Shea 2360, in deep blue boards with the title, "W. B. Yeats", and "The Macmillan Company" imprinted in gold lettering on the spine; it contains blue ink alterations made with a worn nib and not in WBY's hand.

PK ABY (2) [THE HOUR-GLASS / A MORALITY] A copy belonging to Anne Yeats of the English edition of *The Hour-Glass, Cathleen ni Houlihan, The Pot of Broth: Being Volume Two of Plays for an Irish Theatre*, published in London by A. H. Bullen in 1904 (Wade 53, O'Shea 2362). Some of the pages are stamped "The National Theatre Society Ltd. / Abbey Theatre / Dublin." *The Hour-Glass* occupies pp. 3–32. The copy seems to have been used as a prompt copy—it has pencil marks showing which words should be stressed in a number of speeches and crosses against several speeches by different characters as if these were found to be trouble spots in rehearsal. There are modifications bringing the text in line with a number of the modifications made to the 1907 theatre edition, some of these written by WBY in black ink fading to grey.

PKa NLI (6) MS. 30,381 A sheet of ruled three-hole loose-leaf notebook paper identical to that used for pp. 150–151 of VQ. Using the verso of the page and ignoring the ruled lines, Yeats wrote in blue-grey ink the words of the lyric "I was going the road one day."

PL ABY (3) [THE HOUR-GLASS / A MORALITY] A copy belonging to Anne Yeats of the Dublin edition of PK ABY (2), printed by Maunsel and Co., Ltd. in 1905. It is Wade 54, O'Shea 2363, in purple boards with Elinor Monsell's design on the cover in black of a girl restraining a wolf-hound. *The Hour-Glass* occupies pp. 3–32. Pages 3–8 are unopened; the sheet with pages 9–10 is torn at the top. WBY made a number of unique alterations to the text in black ink, some of which has faded to a grey with green-blue tone. The uncancelled insertion on p. 20 (ll. 244–246) is circled in red ink.

PM Berg (4) [THE HOUR-GLASS: A MORALITY.] A theatre edition published by A. H. Bullen in 1907, signed as "correct / W. B. Y." and with his handwritten alterations. Inside the front cover is a bookplate: "ex libris / Freelands / 1920 / W. T. H. Howe", and beside it a signature: "S. B. Jackson / 15/11/22".

PN ABY (4) [THE HOUR-GLASS: /A MORALITY / BY W. B. YEATS] A theatre edition belonging to Anne Yeats, published by A. H. Bullen in 1907. It is Wade 67, O'Shea 2361, in brown-grey boards with blue lettering and contains only *The Hour-Glass*. A note in ink on a slip reads "Proof corrections." Although there seem to be some errors (possibly at ll. 270–271 and certainly at l. 376, for example), the main changes suggest that it was proof for Wade 92, *Plays for an Irish Theatre* (A. H. Bullen, 1911). WBY annotated it in black ink. On p. 10 "I want somebody who has not changed" was originally written above the line, then erased.

PO ABY (5) (6) (7) [THE HOUR-GLASS: / A MORALITY / BY W. B. YEATS] Three further copies of the theatre edition of 1907 (Wade 67), belonging to Anne Yeats, all with slips reading "Proof corrections." WBY made almost identical changes in ink to all three; they are also close to PM and PP. Where the readings are identical in all three copies, they are cited simply as PO; copy 1 is POi, copy 2 POii, and copy 3 POiii.

PP Kansas Y164 [THE HOUR-GLASS: A MORALITY.] A theatre edition published in

London by A. H. Bullen in 1907, with revisions by Yeats in black ink, and with marginal crosses and underlined letters in pencil, perhaps by Yeats. There are also two marginal annotations on p. 15 in pale grey ink in a hand other than Yeats's. On the cover is a penciled note: "Revised text 16.xii.1910". The copy belonged to P. S. O'Hegarty and was obtained by the Kenneth Spencer Research Library in 1950.

PQ NLI (2) MS. 8763 (2d) A single page in prose of the play's ending. It uses the apron stage and steps from the auditorium introduced by Nugent Monck late in 1911 or 1912. Yeats wrote it in black ink on an inverted sheet of the narrow paper used in NLI 8763(2)—see VA–VD, below.

PR NLI (5) MS. 30,006 [THE HOUR-GLASS: / A MORALITY] Page proofs for Vol. 3 of the unpublished Coole edition of *Plays*. Pages [133]–152 of the volume contain the prose version of *The Hour-Glass*. The first play in the volume, *The Countess Cathleen*, was stamped "FIRST PROOF" and "27 Oct 1931" by the printer. On the same page is a pencil note, "Marked by W B Y". On the title page to *The Hour-Glass* WBY wrote "1903" in response to the query "Date?". Below this the editor noted: "To precede The Pot of Broth." There was at one time a pencil note scrawled in the bottom right corner which read, "Not to go in Collected Plays". This has been virtually erased. There is a note in ink, not in the hand of Thomas Mark (Macmillan's editor), reading "Marked Proof" on the top of p. 145. Corrections and queries by Thomas Mark were made in deep blue ink. Yeats used a slightly darker ink and generally responded to queries by crossing out the question marks or by inserting the necessary change. The manuscript was given to the NLI in 1985 by Senator Michael Yeats.

PS Texas (1) [THE HOUR-GLASS. / A MORALITY / (IN PROSE)] Vol. 3 of the abandoned Scribner edition. Pages of the prose version from *Plays in Prose and Verse* (London, 1922) with two modifications. On p. 37, the title page of the prose play, "A MORALITY" is deleted in ink and replaced by "1903", and on p. 57 a phrase from one of the Fool's speeches is deleted in pencil.

P–VQb NLI (4) MS. 13,571 Typed notes to the individual plays for *Plays in Prose and Verse* (1922) on sheets measuring 25.4 x 20.3 cm of buff typing paper without watermark. Corrections were made in black ink probably by WBY. Sheets 6 and 7 contain the note to the prose version of *The Hour-Glass*. The manuscript was given to the NLI by Senator Michael Yeats.

THE MIXED VERSION

VA–VD, VF–VH NLI (7) MS. 8763(2) A collection of holograph fragments written in black ink with two pages in pencil (VH). They are mostly from the play's opening and final scenes. Few of the pages are numbered. Two different sorts of paper were used: (1) wide, three-hole, loose-leaf sheets measuring 20.3 x 16.5 cm with 31 lines per page (0.5 cm apart), a double pink rule near the top and the watermark WALKER'S / LOOSE / LEAF and (2) narrow sheets measuring 20.3 x 12.7 cm with identical characteristics. MS. 8763(2) was given to the NLI by Mrs. Yeats in September 1957.

VE NLI (15) MS. 30,385 A dark green loose-leaf binder with "WALKER'S / LOOSE-LEAF / TRANSFER CASE / No.-T, 8" on the cover holding nineteen leaves of ruled three-hole loose-leaf notebook paper with 31 lines 0.5 cm apart and a double red rule at the top. The watermark is WALKER'S / LOOSE / LEAF and the pages measure 20.3 x 16.5 cm. These contain passages from several plays (*The Player Queen*, *The Countess Cathleen*) written by Yeats in black ink. The last leaf has on recto and verso part of the dialogue between the Wise Man and his Pupils from the mixed version of *The Hour-Glass*. The sheet is torn and at one time was evidently crumpled up. Senator Michael Yeats gave the manuscript to the NLI in 1985.

VI NLI (8) MS. 8763(2a) [Hour Glass] An almost complete working draft of the entire play, probably written in 1912. It uses a combination of 37 sheets of the wide and narrow paper of NLI 8763(2). VI 21^{r} was originally found with NLI 8758(8) and (9).

VJ Texas (2) A draft of thirty-seven pages, housed in the Humanities Research Center of the University of Texas. It appears to predate the prompt copy and was written on paper similar to the narrow pages of NLI (7). Most of the pages were inverted; all were written in black ink and subsequently numbered. There were several stages of composition, and pages numbered 6, 8, 14, 16–17, 19–21, 36, and 37 may well replace pages no longer extant. Yeats signed the final page. The copy was purchased from William M. Roth in May 1950.

VK NLI (12) MS. 21,504 [THE HOUR-GLASS] A prompt copy of twenty-seven pages with an additional title page and a final blank page. Pages 25–27 are ribbon copy, unrevised. The rest are carbons, altered in black ink and pencil by Yeats. On the cover someone has marked: "Prompt copy corrected by W. B. Yeats". The green boards and edges of the pages were singed by the 1951 fire in the Abbey Theatre. The pages, measuring 26.5 x 20.2 cm, are clipped together in the upper left corner. All carry the watermark JOHN M^{C}DONNEL & C^{O} L^{TD} / SWIFT BROOK. The copy was among the Abbey Theatre papers given by the theatre to NLI in 1976.

VL NLI (17) MS. 30,761 A single holograph sheet containing on the recto the draft of a preface to the revised version of the play. Yeats wrote it in black ink, now faded blue-grey, on a leaf of ruled loose-leaf notebook paper with three holes, measuring 20.3 x 12.7 cm with the watermark WALKER'S / LOOSE / LEAF. There are 31 ruled lines 0.5 cm apart with a double pink rule at the top, the same type of paper as the narrow sheets in NLI 8763(2).

VM NLI (10) MS. 8763(2c) [The Hour Glass.] A single page holograph in black ink on which the note to the play in *Responsibilities* (1914) was drafted. Yeats used for it an unlined sheet measuring 22.8 x 17.8 cm with the watermark MUDIE & SONS / 15 COVENTRY S^{T}. W.

VN Yale ZA5586 [THE HOUR-GLASS / NEW VERSION] A typeset version in the style of the Cuala Press, marked up as proofs by Yeats and Ezra Pound in black ink, probably while Pound was acting as "secretary" to Yeats at Stone Cottage. They did not catch all the printing errors and there may well have been a later set of proofs. The changes were incorporated in both *The Hour-Glass* (Cuala Press, 1914) and *Responsibilities: Poems and a Play* (Cuala Press, 1914). The page numbers, from 16 to 50, however, differ from both. The copy was part of the Pound Archive acquired by the Beinecke Library at Yale in 1973.

VO NLI (9) MS. 8763(2b) Four sheets of holograph revision, written in black ink, of the ending of the play. They revise the version in *Responsibilities: Poems and a Play* (1914), but some of the changes do not appear in any printed text. They were written on cut-up sections of unlined writing paper measuring 17.5 x 13.7 cm with the watermark HANOV[ ] THE TIME[?] in an oval around a crest. Two holes were punched at the top of each page.

VP Emory (2) PR5904 R3 [THE HOUR-GLASS / NEW VERSION — *1912* [pencil]] in *Responsibilities: Poems and a Play*, first edition, number 11 of 400 copies published by Cuala Press in 1914; original linen-backed boards, uncut. It is Yeats's copy with his bookplate [Wade 107] with a few changes written by Yeats in black ink and the date and alterations to the printing of the title marked in pencil. The changes may have been made for *Responsibilities and Other Poems* (London, 1916), although that edition incorporated additional alterations in punctuation. The copy, which formerly belonged to Senator Michael Yeats, was purchased by the Robert W. Woodruff Library in May 1980.

VQ NLI (14) MS. 30,251 [THE HOUR-GLASS] Two copies of *Responsibilities* (London, 1916) were taken apart and pasted onto larger sheets of translucent unruled three-hole loose-leaf notebook paper to make one copy of the play. The backing sheets have the watermark WALKER'S / LOOSE / LEAF and measure 22.7 x 18.1 cm. Yeats transcribed onto them in pale grey-black ink and pencil the passages in Latin for *Plays in Prose and Verse* (1922). Much of the revision was done before the pages were pasted onto the loose leaf; but the changes on pp. 152 and 159 were made afterward, and pp. 150–151 were replaced by Yeats's holograph passage in black ink on ruled, three-hole WALKER'S / LOOSE / LEAF paper measuring 22.8 x 18.1 cm. It has 35 blue lines 0.5 cm apart and a double pink rule at the top. Page 132 has a note written in red pencil in another hand: "Page 131 awanting / (Set from other side)"; it can be read through the backing sheet. The copy was given to the NLI by Senator Michael Yeats in 1985.

VQa NLI (16) MS. 30,487 It consists of two sheets of buff paper with no watermark measuring 20.3 x 16.7 cm with two holes punched along the left side. On them Alan Porter wrote very legibly in black ink the passages in Latin for the 1922 edition of *The Hour-Glass* in verse. This manuscript is not transcribed separately in this edition, but the one deviation from it in the Latin WBY wrote into VQ has been noted. The manuscript was given to the NLI by Senator Michael Yeats.

VQb NLI (11) MS. 13,571 Typed notes to the plays for *Plays in Prose and Verse* (1922). The paper is the same as for P–VQb NLI 13,571. The note to the verse version of *The Hour-Glass* is on p. 17. It is corrected in black ink and the date may have been added by WBY.

VR NLI (13) MS. 30,007 [THE HOUR-GLASS / (IN VERSE)] Proofs in quires marked up for Vol. 4 of the unpublished Coole edition of *Plays*. "The Hour-Glass" occupies pp. [1]–35. Its title page and pp. 17 and 33 have a purple stamp, "[?]ARK, Ltd. / 27 NOV 1931 / EDINBURGH". On the title page there is a note by Macmillan's editor, Thomas Mark, in pencil at the top: "Remember to send to WBY". Over this he wrote in ink "Marked by author". Below the title Yeats wrote in black ink "1903 [cancelled] 1914" in reponse to query about the play's "Date", and over Mark's ink list of the fourteen plays for the volume he noted, "I think I had better see a revise of [?~~to~~] this volume, WBY". This was lightly cancelled in pencil and he then wrote, "I think I should get a revise of pages ~~143 to~~ 97 to 144" [all cancelled]. The tops of pp. 17 and 33 have "Marked Proof" not in Mark's hand. Most of the annotations are by Mark, in deep blue-black ink, grey when it is thin; many of the questions he raised he subsequently answered himself with ticks. WBY appears to have used a blacker ink with a purple sheen, and as in NLI 30,006 he responded to many of the queries by cancelling question marks or inserting the necessary change. The copy was given to the NLI by Senator Michael Yeats in 1985.

Index of Manuscript Abbreviations

Manuscript	Abbreviation
ABY (1)	PJ
ABY (2)	PK
ABY (3)	PL
ABY (4)	PN
ABY (5)	POi
ABY (6)	POii
ABY (7)	POiii
Berg (1)	PA
Berg (2)	PB
Berg (3)	PD
Berg (4)	PM
Emory (1)	PH
Emory (2)	VP
Kansas	PP
LCP	PCi
NLI (1) 8763(1)	PCii
NLI (2) 8763(2d)	PQ
NLI (3) 10,950	PE
NLI (4) 13,571	P–VQb
NLI (5) 30,006	PR
NLI (6) 30,381	PKa
NLI (7) 8763(2)	VA–VD; VF–VH
NLI (8) 8763(2a)	VI
NLI (9) 8763(2b)	VO
NLI (10) 8763(2c)	VM
NLI (11) 13,571	VQb
NLI (12) 21,504	VK
NLI (13) 30,007	VR
NLI (14) 30,251	VQ
NLI (15) 30,385	VE
NLI (16) 30,487	VQa
NLI (17) 30,761	VL
Quinn (1)	PF; PF add
Quinn (2)	PI
Quinn (3)	PGi
Quinn (4)	PGii
Texas (1)	PS
Texas (2)	VJ
Yale	VN

Introduction

Yeats first encountered the story of *The Hour-Glass* in 1888, when collecting material for his book *Fairy and Folk Tales of the Irish Peasantry*, published in the Camelot series. The tale, called "The Priest's Soul," was included in Lady Wilde's *Ancient Legends, Mystic Charms, and Superstitions of Ireland* (London, 1887), a volume that Yeats initially considered "delightful" but which he later felt was too much influenced by English literary traditions.[1] "The Priest's Soul" was noticed by John Eglinton, who suggested to Yeats that it was a possible subject for a play,[2] something Lady Wilde had asserted in her introduction to the story (see Appendix I). The prose scenario that Yeats customarily wrote before embarking on a play is not extant for *The Hour-Glass,* but in it (if we can judge from the available material) he would have been moving away from "The Priest's Soul" in several ways. First, the priest, whose capacity for argument had arrogantly led him to disprove the existence of God and men's souls, was transformed in the play into a teacher who genuinely believed that he was ridding the community of superstition. Yeats kept in modified form the priest's three central dialogues: first with the Angel, who allows him twenty-four hours in which to find a believer and thereby win salvation for his soul after purgatory; second with his pupils, who only show how thoroughly he has converted them; and third with his wife, who likewise cannot help him since she has replaced her beliefs with his. The violent ending Yeats altered considerably. In the tale the priest leaves his house and questions all he meets only to discover how widely his influence has spread. "Half mad with fear" he flings himself on the ground and is then greeted by a passing child with "God save you kindly." The child, a foreigner, suggests that since life is invisible and yet plainly exists, the same may be true of the soul. The priest tells the child his story and then says, "Take this penknife and strike it into my breast, and go on stabbing the flesh until you see the paleness of death on my face. Then watch—for a living thing will soar up from my body as I die, and you will then know that my soul has ascended to the presence of God." The priest takes an agonizing twenty-four hours to die, but then a butterfly—the first to be seen in Ireland—emerges from his mouth; "and now all men know that the butterflies are the souls of the dead waiting for the moment when they may enter Purgatory, and so pass through torture to purification and peace." The tale ends: "But the schools of Ireland were quite deserted after that time, for people said, What is the use of going so far to learn when the wisest man in all Ireland did not know if he had a soul till he was near losing it; and was only saved at last through the simple belief of a little child?"

In his note to the play Yeats wrote that "my own meaning was personal and sincere,"[3] and

[1] *The Collected Letters of W. B. Yeats*, Vol. I, 1869–1895, ed. John Kelly (Oxford, 1986), pp. 87, 443.

[2] See Appendix III, VM.

[3] Ibid.

in his articles of the time he makes quite clear his keen opposition to materialism or to any rationalist insensitivity to the value of imagination and the supernatural, an opposition expressed in the play's ending.

As well as wishing to express his own beliefs, Yeats had practical demands on him. In 1902 he began to write plays for a group of actors soon to be known as "W. G. Fay's National Dramatic Company." They performed the first of his one-act plays, *Cathleen ni Houlihan*, in April of that year. A week later Yeats wrote to Lady Gregory about what was to become *The Hour-Glass*, "I have a plan for a little religious play in one act with quite as striking a plot as Kathleen—it cannot offend anybody and may propitiate Holy Church,"[4] the vituperation directed against his *Countess Cathleen* (1899) evidently still rankling. According to William Fay, Yeats wrote *The Hour-Glass* so that the players would have something to offer their audiences in the "holy season."[5] Yeats explained to A. B. Walkley that although he felt that writing prose was a departure from his proper work of plays in verse, the prose drama was required for the theatre.[6] He later added, "Our Irish Dramatic movement was just passing out of the hands of English Actors, hired because we knew of no Irish ones, and our little troop of Irish amateurs—as they were at the time—could not have too many Plays, for they would come to nothing without continued playing."[7] This is important, for *The Hour-Glass* is not a play of the study but a work started at the beginning of Yeats's "apprenticeship" in a working company, and the development of the drafts cannot be understood without awareness of the fact. Yeats's observation of the success of Douglas Hyde's *Twisting of the Rope*, the approbation given the recent revival of *Everyman,* and his collaboration with Lady Gregory in a pageant called *The Black Horse*[8] were experiences that offered alternatives to the elaborate and exaggerated productions of the commercial theatre of the day which Yeats so disliked. He experimented with *The Hour-Glass*'s scenery, with restricting actors' movements, even with attempts to dictate the cadence of some of the dialogue; he was quick to test the new possibilities provided by alterations to the stage and scenery and, throughout the play's evolution, worked repeatedly at the relationship of visual picture to words. "Nothing," as James Flannery asserts, "more clearly demonstrates Yeats's intention to be taken seriously as a 'practical dramatist' than his continual efforts to make his plays philosophically significant and stylistically coherent, but above all, stageworthy in terms of the practical demands of the theatre."[9]

On 13 June 1902, about a week before returning to Ireland from a visit to London, Yeats wrote to Lady Gregory that he had almost finished the first draft of "The Fool and the Wise Man."[10] He hoped, he said, that it would be performed by the Fays in October with *Cathleen ni Houlihan*. The altered title suggests Yeats's change of emphasis, from the fate of one man in "The Priest's Soul" to the embodying of a debate between two representative figures. This new emphasis is clearest in the early version where the even-handed treatment of the

---

[4] *The Letters of W. B. Yeats*, ed. Allan Wade (London, 1954), p. 370. Hereafter cited as *Letters*.

[5] William Fay, "The Poet and the Actor," in *Scattering Branches: Tributes to the Memory of W. B. Yeats*, ed. Stephen Gwynn (New York, 1940), p. 129.

[6] *Letters*, p. 405.

[7] W. B. Yeats, preface to *The Unicorn from the Stars and Other Plays* (New York, 1908).

[8] Lady Gregory later developed this into *The Travelling Man*. See *The Wonder and Supernatural Plays of Lady Gregory*, ed. Ann Saddlemyer (New York, 1970), p. 5.

[9] James Flannery, *W. B. Yeats and the Idea of a Theatre* (New Haven, 1976), p. 295. Hereafter cited as Flannery.

[10] *Letters*, pp. 375–376.

contrasting values also differentiates the play from *Everyman*, with which the subtitle, "A Morality," was to prompt comparison.

Of the play's earliest handwritten version, mentioned in the letter to Lady Gregory, only a three-page fragment remains, containing the Wise Man's rationalization for his previous lack of belief and the Angel's response before starting to relent. Yeats was not an orthodox Christian and was interested in exploring a more general problem that he saw lying behind the encounter, that of mortal and immortal having experience so different that mutual understanding is impossible: "You cannot know what a life men live," the Wise Man says, "storms, death, . . . the grass rotting, many sicknesses. . . . You live in the country people only see in dreams. . . . You cannot know those [?facts] it shows to us. It is as hard [?for] you to understand our temptation as for us to believe in you." The Angel's reply, "You were given thought & five senses," is too simple a reaction and Yeats cancelled it, although he retained the Wise Man's argument, with which he agreed, throughout the play's evolution.

From Dublin Yeats went to Coole Park, Lady Gregory's home near Gort, where the first of the play's typescripts was probably made. Because he suffered from eyestrain at this time, much of the development of the prose play occurred in typescripts. George Moore had proved to him that it was possible to write books by dictating to a typist, and in April Yeats had dictated to him one of the acts of their collaboration, *Diarmuid and Grania.* He also made use of professional typists who, with some difficulty in deciphering his handwriting, typed up a few of the finished sections of his novel, *The Speckled Bird.* In the dedication to *Where There Is Nothing* (1902) Yeats mentions that while he was at Coole he spent most mornings dictating to Lady Gregory, a process that was to develop into an efficient partnership. But he later noted that *The Hour-Glass* was almost wholly his because "the speech there is far from reality" and so "I needed less help."[11] MS. PB (the earliest version to survive) may just pre-date Lady Gregory's participation in the wording of the plays. It seems likely that the typescript, not typed by a professional, was done rather hurriedly by Lady Gregory, probably from Yeats's manuscript draft, while he was at Coole in June 1902. He subsequently revised all of it by hand. The typescript was accompanied by a list of stage directions in Lady Gregory's hand, which, although it could have been placed with the copy later, more probably belongs to the same period as the draft, showing again the evolution of the play within the constraints and demands of an active theatrical company.

MS. PB begins *in medias res* with the Wise Man reading through the lesson he is to teach to the pupils, a realistic touch that was cut from subsequent versions. The door opens and the Fool comes in asking for money. It takes three requests before the Wise Man responds, but with his question "What do you know about wisdom?" Yeats initiates the debate between simple faith and learning that lies at the heart of the prose version. In the legend no proof had been offered of the priest's wisdom, although Lady Wilde's postscript to the tale emphasized that Ireland had been a center of learning, something that would have appealed to Yeats. Wanting his Wise Man to display genuine medieval knowledge, Yeats made him mention books by Simonides and Tertullian and gave him a speech modeled on passages from Dante which he mentioned in *Autobiographies* and *A Vision.*

Though they call him Teigue the fool, he is not more foolish than everyone used to be.

[11] Preface to *The Unicorn from the Stars and Other Plays* (New York, 1908).

> . . . But I have overthrown their three worlds with the seven sciences. . . . With philosophy that was made by the lonely planet I have made them forget Theology; with Architecture I have hidden the ramparts of their cloudy Heaven, a[n]d with Music, the fierce planet['s] daughter whose hair is always upon fire; and with grammar daughter of the moon I have made them shut their ears to imaginary harpings and the speech of the angels; and with Arithmetic I have made formations of battle that have put the hosts of Heaven to the rout; But Rhetoric & dialectic that were made by the light star & the amorous star, you have been my spearmen and my catapults. . . . 'Dialectic is under Mercury for Mercury is the smallest of the planets'.
>
> (PB 5, ll. 6–22)

Yeats explained to Frank Fay, "The astrological allusions are out of the Paradiso [more probably *Il Convivio*] of Dante. He attributes the seven sciences to the seven planets and for the most part for reasons that are obvious to an astrological student but would take too long to explain. For instance Saturn who presides over the birth of contemplative natures has philosophy attributed to him and so on."[12] In rehearsal, however, A.E. (George Russell) remarked that such references were out of keeping with the Wise Man's rationalist stance. "Of course," he said,

> in astrology the planets are gods, and when he speaks of the "amorous star" he speaks of the spiritual power which it symbolises. I do not think it is logical to disbelieve in God and the angels and to believe in the divine influence of the planets. I think he should be sceptic of these things also and tell how men before he came believed in love coming from the "amorous star" but that now it is simply a comely presence and the promise of bodily beauty which awakens love.[13]

But Yeats wanted to establish a Renaissance setting and he was in any case generally happy with eclectic schemes, so he left the passage in the prose version. It did not appear in the mixed version, but there the Wise Man was given mythological allusions more vulnerable to A.E.'s criticism and probably included for their poetic and mysterious qualities.

In writing his play Yeats not only removed the more violent aspects of the tale but also moderated the sins associated with the questioning of religion. The Fool's challenge to the Wise Man, in which he indirectly blames him for the decline in religious observance, frees him from the suggestion in the tale of personally dissolute behavior; the general "changes" to which the Fool alludes even have a humorous touch: "people snoring" in bed instead of going to church, priests "obeying their wives." Of the central sections, Yeats simply expanded Lady Wilde's dialogue between the Wise Man and his wife, Bridget, with its deadpan comedy. Only in handwritten modifications to one copy did he attempt to give Bridget and her relationship with the Wise Man any depth. This was in the Dublin edition of 1905 (ABY 3, PL) but, perhaps finding the realism out of place in the play, he never printed it. The exchange between the Wise

---

[12] W. B. Yeats to Frank Fay, typed letter sent from Coole Park, 15 Sept. [1902], in University College, Dublin (MS. CUR. L. 4).

[13] A.E. to W. B. Yeats (March 1903) in *W. B. Yeats: The Critical Heritage,* ed. A. Norman Jeffares (London, 1977), pp. 130–131. Hereafter cited as *Critical Heritage*.

Man and the Angel he modified to provide a wittier close in which the Angel trounces the logic of the Wise Man. In this Yeats may have been marginally swayed by the thought of the reception given to *The Countess Cathleen*, an idea that may also have been part of the reason for the innovation of a fourth dialogue, between the Wise Man and his children, which turns the Wise Man into a more domesticated figure and allows for the expression of more poignant regret for his past behavior.

MS. PB shows that Yeats was already adept at using the physical picture in his structuring of the plot. For instance, the Wise Man's assertion that religious belief is simply superstitious folly is immediately refuted by the entrance of the Angel. And, later, when the Wise Man believes that his last hope of finding a believer has gone, he moves to the hour-glass to cover its dominating presence only to find the Fool—his rescuer—sitting obliviously beside it; this positioning of the character allows a natural flow into the plot's final phase. The Wise Man then pushes the Fool to articulate his belief and he responds with "I wont tell you what is in my mind, and I wont tell you what is in my bag. You might steal away my thoughts," clearly equating the physical reality of his pennies with the abstract but equal reality of thought. It is very much the same equation as that drawn by the child in the legend when he declares that since life although invisible clearly exists, so may the soul. Yeats expresses the idea not as the legend does, in adult terms placed in the mouth of a child, but through dramatic and sympathetic exploration of the character of the Fool and his concerns. The draft breaks off at the point where the Fool starts to tell the story of his knowledge of the angels in traditional terms: "Once I was alone out on the hills, and an angel came by and . . ."

The principal difference between MSS. PB and PC is that the latter finishes the play, picking up allusions made earlier to a metaphysical scheme of fixed and wandering stars and bringing to fruition the suggestion that the Fool become teacher of the pupils, a suggestion that was omitted in the published versions. The pupils return, summoned by the Fool, to see the butterfly, which one of them recognizes as the Wise Man's soul.

By 25 July 1902 the play was sufficiently advanced that Yeats sent it to Frank Fay with suggestions about casting. He seems to have been writing it with particular actors in mind and with the intention of evening out the balance between the Wise Man and the Fool. He stipulated that Frank Fay play the part of the Fool, which is significant because Frank usually took heroic roles. For the Wise Man Yeats chose the handsome Dudley Digges, who soon afterward left the company for the United States. He stressed that "Digges should not make up too old. The wise man is a man in the full vigour of life."[14] The version that Yeats sent and that was used for the first performance was MS. PC (i and ii). This version (like MS. PB) mentions the Fool's skin clothes to which Yeats alluded in a letter, and omits the Latin words for the Wise Man's prayer, which Yeats sent in the same letter. PCi was produced at Victoria Hall West in London on 20 October 1902 in order to satisfy the Lord Chamberlain's license requirements. PCii has handwritten alterations that take the play a step further in its evolution. Among these is an additional handwritten speech for the Wise Man explaining why he cannot leave the room to search for a believer himself. This drafted speech, dictated to or transcribed by Lady Gregory, was probably written in response to a criticism A.E. made while the play was in rehearsal: "It struck me that it was a little difficult to understand why the Wise Man remains lamenting in his room though there are crowds without. He has only a few moments to find his believer and he

---

[14] *Letters*, p. 378 (7 September 1902).

sends messengers and remains himself. It is a little hard to believe."[15] The prompt copy (PE) and MS. PF give revised, and stronger, versions of the rationalization.

By the autumn of 1902 Yeats was busy with both the scenery and the costumes for the play. The 1903 production showed the results of theories he set out in articles written for *Samhain* in 1902 that "poetical drama" should be "staged with but two or three colours. The background, especially in small theatres, where its form is broken up and lost when the stage is at all crowded should, I think, be thought out as one thinks out the background of a portrait."[16] T. Sturge Moore and Robert Gregory devised the working details of the scene. Yeats wanted a set that would not impose on his play an "emotion of reality" at odds with it. The color scheme chosen was primarily green and purple with touches of a reddish brown in the furniture, Bridget's dress, and the Fool's costume, and a brighter red in his wig and the Angel's robe. The set for the first performance on 14 March 1903 seems to have been somewhat simpler than Yeats had originally intended. Wanting symbols of different types of learning associated with the Renaissance, he listed "an astronomical globe. A blackboard. A large ancient map of the world on the wall. Some musical instruments." These all appear in the prompt copy (MS. PE) and in subsequent printings but not in the accompanying properties plot, and none of the descriptions of performances mention them (they were deleted from PF, a typescript that may well have been modified in the light of performance). The design also differs slightly from that of Sturge Moore, who listed a lectern and high stool in place of the desk and chair. That Yeats was observing everything critically is clear from his complaint that the bright brown chair back had annoyed him intensely during the first performance.[17] The color was subsequently made less obtrusive, and in 1905 Yeats campaigned successfully to have the chair with its high straight back replaced by a more ornamental one with gently curving legs and arms.[18]

The play was performed not only on tours in Ireland but also in Scotland and England. A. B. Walkley's review in *The Times* of a performance of May 1903 treated the play seriously as "experimental theatre." "We are," he said, "listening to English spoken with watchful care and slightly timorous hesitation. . . . That at once ennobles our mother-tongue, [and] brings it into relief."[19]

> The next pleasure is for the eye. . . . The speaker of the moment is the only one who is allowed a little gesture. . . . When they [the actors] do move it is without premeditation, at haphazard, even with a little natural clumsiness, as of people who are not conscious of being stared at in public. Hence a delightful effect of spontaneity. . . . Add that the scenery is of Elizabethan simplicity . . . and you will begin to see why this performance is a sight good for sore eyes—eyes made sore by the perpetual movement and glitter of the ordinary stage.

---

[15] *Critical Heritage,* p. 130.

[16] W. B. Yeats, "Notes" prefaced to *Samhain* 2 (October 1902), reprinted in *Explorations,* selected by Mrs. W. B. Yeats (London, 1962), p. 88.

[17] *W. B. Yeats and T. Sturge Moore: Their Correspondence 1901–1937*, ed. Ursula Bridge (London, 1953), p. 5. Hereafter cited as *Sturge Moore*.

[18] There is printed in several books a photograph showing the early set and generally identified as being of the Fays in 1903 (Flannery, plate 5, for example), although it appeared on the 1908 program in which A. Sinclair played the Wise Man and J. A. O'Rourke the Fool (W. H. Henderson Press Cuttings, NLI MSS. 1729–32).

[19] A. B. Walkley in *The Times* (8 May 1903), reprinted in Liam Miller, *The Noble Drama of W. B. Yeats* (Dublin, 1977), pp. 86–87. Hereafter cited as Miller.

Walkley did, however, express the hope that the slight self-consciousness of the group would ease in time. Like *The Pot of Broth,* the early version of the play could be successful if played in a very simple, unpretentious way, but whereas *The Pot of Broth* needed a light touch because of the slight nature of its story, *The Hour-Glass* required a sense, as in the acting out of fairy tales, that each character was consciously adopting a role in order to present a story whose superficial simplicity pointed at more profound truths. This deliberate avoidance of realism may be one reason why the pupils, for example, described as Young Men and given actions of very young men, were always played by adults. Yeats mentioned that what he saw in the legend was something "charming"; his concern was that this became a platitude on the stage.

In addition to experiments with scenery and the movements of the actors, Yeats implemented a third innovation in *The Hour-Glass*, derived from his experiments with Florence Farr in intoning his poetry to the psaltery, something he initiated because he knew with each of his poems exactly how he wished it to be read and wanted to record the tune and rhythm. For his plays he made a more restricted use of the technique, writing in 1904, "When one wishes to make the voice immortal and passionless, as in the Angel's part in my *Hour-Glass,* one finds it desirable for the player to speak always upon pure musical notes, written out beforehand and carefully rehearsed. On the one occasion when I heard the Angel's part spoken in this way with entire success, the contrast between the crystalline quality of the pure notes and the more confused and passionate speaking of the Wise Man was a new dramatic effect of great value."[20] This again shows how clearly Yeats was envisaging the overall effect of the play. The early versions show that he initially thought of the Angel as male, but finding that women could more frequently come closer to the "pure notes," he often allowed the role to be played by women—so often that he altered the pronouns in the printed versions.

Although in many ways today *The Hour-Glass* may be seen as somewhat slight and of small contemporary relevance, the religious question at the center of the prose version was highly controversial at the time the play was written. Before the first performance Yeats thought it necessary to make a speech pleading for "freedom from religious and political censorship."[21] Frank Fay commented to him, "I think *The Hour-Glass* very fine though I do not like the holding of an unbeliever up to the scorn so to speak of this pretentiously pious country. Of course I know that it would be impossible to plead for unbelief in a play here; but I know that unbelief is a sincere thing. You, I am glad to see, draw your unbeliever with sympathy for him."[22] But Fay overstates Yeats's support for the Wise Man. Although the first drafts drew him with sympathy, this dwindled as the prose versions grew, and when Yeats saw the first performances, he decided that he had gone too far. For him the Wise Man's discrediting came to mean that "my own [?special] meanings had vanished & I saw before me a cowardly person who seemed to cry out the wisdom of this world is foolishness & to understand the words not as may a scholar and a gentleman but as might some ignoramus of the pulpit."[23] He set about revisions that ultimately produced the mixed version.

---

[20] W. B. Yeats, "The Play, the Player, and the Scene," *Samhain* (1904), reprinted in *Explorations,* selected by Mrs. W. B. Yeats, p. 174.

[21] Flannery, p. 328.

[22] Richard J. Finneran, George Mills Harper, and William M. Murphy, eds., *Letters to W. B. Yeats*, vol. 1 (New York, 1977), p. 100.

[23] See Appendix III, VL.

By 1910 several new factors were to lead to more radical revision. In 1909 Yeats had turned *The Golden Helmet* into verse and found that he was much more satisfied with it than he had ever been before. It was also in that year that he renewed his acquaintance with Edward Gordon Craig. They discovered that they both opposed realism, and Craig agreed to make a model for Yeats of a stage with his new high jointed screens of various widths so that Yeats could experiment with the staging of his plays as he wrote them. It was also agreed that Craig would design the costumes and a set that used the new screens for one of Yeats's plays. The play chosen was *The Hour-Glass*, which Craig had admired in 1902, almost as soon as it had been written. It is evident from their correspondence that not only Yeats, but Craig too, was exploring the new scenery. Craig applied for a patent in February 1910, the month in which Yeats received his model. Of the new scenery Yeats said, "The primary value of Mr Craig's invention is that it enables one to use light in a more natural and more beautiful way than ever before."[24] The intensity of lighting could be used to evoke a mood rather than suggest times of day, and, because the set was not realistic, there was no optical illusion to be broken with falsifying shadows. The importance of this change in set is clear from Yeats's Preface to *Plays for an Irish Theatre* (1911), a volume that included *The Hour-Glass* and in which four of Craig's designs appeared. "It was," he said, "only by watching my own plays that I came to understand that this reverie, this twilight between sleep and waking . . . is the condition of tragic pleasure, and to understand why it is so rare and so brief. If an actor becomes over emphatic . . . if an electric lamp that should have cast but a reflected light from sky or sea, shows from behind the post of a door, I discover at once the proud fragility of dreams." Craig's design for *The Hour-Glass* divided the stage so that on the audience's right there was an alcove a third of the way back from the edge into which the Wise Man's desk fitted so that he faced toward the center of the stage. On the left side of the stage was a wide corridor that curved out of sight behind the alcove. This device created additional interest by allowing for several independent groups of characters and differences in the lighting on them. Watching the 1911 performance of the prose play in this set a critic commented, "The new arrangements served to strip away everything that could distract from the emotional and dramatic unfolding, and to underline the most significant events of the play."[25]

The collaboration made Yeats aware of Craig's theories of costuming, in which the most important feature was a mask designed to convey complex character traits: "a barbaric man who is both bold and tender," for example.[26] Of the Fool's costume, which consisted of a plain, floor-length robe and a three-quarter face mask, Craig wrote beside his sketch that it was to show "a hint of clown / a hint of Death / and of sphinx / and of boy."[27] One may be dubious about whether so much could be conveyed in a costume, but the mask seems to have made Yeats more aware of the representative nature of Teigue than ever before. It is clear from his letters to Craig in 1910 that his use of folk characters such as the Fool was changing. If the masks for *The Hour-Glass* worked well, he said, he would consider using them for the Fool and the Blind Man in *On Baile's*

---

[24] W. B. Yeats, *The Mask* 3, nos. 10–12 (April 1911): 191.

[25] *The Irish Times*, 13 January 1911.

[26] Edward Gordon Craig, "The Artists of the Theatre of the Future" (cont.), *The Mask* 1, nos. 3–4 (May–June 1908): 64; reissue, New York, 1966.

[27] Collection Gordon Craig, Bibliothèque Nationale (3 November [1910]). This design is reproduced in several places; see, for example, Miller, p. 163.

Strand. It would, he claimed, give

> a wildness and extravagance that would be fine. . . . It would put them into a world of mythology, and that idea delights me. . . . One could put a terrible mask on the blind man for he like the fool is a symbol, a god. He is the shadow of Concubar, the High King as the Fool is Cuchulain's shadow. In a sense they are reason and impulse, policy and heroism, the cold and the hot, the mind and the senses and a thousand other things that should suggest themselves to the imagination when the curtain falls. Indeed above all they are the Wise Man and the Fool over again. If the Fool in "The Hour Glass" goes well that mask will do for the other Fool and I will make Bullen [Yeats's publisher] pay for a Blind Man's mask.[28]

The antinomies in *The Hour-Glass*, mentioned by Yeats in his letter, are evident in ideas he sketched on the cover of MS. PD: "Ecstasy—reason / Imagination—argument / Nature—logic / Belief—clerical formulae."

That Yeats saw common characteristics in the two Fools is suggestive. He described the type as the Fat Fool of folklore who is "as wide and wild as a hill" and not "the Thin Fool of modern romance";[29] both his fools occupy a marginal position in society and possess a mysteriousness that inhibits any feeling that they are completely knowable. But there are differences between them too. Unlike the Fool in *On Baile's Strand* who is only a scavenger preying on the unwary, the earlier Fool is integrated into the natural and supernatural worlds. The drafts show that Yeats always called him Teigue, a generic name that does not individualize him. In the early version of the play Teigue was representative of simple faith, but he also had characteristics that made him almost stereotypically an Irish fool. In Craig's costume these were to be subordinated by a design that, while stressing the mysteriousness of the Fool, missed a shyness hidden by Irish loquacity that had been a large part of his charm. Although the qualities remained in the play's words, they were no longer reinforced by the costume. This diminished the Irishness of the play and made the Fool more obviously a symbolic counter in a dramatized debate about the comparative value Yeats saw in learned wisdom and simple faith.

The extravagance and enormously energetic nature of Craig's creativity seem to have reinforced similar traits in Yeats. Although in turning *The Hour-Glass* into a mixed version of prose and verse he kept much of the dialogue between the Wise Man and his pupils, wife, and children, and large parts of that with the Fool, he altered the overall tone radically by introducing highly imaginative, meditative speeches for the Wise Man. He seems to have wanted this character to come at least close to being tragic. What Yeats meant by "tragedy" is evident in his contemporary article "The Tragic Theatre" (1910). In describing the third act of John M. Synge's *Deirdre* he commented on "Deirdre's cry at the outset of a reverie of passion that mounts and mounts till grief itself has carried her beyond grief into pure contemplation. . . . The player, whose art had seemed clumsy and incomplete . . . ascended into that tragic ecstasy which is the best that art—perhaps that life—can give." In "mainly tragic art," said Yeats, "one distinguishes devices to exclude or lessen character, to diminish the power of that daily mood, to cheat or blind its too clear perception. If the real world is not altogether rejected,

---

[28] Collection Gordon Craig, Bibliothèque Nationale (3 November [1910]).

[29] W. B. Yeats, note to *The Hour-Glass* in *Plays for an Irish Theatre* (London, 1911), p. 221.

it is but touched here and there, and into the places we have left empty we summon rhythm, balance, pattern, images that remind us of vast passions, the vagueness of past times, all the chimeras that haunt the edge of trance."[30] Craig's "scene" allowed much greater scope for such a mood, and the changes Yeats introduced turned the play, he said, into "practically a different work of art."[31]

There are nine groups of manuscripts and a number of stray sheets from the period 1910–1912 when Yeats carried out the play's transformation. Most of these cover only a few speeches from the play's opening or close, although together they contain almost all the revisions he made to it. They make the play stronger and better integrated, providing careful preparation for key passages. For example, instead of having the Wise Man converted abruptly by his encounter with the Angel, the conversion is prepared for by the opening speeches, which both introduce hints of the metaphysical scheme that he will come to accept and connect dreams with divine intervention.

On 23 May 1910 Yeats wrote to Gordon Craig:

> I am myself busy with 'The Hour Glass' again. I have put it into verse much to its advantage. I have got rid of the touch of platitudes. I have just done the Wiseman's dying speech in rhyme, and the Fool rings the bell for the pupils and the strokes of the bell come at certain arranged moments of his speech like a Dirge. These kind of effects begin to amuse me more and more. I conceive of the play as a ritual. It must not give all to the first hearing any more than the Latin ritual of the Church does, so long as the ultimate goal is the people.[32]

The specific manuscript Yeats was alluding to may be VG (VH is similar), in which not all the lines rhyme but a bell does punctuate the Wise Man's speech. It is possible that VD, although more polished, may belong to the same draft as VG, most of which has disappeared. There is also an extensive draft (VI), called the "Complete Copy" by Richard Ellmann, to which Yeats may have been referring in a letter to his father in March 1912 when he said that he was busy with "the re-writing of old work, *The Countess Cathleen* and *The Land of Heart's Desire* and *The Hour-Glass*, to get them as effective on the stage as possible."[33]

Flannery suggests that it was while Nugent Monck was director that Yeats came closest to having his plays realized.[34] Monck was brought in from a Norwich theatre group specializing in medieval plays specifically to experiment with productions using Craig's screens. He sometimes used hymns and incense in the foyer to instill an appropriate mood in the audience before a play had begun. He extended the stage into the orchestra, creating an apron with stairs leading down from it into the auditorium, which meant that actors could now enter through the auditorium as well as using the more conventional stage entrances. Monck utilized this access for processions. A page from a prose draft (PQ) shows clearly Yeats's exploration of the change, probably in late 1911 or early 1912. The prose version of the play continued to be the

---

[30] Reprinted in *Essays and Introductions* (London, 1961), pp. 239, 243.

[31] *Letters,* p. 576 (22 February 1913).

[32] Collection Gordon Craig, Bibliothèque Nationale (23 May 1910), reprinted in Flannery, p. 315n.

[33] *Letters*, p. 567.

[34] Flannery, p. 236.

one most often performed, and Yeats stated in the note to the new version of the play published in *The Mask* in 1913 that he would let the promising "second company" of young actors (whom he described to his father as being better at his plays than the old company) "go on playing the old version" amended to make the Wise Man submit to his fate and recover his courage. Monck played the role of the Wise Man in the first production of the new, mixed version, a performance Yeats admired. But Flannery's assertion that Nugent Monck and the Abbey Second Company were influences in the writing of the new version seems to be refuted by the drafts, which show that Yeats had already made the major changes to the play in 1910, a year before Monck arrived.[35]

Although the final form of the mixed version discarded the dialectic between atheistic rationalism and simple piety in favor of a discrimination between simple faith held by a simple being and a leap into faith by a skeptical, educated being, the drafts show that Yeats moved gradually to this discrimination. Initially, for example, he introduced ideas about the worth of simple people as opposed to the more sophisticated, using an Irish tale: in VA he had one of the pupils mention a story of a man learning the talk of the beasts and marrying the king's daughter, such a marriage being one of the traditional ways that fairy tales indicate the hero's success. Yeats's source for the allusion may have been a story Jeremiah Curtin records, called "The Widow's Son, the Devil, and the Fool,"[36] in which a widow's foolish son, a blessed simpleton, overhears two magical cats discussing the illness of a princess and agreeing upon the method by which she can be cured. The young man decides to put his newly acquired knowledge into practice and, of course, eventually marries the princess with her grateful father's blessing. As he revised the play Yeats came to view the value of the blessed simpleton more critically and omitted the tale from subsequent versions. He may well have decided that it would require a disproportionate amount of space to make the allusion clear for the overall balance he was trying to achieve between the values of simple faith held unquestioningly and the faith possible to those who experience doubt.

Correspondingly, Yeats's depiction of the personality of the Wise Man changed as the play evolved. Although from the first the Wise Man had been made more idealistic than the priest of the legend, in the early typescripts he had been an unsympathetic character, and in MSS. PB and PC was given speeches that clearly ran contrary to Yeats's own beliefs. He had something of the blustering bully in him, like the sort of hedge-school master depicted in William Carleton's stories.[37] In the drafts of the mixed version Yeats increased the Wise Man's efforts to seek the co-operation of his pupils and gave them speeches expressing affection for him, thereby turning him into a more sympathetic character whose fate might be seen as tragic. The Wise Man shows a concern for Teigue and anxiety about the one who may be coming to drag him away that suggest Yeats may have been modeling him in part on Marlowe's Faustus. Most important, the emphasis was altered from his materialistic disbelief to his developing comprehension of a radical metaphysical scheme.

This scheme is broached by the passage, on which the pupils chance, on the visible and

---

[35] Ibid., p. 307.

[36] Jeremiah Curtin, in *The Sun* (New York), 21 May 1893, reprinted in *Irish Folk Tales*, ed. Seamus O Duilearga (Dublin, 1943), pp. 75–84.

[37] William Carleton, "The Hedge School," in *Traits and Stories of the Irish Peasantry*, 2 vols. (London, 1843), 1: 271–324.

invisible countries. It was first introduced in PF and comes from a genuine folk belief mentioned several times by Yeats, by Lady Wilde in the *Ancient Legends,* and in Lady Gregory's *Visions and Beliefs in the West of Ireland,*[38] a book that contains most of the folklore she and Yeats gathered together. The substance of the belief is that the fairies, who may be angels thrown out of heaven for rebelling with Lucifer, live in a land that normally mortals may not visit. Although opinions about the location of the country vary—with some versions suggesting it is an island, others that it lies below the earth or within mountains or is simply invisible—its main distinguishing feature is that it is in some ways the inverse of the earth: for instance, when earthly crops are plentiful, there is famine in the invisible country, hence suggestions in some versions that food should be left for the fairies. Conversely, when there is famine on earth it is said to be because the fairies have stolen the goodness from the crops. Although the belief is often interpreted as a simple reversal of seasons, it is also inevitably sometimes seen as symbolic of life and an afterlife. In PF, Yeats wrote of a moment, at the point of death, when one perceives life from a new perspective: "One sinks in on God, we do not see the truth, God sees the truth in us. . . . Tell them Fool that when the life & the mind are broken the truth comes through them like the peas through a broken peascod." Later, in emendations to the 1907 theatre edition, a similar idea is attributed to Plato: "Go and call my pupils again. I will make them understand. I will say to them that only amid spiritual terror or only when all that laid hold on life is shaken, can we see truth. There is something in Plato, but—No, do not call them. They would answer as I have bid" (variant of l. 295 of the *North American Review* text, PM, PN, PO, PP, PR). In the mixed version the idea is given much greater importance, occupying a large part of the Wise Man's speeches. He explains to his pupils, for example:

> . . . there is a spiritual state
> That can alone be touched & known & [?tastes]
> When all the faculties where by our minds
> Are masters of their state, when all the life
> We know or ever shall know is burnt out
> Withers, as though in Autumns wind
> And that we mount into reality
> Not by laborious, cold deliberate thought
> But in a frenzy.
>
> (VCii 9^r, ll. 2–10)

The idea appears with different imagery at several points. For example, in the dialogue with Bridget the Wise Man says that "Nature would lack all at her most need / Could not the soul find truth in a flash / Upon the battlefield, or in the midst / Of overwhelming waves" (VI 30^r). It is also found in the Wise Man's closing meditations. That the Wise Man was expressing something important to Yeats is suggested by the later inclusion of the idea in *A Vision*: "Belief comes from shock" and "is renewed continually in the ordeal of death."[39] The Wise Man's attitude to death, "perishing is but exaltation," not only embodies Yeats's ideal of the death of

---

[38] Augusta Gregory, *Visions and Beliefs in the West of Ireland* (Gerrards Cross, 1970; reprint of the 1920 edition), pp. 225, 262, 317, 338.

[39] W. B. Yeats, *A Vision* (London, 1937), p. 53.

the hero but shows another similarity of his ideas to those of Craig, who described death as "that mysterious, joyous, and superbly complete life which is called Death."[40] The Wise Man's final speeches in the mixed version are colored by remnants of the medieval world picture of the prose play. For example, he states that he knows "what gave the stars their station / And the disordered cloud its way" (VF 3^r, ll. 22–23), recalling *Paradiso* (ii. 12; viii. 97–99), in which the stars and their spheres are seen as the instruments of God's providence ordained to mold the destinies of Earth. Yeats may also have been drawing on Faustus's plea, "Stand still, you ever-moving spheres of heaven that time may cease . . . / in the firmament! . . . You stars that reigned at my nativity" (V. ii. 134–135, 143–144, 155).[41]

The most radical adjustment to the balance between the Fool and the Wise Man occurred when Yeats made the Wise Man discard his concern with the Fool's belief and declare himself indifferent as to whether he is saved or not. This change was made to the first extant draft of the mixed version but not incorporated into the prose version until 1922. The new version retained the Fool's offer to tell the Wise Man of his belief, and in VF there was a suggestion that an angel, perhaps of God's mercy, had told him to tell the Wise Man of his faith. In this draft the Fool declares that the Wise Man has not discovered that he, Teigue, has been "the one who believed, & that he had found me" (VF 4A^r, ll. 19–20). Yeats cancelled the second suggestion, instead presenting the information that the Wise Man's soul is saved through Teigue's statement that the Angel will release the butterfly in the Garden of Paradise. The ending of the single sheet of prose from 1911–1912, like that of the prose version of 1922, is more pessimistic. In it, the possibility that the pupils will regain their faith is squashed, bearing out the Angel's assertion that the Wise Man cannot undo what he has done. Such an ending, of course, also undermines the importance of the Fool by depriving him of his role of guiding the pupils to religious truth. From early in the play's evolution (PC) the Wise Man had said that the Fool's prayers needed for the salvation of the pupils were better than his own. But in the later versions Yeats not only cut this speech but inserted a bit of by-play diminishing the dignity of the Fool by making him appear to be a puppet obeying orders from the Wise Man to sit, stand, and move about— a striking contrast with his freedom and independence in earlier versions.

In contrast with the belief of the Fool, which is uncritical, the Wise Man arrives at a faith close to that Yeats praised in "Anima Hominis." "We must not," he said, "make a false faith by hiding from our thoughts the causes of doubt, for faith is the highest achievement of the human intellect, the only gift man can make to God, and therefore it must be offered in sincerity."[42] However, the metaphysical scheme of *The Hour-Glass* is more eclectic, combining elements of Christianity with Far Eastern and Plotinian schema, a world picture in which Yeats expressed interest through much of his adult life. The picture that emerges from the scattered hints in the various drafts is of a cyclical system in which man experiences reincarnations, realizes only at the point of death that earthly "reality" is but a dream, and on dying is re-absorbed with loss of individuality into the supra-mundane.

Yeats revised his early plays in 1911—*The Hour-Glass* in January, *The Land of Heart's Desire* in February, and *The Countess Cathleen* in December. The Texas manuscript (VJ),

[40] Edward Gordon Craig, "The Actor and the Uber-Marionette," in *The Mask* 1, no. 2 (April 1908): 9; reissue, New York, 1966.

[41] I am grateful to Mrs E. E. Duncan-Jones for bringing the resemblance of Yeats's play to *Faustus* to my attention.

[42] *Mythologies* (London, 1959), p. 332.

which probably belongs to this period, differs little from the complete copy except at the end where the Fool is made more articulate than in earlier versions. It is neatly written; some of its revisions may have been intended to make words more legible as if in preparation for a typist, but others show that Yeats was still modifying the text. The revised plays were then restaged the following year—*The Land of Heart's Desire* in February, *The Countess Cathleen* in September, and *The Hour-Glass* from 21 November 1912. The prompt copy for this production of *The Hour-Glass* (VK) survives, singed by the 1951 fire at the Abbey Theatre. For it and the Texas manuscript Yeats reinserted several lines from drafts earlier than the "complete copy." For instance, the Wise Man's dramatic speech about frenzy beating a drum, shouting aloud, and screaming is incorporated from VC, as is the statement about everybody being a fool while asleep and dreaming. In addition, a number of small but subtle alterations, first made to VJ, were incorporated in the prompt copy. The Fourth Pupil's expression of doubt at the dismissal of God was expanded to include a suggestion that he had dreamed that he was instructed to correct the Wise Man (VJ 1–2), and Yeats added a new close to the play in which the Fool remarks that he and the Wise Man are "the two fools / We know everything but we will not speak" (VJ 37). The prompt copy modified the passage before this to provide a smoother approach to it in which the Fool, on reentering the room after the Wise Man has died, suddenly realizes that the Wise Man cannot give him the penny he asks for and says, "No, no you will say nothing. You and I, we are the two fools, we know everything, but we will not speak" (ll. 587–589). VJ and the prompt copy contain much the same material in the final speeches but it is slightly differently arranged, with more dialogue between the Fool and the Angel in the prompt copy, where the Angel enters and "removes" the imaginary butterfly in a casket rather than in his hands. The prompt copy also contains an innovation in its final line, giving the play the crispest of its endings: Teigue closes the stage curtains, saying: "He is gone, he is gone, he is gone, but come in everybody in the world and look at me:— / I hear the wind a blow, / I hear the grass a grow, / And all that I know, I know, / But I will not speak, I will run away."

In marking up a copy of the 1914 Cuala Press edition of *Responsibilities: Poems and a Play* (VP) for the 1916 London edition (*Responsibilities and Other Poems*), Yeats made a significant alteration: he cut the Wise Man's action of kneeling to the Fool. A letter written that year to Sturge Moore offering advice about a play Moore had just written may indirectly suggest his reasoning:

> It just wants to have those things taken out which as a matter of course are taken out of practically every prose play in rehearsal. The moment one goes into rehearsal one discovers, among other things, that the stage picture is so much more powerful than the words that there are whole passages which lose their weight. A shifting of the centre of gravity takes place and this involves minor changes.[43]

For the 1922 revision of *Plays in Prose and Verse*, Yeats, with the help of Alan Porter, turned many of the speeches in the mixed version into Latin. He explained that the repetition in the play, which had been acceptable in prose, grated when all the first half was in verse: "We listen more intently to verse than to prose, and therefore notice verbal repetition more quickly. Nothing said in latin, necessary to the understanding of the play, cannot be inferred from who

[43] *Sturge Moore,* p. 24 (26 January 1916).

speaks and who is spoken to."[44] The addition of Latin further differentiated the mixed version from the prose play, making more sophisticated what was already the more subtle and philosophically difficult version.

In estimating the importance of *The Hour-Glass* there are several things to be considered. Clearly the play was personally significant to Yeats in asserting values in which he believed. It was also vital to his development as a dramatist. Flannery remarks, "One may ask whether *The Hour-Glass* is theatrically as successful as *Purgatory,* but without question its revisions prepared the way for the success of his later plays."[45] The later manuscripts presented in this edition hold a magnifying glass over that turning point in Yeats's career. Similarly, the early drafts show how Yeats's awareness of the essentials of theatrical performance evolved until he was ready to cut away, in the mixed version, and even more in the dance plays, all that simply distracted from words and movement.

[44] See Appendix III, VQb.

[45] Flannery, p. 315.

Transcription Principles and Procedures

When writing a draft, Yeats was jotting down for his own convenience a record of the stage to which composition had come. His hand, which was almost always difficult to read, could come close to an unsystematic shorthand, with endings of words unfinished, whole words represented by an approximate line or omitted altogether, haphazard spelling and punctuation. Consequently, in the presentation of these manuscripts there is a degree of interpretation. The principles by which that interpretation has been done are listed below:

1. Where it seems clear that Yeats intended a word, even though letters may seem to be missing or run together at the end of it, the word is transcribed in full. In many cases, Yeats's actual spelling cannot be determined, and in such cases a standard spelling is given. On the other hand, Yeats's spelling is preserved when clear, even if it is incorrect, as, for instance, "know" for "now" (VA 7^{r}, l. 18), "sollid" for "solid" (VA 7^{r}, l. 16). In *The Hour-Glass* Yeats uses two different spellings for the Fool's name, both "Teig" as in *Countess Cathleen*, and "Teigue." These are not regularized.

2. Yeats frequently broke words at unusual points, or broke words not normally divided. He was also inconsistent in whether or not he broke certain words. Thus instances can be found of "bed side" within a few lines of "bedside" (VI 17^{v}, ll. 9 and 11). Where the space between "syllables" is as large as Yeats left between words the space has been preserved in transcription. Although it is possible that Yeats regarded certain words as hyphenated without inserting the hyphen—see "no one" (VB 1^{r}, l. 23), for example—it is also conceivable that he spelled syllabically or in units, and that this was sometimes reflected in his writing.

3. Symbols used for illegible words and editorial conjectures are as follows:

[?]	a totally undeciphered word
[? ? ?]	several undeciphered words
[~~?~~]	an undeciphered word that was canceled
[?world]	a conjectural reading
[?world/would]	equally possible conjectural readings

4. Overwritings are shown thus: ha$\left\{\begin{array}{l}\text{s}\\ \text{ve}\end{array}\right.$ = "have" amended to "has."

5. Obscure marks whose significance has not been determined are silently omitted in transcription.

6. Cancellation of single lines or of words within a line is regularized to horizontal cancellation lines. Parallel lines are used to indicate cancellation first of a word or phrase and then of the entire line or a greater portion of it. Where Yeats intended to cancel an entire word

but only struck through part of it, the cancellation line in the transcription extends through the entire word. However, even when it seems likely that Yeats meant to cancel an entire phrase or line, no word that he did not at least partially cancel is cancelled in the transcriptions.

7. Cancellation of an entire passage is indicated by a vertical bracket in the left margin. Where typographical limitations make it impossible to print a marginal revision in its actual position, it is given immediately below the transcription of the page on which it occurs. Arrows leading from such passages are not reproduced.

8. Yeats's "stet" marks are preserved, as are his underscorings to indicate the passage to which "stet" refers.

9. Spacing and relative position of words and lines approximate the originals insofar as printed type can reproduce handwritten material.

10. Most of the holograph pages are unnumbered, and they have here been numbered sequentially; superscript "r" and "v" refer to the recto and verso of each sheet as Yeats used it. The assigned leaf number is followed by bracketed line numbers that relate the passage on each page approximately to the numbered lines in *The Variorum Edition of the Plays of W. B. Yeats*, edited by Russell K. Alspach (London, 1965, 1966). In the left-hand margin of each transcription, numbers have been assigned to every line to make possible references in notes. These line numbers differentiate sequential attempts at a line from subsequent interlineated revisions of it.

11. In the transcriptions of typescript material, minor and obvious typing errors such as strikeovers may not be recorded; possible spelling errors, emendations of capitalization and punctuation, and alterations that turn one word into another are indicated.

12. In the *apparatus criticus*, such as that which records variants from MS. PD (pp. 37–53), variants are shown from the final version of PD. Where PCi and PCii read identically, the reading is cited as PC; where they differ, PCi and PCii are used. The same pattern is followed for PGi and PGii and POi, POii, and POiii. The abbreviation "del to" indicates "is deleted and revised to." Details of the exact form of character identifications and stage directions for each typescript or printed version are described at the beginning of the listed variants and are not subsequently included individually. For example, the stage directions of PG are underlined; this is noted at the beginning and not subsequently counted as a variant.

13. The following typographical conventions have been used:

roman	ink
italic	pencil
boldface	typescript or print

The Hour-Glass

Transcriptions

The Prose Version

The three-page holograph (PA) of the dialogue between the Wise Man and the Angel is the earliest fragment of the play we have, and it provides the most moving of the Wise Man's pleas to the Angel. On the first page is an asterisk but the passage to be interpolated at that point is no longer extant, and page 3 is most probably a revision of a sheet now missing.

The only other holograph fragment of the prose play is a single page (PQ) from 1911–1912 containing the final speeches and showing Yeats experimenting with the extended stage and steps from it into the auditorium which Nugent Monck introduced. It is written on inverted sheets of a narrow, lined paper, similar to that used in much of the mixed version.

There are eight typescripts of varying degrees of completeness:

(1) The earliest of these is PB, of which fifteen pages are extant, numbered 1 to 12, with three additional pages of revisions and interpolations. Accompanying the typescript is a page in Lady Gregory's hand setting out the "scene." The draft is almost complete, missing a little over one page of material. It ends at the point where the Fool begins to tell the Wise Man what he knows of Angels. The draft was not typed by a professional and may well have been done by Lady Gregory, who probably also wrote in the phrases in pencil at Yeats's dictation. He subsequently revised the draft in black ink, either using nibs of two different thicknesses or quite possibly using the front and back of a single nib. There are two pages numbered 1. That beginning "The wise man . . ." seems to be modified by the second page numbered 1 and an additional page (2). This gives the play a more leisurely opening, which was then used in MSS. PC, PD, PF, and the prompt copy (see ll. 1–32; all line numbers quoted refer to PD). There are two pages numbered 3; the first of these was abandoned and replaced before the next page was typed.

(2) PCi is the copy submitted to the Lord Chamberlain's Office for a license, which was granted on 20 October 1902. This version was performed at Victoria Hall West. Most pencil corrections to PCii were transferred to PCi with the same carbon still in place.

(3) In the National Library of Ireland there is a sixteen-page typescript (PCii); p. 6 has a piece pasted onto the foot, making it longer than the others. The strip was added for the insertion of ll. 167–169 ("For . . . threshing floor"), which the typist had omitted. The number of differences between PB and PC suggests that there was probably an intermediate typescript that is no longer extant, perhaps a modified carbon copy of PB.

(4) The Berg Collection houses PD, a complete typescript of seventeen numbered pages, which is a carbon of PF [Quinn (1)]. The typing of this may have been done by a professional typist but done in a hurry since it introduces errors that were only gradually removed from the play, such as ll. 151–153 from the dialogue between the Wise Man and the Angel, which [PB, PC] read: "those are the messengers that come to men. . . . You carry the pardons of the Most

High, give them to me." PD turns this into "come to me. . . . pardon . . . give them." Similarly ll. 302–303 read: "There is nobody . . . who has enough belief to fill a pipe with." PD turns this into "nobody . . . who had," an error that remained in the play until the English edition of *Plays for an Irish Theatre*, vol. 2, 1904 (Wade 53). PD could have been typed from PC after some but not all of the corrections to PC were made, since it does not follow the earlier typescript in every respect; in general it is more heavily punctuated and some changes seem to be improvements, such as l. 104 where "an Angel . . . having a blossoming apple bough" is altered to "carrying a blossoming apple bough," and l. 106 where "I am going to expound this great Saracen, but I must refute that passage in Tertullian" becomes "and I must refute." It incorporates some of the slips of PC, omitting the comma in l. 336 between "five" and "six" as the Fool blows the dandelion to find out what the time is, and in l. 107 splitting "Ter tullian." A page turn from pages 7–8 at the end of a sentence and partway through a speech in PC led the typist to repeat "W.M." In PD (and PF of course), where the page turn no longer split the speech, this repetition is faithfully followed although it is unnecessary, and the mistake was repeated in PG and the prompt copy. There are a few corrections and a few revisions, the most significant of which clarifies the allocation of the children's speeches and the points at which various characters enter, although it does not incorporate PCii's handwritten distribution of the young men's speeches, which may have been inserted after PD was typed. Most of the changes were made by Yeats in blue-black ink. The copy is signed but undated.

(5) The National Library of Ireland also houses a typed prompt copy (PE) from 1903 with handwritten alterations in several hands, including that of Yeats. It may have been typed from PD, certainly from a text at that stage of the play's evolution, although the punctuation of PD is not followed exactly and there are small textual differences. In ll. 152–153 "men" is restored, but the illogical "pardon . . . give them" remains. Again there is an interpolated passage explaining why the Wise Man cannot leave the room. The children's speech "there is no Heaven there is no Hell" was altered to the less contentious line "There is nothing we cannot see, there is nothing we cannot touch." Bridget's speeches about her daily occupations were made less comical with two revisions not incorporated into the printed text until the English edition of *Plays for an Irish Theatre* (1904). The butterfly mentioned at the end of the play was amended to a more practical "white flame." The copy is accompanied by a handwritten list of properties, two sets of costume descriptions in different writing, and a typeset properties plot. The properties plot, suggesting that the copy was used for a number of productions, reads:

> National Theatre Society Ltd. / "THE HOUR GLASS." / PROPERTY PLOT. / STAGE: — Table R. Chair L. of Table. Book in Stand on Table. Hour Glass on Stand R. C. Over-Door, fixed, C. Bell Rope L. Three-legged Stool L. C. / HAND:—Bell in P.C. Shears for Fool. Pennies in Bag for Wise Man. Duster for Wife. / Those underlined we carry.

There are also two additional properties plots written in different hands. The first of these, in black ink, reads: "Properties / Hour Glass—Book—Desk—Chair—Stool—/ Stick (Wiseman)—Shears (Fool)—Bell—/Bag (Fool)—Money (Wiseman)—money for / students—Flowers (Fool)—Cover for Hour Glass." Below this, written in another hand in blue ink, is:

> Dresses / Wise Man Blue purple cloak. Black / half-flow wig / Fool Long haired red

wig, blue tunic / & trews, skin pampooties, leather bag / & belt, shears, dandelion; cross-gartering / 3 Pupils Tunics, trews, pampooties, crossgartering, half flow wigs, belts / 2 children Tunics, trews, pampooties, crossgartering.

The second properties plot is on the verso of a sheet measuring 20.5 x 15.7 cm with the watermark [ ]ift Brook /AIR-DRIED / [ ]r fine Vellum. Written in pencil is:

The Hour Glass / Wise Man Blue purple Cloak. Black Wig / Fool Long haired reddish wig / Blue tunic & trues Skin / Pampooties Leather Bag / & Belt. Shears Dandelion / Cross Gartering Apron. / Pupils (3) Tunics Trues Pampooties / Cross Gartering Longhaired / Wigs, Belts / Children (2) Tunics Trues Pampooties / Cross Gartering

(6) The John Quinn papers in the Manuscript Division of the New York Public Library include three typescripts of the prose version of the play. One of these, PF, is the ribbon copy of PD. The text, however, contains significant revisions in Lady Gregory's hand, carrying PF beyond PD in the play's evolution. The largest revisions are to the opening of the play and to the exchange between Bridget and the Wise Man, and may reflect what was found to work in performance. "Wise Man" was written on the cover sheet, suggesting that the copy may have been used as a script. Two additional sheets belonging to the typescript, designated PFadd, are housed with Quinn (3). The revised text is substantially that of the first printed version.

(7) The second of the Quinn typescripts [Quinn (3) PGi] may well have been typed from the modified PF. It follows its text with few changes and, in general, improves its punctuation. One slip that occurred in PF/PD and that suggestively appears in PG is an unnecessary indentation at l. 67, corrected by hand.

(8) Quinn (4) PGii is a carbon of PGi from which, although separately revised, it differs little. The first printing, in *The North American Review*, could well have been made from PGii, in which considerable care seems to have been taken to achieve a version with correct punctuation. Not all errors were caught, however. What differences there are between PGii and NAR could have been introduced during the checking of proofs.

There are a number of printed copies with Yeats's handwritten alterations:

(1) The first of these (PH) was a copy of the first printing in *The North American Review*, belonging to Lady Gregory. It was signed by Yeats, slightly revised, and given a new ending that expands the description of the butterfly. It was incorporated in PM and PP and makes the saving of the Wise Man's soul more explicit. The ending was typed on a slip of paper in preparation for a pamphlet where, bound with *The Golden Helmet*, it was published to establish copyright.

(2) PK, a copy of the English edition of *Plays for an Irish Theatre* (1904), evidently used as a prompt copy. Some of the modifications made in it by Yeats are the same as those made to the theatre edition of 1907. Inside the cover is a folded piece of paper measuring 20.3 x 18.4 cm with a watermark: UNIQUE NOTE/ SBM. On it WBY wrote in black ink:

Notes. / 'The Hour Glass' was first produced at the Molesworth Hall Dublin on 14 March 1903 with the following cast / The Wise Man J Dudley Digges / Bridget (his wife) Maire T Quinn / Her Children. Eithne and Padragur Nic Shiubhlaigh / His pupils.

. . . P J Kelly / Seamus O Sullivan / P Columb / P Mac Shiubhlaigh / The Angel Maire Nic Shiubhlaigh / The Fool. F J Fay. / The play has been received many times since then & is in the repertoire of The Abbey Theatre Dublin.

Pasted on the title page is a printed note and copy of the music of the ballad "The Gruagach Uasal," with Gaelic words. The note reads, "[This ballad was taken down in Donegal by Mr. E. E. Fournier, as well as the music to which it was sung, and which the people told him was music of the Sidhe. Mr. Jack Yeats has made a drawing for it, and I have made a rough translation of it. 'The Gruagach Uasal,' literally the Noble Enchanter, is used for some strange, unearthly, unfriendly, being. — Augusta Gregory.]"

(3) PL is a copy belonging to Anne Yeats of the Dublin edition of the same volume. This has unique readings, including the only sympathetic and realistic speeches by the Wise Man about his wife in the prose version.

(4) There are six marked-up copies of the theatre edition published by A. H. Bullen in London in 1907. What is possibly the earliest of these (PM) is owned by the Berg Collection. It is signed as "correct / W. B. Y." and has Yeats's handwritten alterations, most of which are in the second half of the play. Several of these combine to alter the emphasis on the pupils' beliefs to a concern with whether or not they have been changed by the Wise Man's teaching. Four further copies of the theatre edition belong to Anne Yeats. One of these (PN) is marked "First proofs" and will be dealt with later; the other three have almost identical modifications and are designated POi, POii, and POiii. The substantive changes are close to those made to the theatre edition of 1907 (PP) owned by the University of Kansas, which has a penciled note on the front cover: "Revised text 16.xii.1910." This modified text is that of *Plays for an Irish Theatre*, published in January 1911. It shows significant moves toward Yeats's interests in the mixed version, in that more attention is paid to the Wise Man's feelings, and the delusory nature of the physical world may be foreseen in the description of it as "A / the dying world."

There are also three sets of proofs:

(1) PI [Quinn (2)], an incomplete set stamped "1st Rev.", probably for the 1904 edition of *The Hour-Glass and Other Plays* (Wade 52). The revisions are not in Yeats's hand, and the text breaks off after l. 306: " . . . [Goes out and shouts".

(2) PN, a modified copy of the theatre edition of 1907 owned by Anne Yeats. Although it contains one or two errors, it was probably used as a proof or record of proofs for *Plays for an Irish Theatre* (A. H. Bullen, 1911, Wade 92).

(3) PR [NLI (4)], a set of proofs vetted by Yeats in 1931–1932 in preparation for the unpublished Coole edition of his plays. Most of the queries are of capitalization or punctuation, but Yeats made modifications of the play's ending that show the influence of the mixed version. PR takes further than the mixed version the Wise Man's self-abandonment to God, for instance, and graphically confirms the Angel's assertion that he cannot undo what he has done, by ending the play with one of the pupils declaring that there is no one in the doorway.

MS. PA

Transcriptions, with facing photographs

[MS. PA, 1r; 173–181]

[MS. PA, 1^{r}; 173–181]

1 I have denied everything, but what my
2 five senses have told me of, & I
3 have taught others ~~to den~~ ~~deny~~
4 think as I did. But pardon me
~~Let me live & I will d undo all that I have done.~~
5 pardon me.^ (He kneels) *
Angel.
6 You should have asked for Pardon years
7 ago, & not know ~~when~~ in the hour
8 of death.
Wise man.
9 Do not send me to wander through eternity
Angel.
Those who do not build up houses
10 It is in life that we build up up the
11 houses, where our soul lives after
for [?the/their] soul in [?the/their] life time ~~become~~
12 death.
become like the wind.
Wise man.
as I see it now
13 Had I seen your face^O beautiful
14 angel I would have believed, ~~but~~
15 ~~my the dreams I had when I was a child~~
16 ~~But~~ But you cannot know what a life

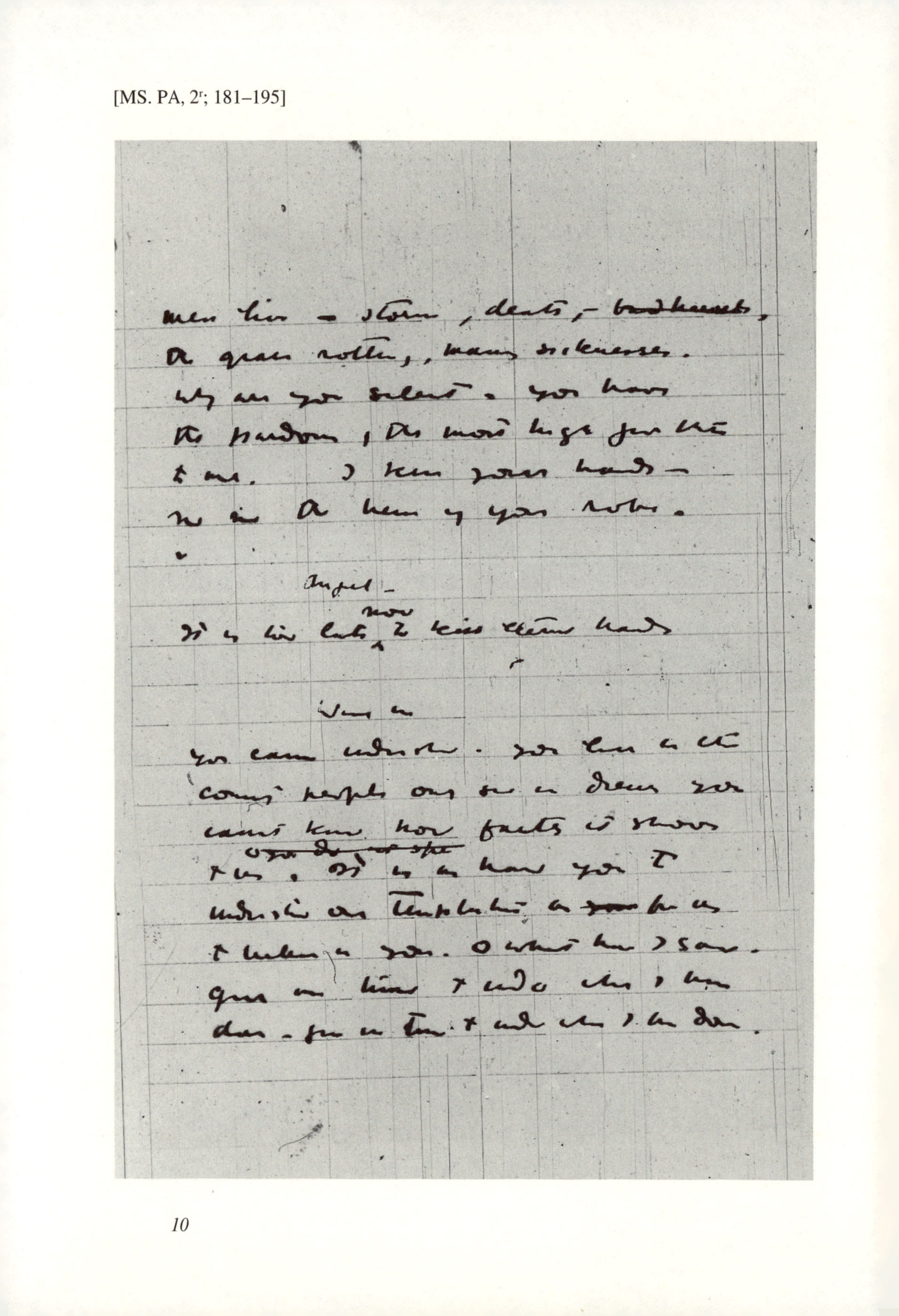

[MS. PA, 2^r; 181–195]

[MS. PA, 2^{r}; 181–195]

men live — storms, death, ~~bad harvests,~~
the grass rotting, many sicknesses.
Why are you silent. You have
the pardons of the most high give them
to me. I kiss your hands —
no no the hem of your robe.

Angel.

now
It is too late^to kiss eternal hands

Wise man

You cannot understand. You live in the
country people only see in dreams you
cannot know those [?facts] it shows
~~O you do not spe~~
to us. It is as hard you to
understand our temptation as ~~you~~ for us
to believe in you. O what have I said.
Give me time to undo what I have
done — give me time to undo what I have done.

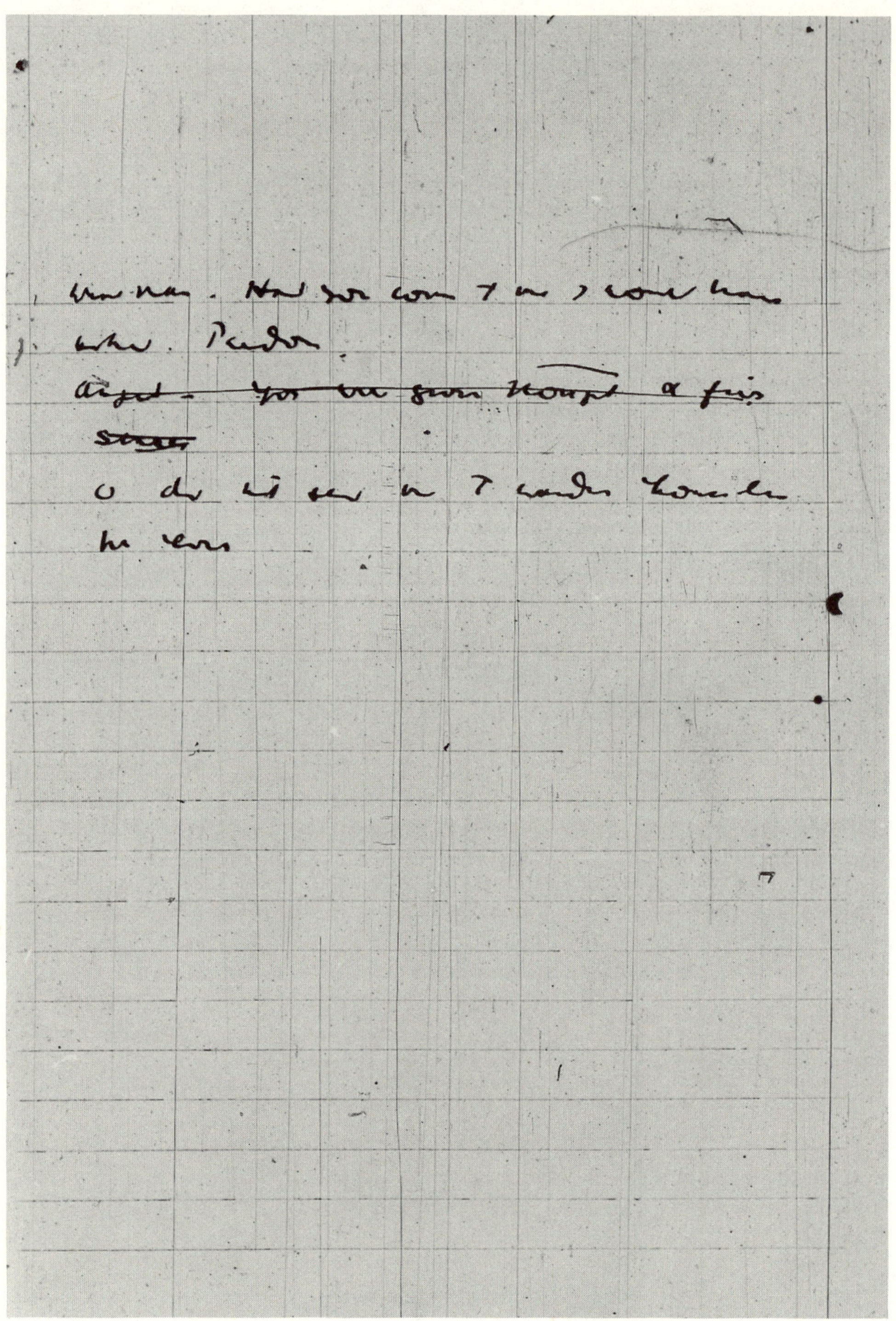

[MS. PA, 3^{r}]

Wise man. Had you come to me I would have
asked Pardon.
~~Angel. You were given thought & five~~
~~senses~~
O do not send me to wander homeless
for ever

MS. PB

Transcriptions, with selected facing photographs

[MS. PB, leaf 1]

A large room with a door at
at the
~~the back and another door each~~ side
into an inner room — A desk
with chair
in middle — An hour glass on a
creepy
bracket on the wall — A stool
near the door. Some benches — An
astronomical globe — A blackboard.
ancient
~~Some maps~~ A large map of
~~and some pictures~~
the world on the wall — Some
musical instruments. Floor strewed
with rushes. A Wise Man
sitting at his desk —

These stage directions are in Lady Gregory's hand.

2 Stet lines entered below "the . . . door"

[MS. PB, page no. 1; 1–23]

1

WISE MAN alone turning over the pages of a book.

W.M. Ah this is the passage. 'There was a time when men thought that the truth could be found through dreams and visions. They imagined that it was quiet and unchanging like the fixed stars and that the mind had to become quiet and unchangin{g / r} too, as it is when sleeping and in trances before it could look on truth. (The Fool comes in. He is dressed in skins. He stands holding out his hat but the wise man does not see him)

W.M. But now we have learned that we come to truth - -

FOOL. Give me a penny.

W.M. ~~Dialectic anb~~ by the activity of the mind. This activity is called. ^dialectic.

FOOL. Give me a penny.

W.M. (goes on reading) ~~dialectic~~ and is under the government of the lightest and all but swiftest of the planets.

FOOL. Wont you gave me a penny.?

W.M. What do you want? The words of the wise Saracen **~~Simonides~~ will not teach you much.**

12, 17 Alterations made by WBY.

[MS. PB, p. 2; 24–40]

Such a great wise teacher as you are will not refuse a penny to a fool.

W.M. What do you know about wisdom ?

FOOL. Oh, I know, I know what I have seen.

W.M. What is it you have seen?

FOOL. When I went by KilCluan where the bells used to be ringing at the break of evey Sunday and every holiday, I could hear nothing but the people snoring in their houses. When I went by Tubbervanagh where there used to be a Station for Confession, the young men were sitting at the cross road playing cards. When I went by Carrigoras where the friars used to be fasting and serving the poor, I saw them drinking wine and obeying their wives. And when I asked what misfortune had brought all these changes, they said it was no misfortune but it was the wisdom they had learned from your teaching.

1

The wise man alone in his teaching room, standing at his desk at
{e {ud {i
an open book. He r{ads alo{d 'And dialect{ec is under Mercury, for Mer-
cury is the smallest of the planets, and dia|lectic is of so light a
{(
body that it can enter through even the littlest crevice ~~'8~~ {) knocking
{o T}
outside) ~~Here are my pupils~~, Wh{i is there. come in. (t}eigue the fool
opens the door. He is dressed in skins and carrying a large rusty
)}
shears (}.
W.M. What do you want. You cannot stay here. I am busy; In a moment
I will have to ring the bell for my pupils., and I must read over the
lesson before they come.
{n
Fool. Wont you gave a pe{eny to Teigue the Fool ? ^
W.M. Run round to the kitchen and my wife will give you something
to eat.
Fool. That is foolish advice for a wise man to give.
W.M. Why, Fool ?
{a
Fool. Wh{tt is eaten is gone; I want pennies for my bag. I must buy
{e
bacon in the shops and nuts in the mark{rt and strong drinks for the
time when the sun is weak. And I want snares to catch the rabbits and
squirrels & hares, & I want ~~a steal~~ pot to cook them in.
~~the little furry beasts that eat the nuts to make my coat for the winter~~
Wise Man. Go away. I have other|n things to think of now than giving
you pennies.
Fool. Give me a penny and I will bring you luck. Bresal the Fisher-
man lets me sleep among the nets in his loft in the wintertime. because
in the summer time
he says I bring him luck; and ^ the wild creatures let me sleep near
their nests and their holes ; it lucky even to look at me or to touch
me, but it is much more lucky to give me a penny. H (holds out his
hat) If I wasnt lucky I'd starve.

18 "steal" written by Lady Gregory; the rest of the insertion is by WBY.
24 Interpolation written by Lady Gregory.

[MS. PB, p. 4; 61–91]

2

Wise Man (touching the shears which the fool has in his hand

have got

together with the hat) What ~~do~~ you ~~carry~~ the shears for

you would drive them away

Fool. I wont tell you. If I told you ~~they would be angry.~~

W.M. Who would ~~be angry ?~~ I drive away?

FOOL. I wont tell you.

W.M. Not if I give you a penny ?

FOOL. No.

W.M. Not if I give you two pennies ?

FOOL. You will be very lucky if you give me two pennies, but I wont tell you.

W.M. Three pennies ?

FOOL. Four, and I will tell you.

W.M. Very well, four. But I will not call you Teigue the Fool any longer.

But first you must promise you will not drive them away (W.M. nods) night

FOOL. Let me come close to you where nobody will heare me. ^**Every ~~day~~ men go out dressed in black and they spread great nets over the hills, great black nets,**

W.M. Why do they do that?

FOOL. That they may catch the feet of the angels. But every morning just before the dawn I go out and cut the nets with my shears, and the angels fly away.

W.M. Ah, now I know that you are Teigu{e/r} the Fool. You have told me that I am wise, and I have never seen an angel.

FOOL. I have seen plenty of angels.

W.M. Do you bring luck to the angels too. ?

FOOL. O no, no, no one could do that. But they are always there if one looks about ~~them~~ one; they are like the blades of grass. I think I saw one coming after me a little time ago. It was the colour of red

All alterations on this page are in Lady Gregory's hand.

[MS. PB, p. 5; 107–149]

embers and there was something shining about its head.

W.M. Well well, there are your four pennines. Run away now, I must ring the bell for my scholars.

FOOL. Four pennies, that means a great deal of luck , Great teacher I have brought you plenty of luck, (He goes out shaking his bag).

W.M. Thought they call him Teigue the fool he is not more foolish than everyone used to be, with their dreams and their visions and their preachings and their three worlds. But I have overthrown their three worlds with the seven sciences, with these seven great books, (he touches the books with his hand as he speaks of them) With philosophy that was made by the lonely planet I have made them forget their grey Theology; with Architecture I have hidden the ramparts of their cloudy Heaven; abd with Music that daughter of the fierce planet whose h The fi the fierce planets daughter whose hair is always upon fire I have filled their ear with such sweet sounds they no longer listen for imaginary harpings; and with Arithmetic I have made formations of battle that have put to rout all the hosts of Heaven; But Rhetoric, dialectic and Grammar, children of the amourous that were made by the light star and the fickle star, amorous star, you have been my trumpeters, my spearmen and my catapults. (He stands again at the open book of dialectic). But most of all He reads out 'Dialectic is under Mercury for Mercury is the smallest of the planets'- O my swift horsemen, O my keen darting arguments it is because of you that have overthrown the hosts that were thought unconquerable , it is because of you that I am called Crochor, the wisest of men. '.

(Enter angel).

W.M.What are you, Who are you-- I think I saw some that were like you in my dreams when I was a child, that bright thing, that dress, that

All interpolations on this page are by WBY with the exception of:

1 "W.M. . . . say it —" and "Glory . . . God" inserted by Lady Gregory, as are:

14 "of"

17 "to the rout"

23 "by them" and "I have"

24 "them"

The clue line moving "daughter" to the beginning of l. 14 was rescinded.

The clue line moves "with Arithmetic" from l. 16 to beginning of l. 17.

[MS. PB, p. 5; 107–149]

3

W.M. You, a fool say Glory be to God. Before I came here
the wise men used to say it —
embers and there was something shining about its head. Glory be to God ^
W.M. Well well, there are your four pennines. Run away now, I must ^
ring the bell for my scholars.
FOOL. Four pennies, that means a great deal of luck , Great teacher
I have brought you plenty of luck. (He goes out shaking his bag).
W.M. Though they call him Teigue the fool, he is not more foolish
than everyone used to be, with their dreams and their visions and their
preachings and their three worlds. But I have overthrown their three
worlds with the seven sciences, with these seven great books, 'he tou-
ches the books with his hand as he speaks of them) With philosophy that
{e
was made by the lonely planet I have made them forg{**rt** ~~**their grey**~~
Theology; with Architecture I have hidden the ramparts of their cloudy
Heaven; abd with Music ~~**that daughter of the fierce planet whose h The fi**~~
~~of~~ and with grammar daughter of the moon
~~^~~ **the fierce planets daughter whose hair is always upon fire** ^ **I have**
made them ~~shu~~ shut their ears to
~~**filled their ear with such sweet sounds they no longer listen**~~ **for**
and the speech of the angels
{n
imaginary harpings ; a{**bd with Arithmetic I have made formations of battle**
^ to the rout &
^ **that have put** ~~**to rout all**~~ **the hosts of Heaven** ^ **; But Rhetoric,** ^ **dialectic**
~~**and Grammar,**~~ ~~**children of the amourous**~~ **that were made by** ^ **the light star**
k & the {r
~~**and the fie le star**~~ ^ , **amo**{**uous star, you have been** ~~**my trumpeters,**~~ **my**
spearmen and my catapults. (He stands again at the open book of ~~**f**~~ **dialec**
tic). ~~**But most of all**~~ **He reads out 'Dialectic is under Mercury for**
Mercury is the smallest of the planets' — O my swift horsemen, O my
~~by them~~ ~~I have~~
keen darting arguments it is ~~**because of**~~ ~~**you**~~ ~~**that have overthrown**~~ **the**
of foolishness them
~~**hosts that were thought unconquerable**~~**, it is because of** ~~**you**~~ **that I**
am called Crochoor, the ~~**waieset**~~ **of men. '.**
(Enter angel).
& I have
W.M.What are you, Who are you — I think I saw some that were like
you in my dreams when I was a child, that bright thing, that dress that

[MS. PB, p. 6; 107–150]

3

emders, and there was something shining about his head, glory be to GOD.

W.M. You a fool say Glory be to God. but before I came the wise men said it. There are your four pennies. Run away now I must ring the bell for my scholars.

FOOl. Four pennies, that means a great deal of luck, great teacher I have brought you plenty of luck. (He goes out shaking the bag).

W.M. Though they call him Teigue the Fool he is not more fllol foolish than everybody used to be, with their ~~dreams~~ and their preachig One would look up and tell another that the stars were holes in the floor of Heaven, while others thought that Heaven waited for them somewhere with gates made out of precious stones; and there were some that dreamt of ~~angels who~~ walked about among golden and silver apple trees ~~and~~ of birds that sang the hours ~~from the branches~~. But I have overturned all that. I have overthrown the ~~armies~~ of foolishness ~~and with nothing but my own wit and the seven sciences for bolt and cata-pult~~

An Angel stands on the threshold. He is dressed in a red garment and has a halo made of metal about his head) Today I am going to expound ~~Simonides the Roman~~. ~~That us better than gold and silver apples.~~

(He goes to the bookshelf and takes down another book) But I must refute that passage in Tertullian we spoke of yesterday. I cannot find it, Ah,here it is. I will give them wholesome bread to eat that will be better than dreams and visions. My name shall be remembered ~~as him~~ that ~~of him who cast~~ ~~folly out of the land~~. ~~It will never return~~(He sees the angel) Who are you ? What are you ? I think I saw some that were like you in my dreams when I was a child. That bright thing, that dress that is the colour of embers, but I have done with dreams, I have done with dreams.

All modifications on this page are by WBY, except l. 4 "so that", in Lady Gregory's hand.

1 "is the colour of" has been omitted at the beginning of the line.

15, 16 Clue line moves insertion to replace canceled lines 7–8. After ll. 15–16 were canceled, a new clue line moved ll. 18–23 "Today . . . visions" to replace ll. 7–8.

24 "It" canceled twice.

28 Clue line moves ink insertion below line to l. 16 after "Thresholds."

3

embers, and there was something shining about his head, glory be to GOD
W.M. You a fool say Glory be to God. but before I came the wise men
said it. There are your four pennies. Run away now I must ring the
bell for my scholars.
FOOl. Four pennies, that means a great deal of luck, great teacher
I have brought you plenty of luck. (He goes out shaking the bag).
[**W.M. Though they call him Teigue the Fool he is not more fllol**
[**foolish than everybody used to be, with their dreams and their preaching**
One would look up and tell another that the stars were holes in the
floor of Heaven, while others thought that Heaven waited for them
somewhere with gates made out of precious stones; and there were some
~~blessed souls that~~
that dreamt of ~~angels who~~ walked about among golden and silver apple
where the & sometimes [? these] angels would come down & stand
trees ~~and of~~ birds that sang the hours ~~from the branches~~. But I have
^ upon the very threshold.
hosts
overturned all that. I have overthrown the ~~armies~~ of foolishness~~and~~
~~Before I came men met angels on the streets~~ & on
~~**with nothing but my own wit and the seven sciences for bolt and cata-**~~
~~their [? very] thresholds~~. ~~The~~ mens hearts ~~& mouths~~ & minds
~~**pult.**~~ & ~~mouths were stuffed with folly~~
An Angel stands on the threshold. He is dressed in a red garment
and has a halo made of metal about his head) Today I am going to
the Great Saracen
expound ~~Simonides the Roman~~. ~~That is better than gold and silver~~ apples.
(He goes to the bookshelf and takes down another book) But I must
refute that passage in Tertullian we spoke of yesterday. I cannot find
it, Ah, here it is. I will give them wholesome bread to eat that will
~~They will never be [? remem]~~
be better than dreams and visions. My name shall be remembered ~~as him~~
for ever but they shall be forgotten. ~~so that~~ ~~They~~
that ~~of him who cast~~ ~~folly out of the land.~~ ^ ~~It will never return~~ (He
sees the angel) Who are you ? What are you ? I think I saw some that
were like you in my dreams when I was a child. That bright thing,
{b
that dress that is the colour of em{ders, but I have done with dreams,
I have done with dreams.
them
I have locked ~~the Angels~~ into their heaven . I have turned the key upon them
the visions up in but before ~~I came mens~~ hearts and minds

[MS. PB, p. 7; 151–188]

4

Who are you what are you
ANGEL. I am the angel of the most High God.
W.M. Why have you come to me?
ANGEL. I have brought you a message.
W,M, What message have you got for me?
Angel **You will die within the hour. You will die when the last grains**
{)
have fallen through this glass. (He turns the hourglass { (
have my (p)
W,M. I ~~hvae~~ a young wife and children that I cannot leave.
^ ^
ANGEL. You must die because no souls have passed over the threshold
of Heaven since you came into this country. The threshold is grassy and
the gates are rusty and the angels that keep watch there are lonely.
W.M. Where will death bring me to to?
ANGEL. The doors of Heaven will not open to you for you have denied
the existence of Heaven, and the doors of Purgatory will not open to you
for you have denied the existence of purgatory.
W.M. But I have also denied the existence of Hell.
{e
ANGEL. H{Ell is the place of those who deny.
W.M. (kneels) I have indeed denied everything, and have taught
others to deny. I have believed in nothing but what my senses told me.
But O beautiful Angel. forgive me—forgive me.
ANGEL. ~~This is not the time to ask~~ You should have asked forgiveness
long ago.
W.M. Had I seen your face as I see it now O beautiful angel ~~I would~~
I would have believed, I would have asked forgiveness. ~~Maybe you do not~~
~~know about the lifeof men~~Maybe you do not know how easy it is to doubt.
those are the messengers that come to men
Storm, death, the grass rotting, many sicknesses. ^ **O why are you silent**
~~take hold~~
You carry the pardons of the most High, give them to me. I would ~~kiss~~
your hands if I were not afraid. No no, the hem of your dress.
{w
ANGEL. It is ~~too late no{e to kiss eternal hands~~. (p)
W.M. You cannot understand. You live in that country people only

---

All revisions in Lady Gregory's hand except "my" and insertion marks in l. 7, stet marks under "kiss" and perhaps "take hold" in l. 26, which are by WBY.

[MS. PB, p. 8; 189–215]

5

only see in ~~your~~ their dreams. You live in a country that is out of
r t
sight, in a c ount{y}y **that we can only dream about. Maybe i**{s}**s is as hard**
for you to understand why we disbelieve as it is for us to believe.
O what have I said, you know everything, give me time to undo what I
have done. Give me a year — a month — ~~a week~~ — a day — an hour! Give me to
this hour's end that I may undo what I have done !
ANGEL. You cannot undo what you have done. Yet I have this power
I
~~have this power~~ with my message. i}**f you can find one ~~that you have~~**
~~ever s~~that believes before the hour's end you shall come to Paradise
i farewell am
after the Purgatorial f{**ore. But now ~~let go my hands~~ for I weary of** the
~~W.M.~~ weight of time.
W.M. ~~(letting go his hands)~~ Ble ssed be the Father, blessed be the
Son blessed be the Spirit, blessed be the messenger they have sent.
~~turning~~
ANGEL. (at the door and ~~pointing at~~ the hourglass.) In a little
while the uppermost glass will be empty.
(Angel goes out).
W.M. Every thing will be well with me, I will call my pupils, they
t w
only say they doub{y. **~~when~~** (pulls the bell.) **They we**}**ill be here in**
a moment I hear their feet outside on the path. They wanted to please,
me, they pretend that they disbelieve. Belief is too old to be overcome
all in a minute. Besides I can prove what I once disproved. (Another
pull at the bell)

All the ink insertions on this page are by Lady Gregory.

7 Period following "done" deleted in ink.

[MS. PB, p. 9; 215–243]

6

pull at the bell) they are coming now. I will go to my desk, I will ~~spek~~ speak quietly as if nothing had happened. (He stands at his desk with a fixed look in his eyes.

(Enter pupils and the fool).

FOOL. Leave me alone, leave me alone, who is that pulling at my cloak, kings son, do not pull at my cloak.

A young man. Did your frien{ds/s} the angels give you that cloak, why done they ^not **give you a better cloak.**

~~Another.~~ Fool. Let go my cloak{,/.} and give me pennies.

A young man|Let go his cloak, it is coming in pieces. What do you ~~who have such friends~~ want pennies for ? With that great bag at your waist?

FOOL. I want to buy bacon in the shops, and nut{s/x} in the market, and strong drink for the time the sun is weak ~~And I want to~~ and snareso to catch rabbits.in. and the squirr{e/i}ls that steal the nuts, and ~~a grea~~ hares and a great pot to cook them in.

A young man. Why dont your friends tell you where buried treasures are ?

ANOTHER. Why dont they make you dream about treasure. If one dreams three times there is always treasure.

FOOL. (holding out his hat) Give me pennies, give me pennies?

(They throw pennies into his hat—He is stan{d/g}ing close to the door that he may hold out his hat to each newcomer)

A young Man. Master, will you have Teigue the Fool for a scholar ?

Another young Man. Teigue the Fool will not be a scholar, Teigue the Fool can teach. Master, will you become a pupil ? What will you teach us Teigue?

W.M.

---

1 "pull at the bell)" repeated because it was unclear on previous page.
All modifications on this page are by Lady Gregory.

[MS. PB, p. 10; 244–280]

7

W.M. Be silent all. (He has been standing silent looking away Sit still in your places, for there is something I would have you tell me.

(A moments pause. They all stand round in their places. Teigue still staying at the door).

W.M. Is there any one amongst you who believes in God ? In Heaven? Or in Purgatory ? Or in Hell?

ALL THE YOUNG MEN. No one master, no one !

W.M. I knew that you would all say that; but do not be afraid, I will ~~be an~~ not be angry. Tell me the truth, Do you not believe ?

, A YOUNG MAN. We once did but you have taught us to know better.

W.M. O teaching, teaching does not go very deep. The heart remains unchanged under it all. You believe just as you always did, and you are afraid to tell me.

A YOUNG MAN. No, No, Master.

W.M. If you tell me that you believe I shall be glad and not angry.

A YOUNG MAN. (to h{i os neighbour) He wants somebody to dispute with.

HIS NEIGHBOUR. I knew that from the beginning.

W.M. If there is one amongst you that believes he will be my best friend. Surely there is one amongst you. '~~THet~~ (They are all silent)

W.M. Surely what you learned at your mothers knees g has not been so soon forgotten.

A YOUNG MAN. Master, until you came, no teacher in this land was able to get rid of foolishness and ignorance. But everyone has listened to you, everyone has learned the truth. You have had your last disputation.

ANOTHER. What a fool you made of that monk in the market place! He had not a word to say.

W.M. (Comes from his desk and stands among them in the middle of the room)

8

~~W.M.~~Pupils, friends, dear friends, I have deceived you all this time. It was I myself who was ignorant. There is a God. There is a Heaven, there is ~~fot~~ fire that passes, and there is fire that lasts for ever.

(TEIGUE through all this scene is sitting on a stool by the door, reckoning on his fingers what he will buy with the money)

A YOUNG MAN (To another) He will not be satisfied till we dispute with him. (To the wise man) Prove it Master. Have you seen them ?

W.M. In a low solemn voice) Just now, before you came in,~~ I hea~~ someone came to the door, and when I looked up I saw an angel standing there

A YOUNG MAN. You were in a dream. Anybody can see an angel in his dreams.

W.M. O my God ! It was not a dream. I was awake. waking as I am now. I tell you I was awake as I am now.

A YOUNG MAN. Some dream when they are awake, but they are the crazy and who would believe what they say. Forgive me Master, but that is what you taught me to say. That is what you said to the monk when he spoke of the visions of the saints and the martyrs.

ANOTHER YOUNG MAN. You see how well we remember your teaching. You have convinced us all.

W.M. Out, out., out from my sight. I want a believer, a believer that I may save my soul from the fire, and you answer me with argument. Out out or I will beat you with my stick. (The young men laugh).

A YOUNG MAN. How well he plays ~~his part.~~ at faith; he is like the monk when he had nothing more to say.

W.M. Out, out or I will lay this stick about your shoulders. Out with you there though~~t~~ you are a kings son. They begin to hurry out.

A YOUNG MAN. Come, come, he wants us to find someone who will dispute

with him. (All go out)

W.M.(alone. He goes to a door at the side)I will call my wife, she will believe; women always believe. (He op opens the door and calls) Bridget ! Bridget ! Bridget comes in wearing her apron, her sleeves turned up from her floury arms)

W.M. Bridget, tell me the truth; do not say what you think will please me. I know what you really think, so do not deny it. You believe do you not that there is a Heaven a Purgatory and a Hell ?

BRIDGET. Oh, I once believed all t a

W.M. Bridget tell me the truth, do not tell me what you think will please me. Do you sometimes say your prayers ?

BRIDGET. Prayers, no, you taught me to leave them off long ago. At first I was sorry but I am glad now, for I am sleepy in the evenings.

W.M. But do you not believe in God ?

BRIDGET. Ah, a good wife only believes what her husband tells her.

W.M. But sometimes when you are alone, when I am in the school and the children asleep, do you not think about the saints, about the things you used to believe in.What do you think of when you are alone ?

BRIDGET. (~~thinking~~ considering). I think about nothing, sometimes I wonder if the pig is fattening well, or I go out to see if the crows are picking up the chicken's food.

W.M. O what can I do ! Is there nobody that believes !

BRIDGET. You want somebody to get up an argument with ?

W.M. Look out at the door and tell me if there is anybody there in the street.

BRIDGET. There is a great crowd of people talking to your pupils.

W.M. O run out Bridget and see if they have found somebody that believes !

BRIDGET.(Wiping her arms in her apron and pulling down her sleeves)

Its a hard thing to be married to a man of learning that must be always having arguments. (Exit, and shouts through the kitchen door) If you two children put yur fingers on the dough I'll give you-(exit

W.M. (kneels down; B{e/r}gins a Latin prayer, breaks off;) I have forgotten it all. It is thirty years since I have said a prayer. I must pray ~~like a~~ in the common tongue like a clown ~~praying~~ ^begging in the market , like Teigue the fool! He prays) Help me Father Son and Spirit. (Bridget enters followed b Teigue the Fool who is holding out his hat to her)

FOOL. Give me something, give me a penn{y/i}ng to buy bacon in the shops and nuts in the market and strong drink for the time when the sun is weak.

BRIDGET. I have no pennies. (To the Wise Man) Your pupils cannot find anybody to argue with you. There is nobody on the whole country who has enough belief to fill a pipe since you put down the monk. Cant you be quiet now and not alway be wantin{g/f} to have arguments. It must be terrible to have a mind like that !

W.M. I am lost. I am lost ~~BRIDGET~~.

BRIDGET. Leave me alone now, I have to make the bread for you and the children.

W.M. Out of this woman ! Out of this I say! will nobody find a way to help me ! but she spoke of my children. I had forgotten them. they will believe. It is only those who have reason that doubt, the young are full of faith. Bridget, Bridget, bring my children to me !

BRIDGET. (inside) Your father wants you, e run to him now.(the two children come in, they stand together a little way from the ~~door~~ threshold of the kitchen door, looking timidly at their father.

W.M. Children, what do you believe ? Is there a Heaven, Is there a

Hell? Is there a Purgatory ?

ONE CHILD. We havn't forgotten, father.

THE OTHER CHILD. Oh no Father. (They both~~e~~ speak together as if in school{)(. There is no Heaven, there is no Hell, there is nothing we cannot see. Foolish people used to think that there were, but you ~~ha~~ are very learned, and you have taught us better.

W.M. You are just as bad as the others, just as bad as the others. Out of the room with you, out of the room ! (The children begin to cry and run away.) or **Go away, go away, I will teach you better.—No I will never teach you again,go to your mother—she will not be able to teach them. Help them O God ! (alone). The grains are going very quickly There is very little sand in the uppermost glass. Somebody will come** or **me in a moment, perhaps he is at the door now. All creatures that can reason doubt. O that the grass and the clouds could speak to me,and I might be saved, for they know where they are rooted and whither they go. I dare not know the moment the messenger will come for me, I will cover the glass. (He covers it). The Fool is sitting by y{t}he door fiddling with some flowers which he has stuck in his hat, he has begun to blow a dandelion head.)**

W.M. What are you doing ?

FOOL. Wait a moment.) He blows)One, two three.

~~O~~

W.M.What are you doing that for ?

FOOL. I am blowing at the dandelion to find out what hour it is.

W.M. You have heard everything ! That is why you want to find out what time it is. T You are waiting to see them come in through the door to carry me ~~aay~~ away. Fool goes on blowing)

W.M. Out out through the door with you ! I will have no one here

[MS. PB, p. 15; 422–458]

12

when they come. (He seizes the fool by the shoulders and begins to force him out by the door, then suddenly changes his ming mind) No, no, I have something to ask you ! He drags him back into the room. Is there a Heaven ? Is there a Hell ? Is there a Purgatory ?

FOOL. So you ask me now. I thought when you were asking your pupils, I said to myself.if he would ask Teogue the Fool, Teigue could tell him all about it, for Teigue has learned all about it when he has been cutting the nets.

W.M. Tell me ! Tell me!

FOOL. I said, Teigue knows everything. Not even the ~~b~~ owls and the hares that milk the cows have Teigue's wisdom. But Teigue will not speak, he says nothing.

W.M. Tell me, tell me! For under the cover the grains are falling.and and when they are all fallen I shall die; and my soul will be lost if I have not found somebody that believes. Speak, speak!

FOOL (looking wise) No no, I wont tell you what is in my mind, and I ~~w~~ wont tell you what is in my bag. You might steal away my thoughts, I met a a bodach on the road yesterday, and he said Teigue, tel me how many ~~o~~ pennies are in your bag,I will wager three o p ennies that there are not twenty pennies in your bag, let me put in my hand and count them' . But I pulled the strings tighter like this; and when I go to sleep every night I hide the bag where no one knows.

W.M. (Goes towards hourglass as if to uncover it) No,no, I have not the courage. (He kneels) Have pity upon me fool, and tell me !

FOOL. Ah! now that is different. I am not afraid of you now, but I must come near you, somebody in there might hear. what the angel told me.

W.M. O, what did the angel t ll you !

FOOL. Once I w as alone out on the hills, and an angel came by and

MS. PD

Transcriptions, with apparatus criticus *of variants in MSS. PCi, PCii, PF, PGi, and PGii*

[MS. PD; 1–12, 16]

THE HOUR GLAS.S.

A Morality. By W. B. Yeats

W.B.Yeats

A WISE MAN.
A FOOL.
SOME PUPILS.
THE WISE MAN'S WIFE AND TWO CHILDREN.
AN ANGEL

SCENE. A large room with a door at the back and another at the side, opening to an inner room. A desk and chair in the middle. An hour glass on a bracket near the door. A creepy stool near it. Some benches. An Astronomical Globe. A Blackboard. A large ancient map of the world on the wall. Some musical instruments. Floor strewed with rushes. A Wise Man sitting at his desk.

WISE MAN. (Turning over the pages of a book) Ah, this is the passage. "There was a time when men thought that the truth could be found through dreams and visions. They imagined that it was quiet and unchanging like the fixed stars and that the mind had to become quiet and unchanging too, ~~and~~ as it is when sleeping and in trances before it could look on truth". (The FOOL comes in. He is dressed in skins. He stands holding out his hat, but the Wise Man does not see him) But now we have learned that we come to truth—

FOOL. Give me a penny.

WISE MAN. (Goes on reading) By the activity of the mind. This activity is called Dialectic—

FOOL. Give me a penny.

Title ...GLASS. / A MORALITY. BY W. B. YEATS. *unsigned PC* *signed on last page, not cover PF* THE HOUR GLASS / A Morality / By / W. B. YEATS / Copyright 1903 by / W. B. Yeats. All / rights reserved. / *all centered. PG*

Dramatis Personae PUPYLS *overwritten with pencil* I *to* PUPILS *PCii, carbon PCi* ANGEL. *PC* Dramatis Personae:, *no periods after* A WISE MAN *etc., all in middle of page PG*

Scene side opening *PG* astronimical *rev with ink* o *to* astronomical *PC* astronomical *PG* globe. A blackboard. . . . wise man *PC, PG* Some benches . . . desk *del PF* *scene and stage directions underlined throughout PG*

Speaker identifications W.M. *after first speech, all idents in caps PC; full ident in caps throughout, no period when stage direction follows PG*

single quotes throughout PC

1 (turning *PC*

5 ~~and~~] an *PC*

6 *single quote, added in pencil PCii, carbon PCi*

7 wise man *PC*

10 (goes *PC* *stage direction underlined in ink PG*

11 dialectic — ' *PC*

12 Wont you give *PGi*

W.M. (Goes on reading) "and is under the government of the lightest and all but the swiftest of the planets".

FOOL. Wont you give me a penny ?

W.M. What do you want? The words of the wise Saracen will not teach you much.

FOOL. Such a great wise teacher as you are will not refuse a penny to a Fool.

W.M. What do you know about wisdom ?

FOOL. Oh, I know, I know what I have seen

W.M. What is it you have seen?

FOOL. When I went by Kilcluan where the bells used to be ringing at the break of every Sunday and every holiday, I could hear nothing but the people snoring in their houses. When I went by Tubbervanach where they used to be a Station for Confession, the young men were sitting at the cross road playing cards. When I went by Carrigoras where the friars used to be fasting and serving the poor, I saw them drinking wine and obeying their wives. And when I asked what misfortune had brought all these changes, they said it was no misfortune but it was the wisdom they had learned from your teaching.

W.M. Run round to the kitchen, and my wife will give you something to eat.

1–14 *del and rev in ink to*

WISE MAN. (turning over pages of a book) Where is that passage I am to explain to my pupils today? Here it is, & the book says that it was written by a beggar on the walls of Babylon — "There are two living countries, the one visible & the one invisible, & when it is winter with us, it is summer in that country, & when the November winds are up among us, it is lambing time there." I wish that my pupils had asked me to explain any other passage, for this is a hard passage — (The Fool comes in & stands at the door holding out his hat — He has a pair of shears in the other hand) — It sounds to me like foolishness, & yet that cannot be, for the writer of this book where I have found so much knowledge, would not have set it by itself on this page & surrounded it with so many images & so many deep colours & so much fine gilding if it had been foolishness —

Fool — Give me a penny —

Wise Man. (turns to another page) Here he has written 'the learned in old times forgot the visible country' — That I understand, but I have taught my learners better —

~~Fool Give me a penny~~ *PF*

So PG but typed and reads (Turning . . . book). . . . Babylon: . . . passage. . . . hat. . . . hand.) . . . knowledge would . . . been foolishness. . . . penny. . . . page). . . . country." That I understand but . . . better.; *double quotes throughout;* Fool *not underlined and* (turns . . . page) *underlined in ink* *commas del after* us *and colon in ink inserted after* has written *PGii*

21 Oh I *PG* seen. *PC, PG*

23 went] sent *PG*

24 Sunday . . . holiday, *del in ink to* day *PF rev adopted PG*

26 they] there *PC*

26–7 they . . . men *del in ink to* the young men used to be climbing the hill to the blessed well, they *PF; rev adopted PG*

27 cross-roads *PG*

33 *no comma PG*

[MS. PD; 43–74]

FOOL That is foolish advice for a wise man to give.

W.M. Why Fool?

FOOL. What is eaten is gone, I want pennies for my bag. I must buy bacon in the shops and nuts in the market, and strong drinks for the time when the sun is weak. And I want snares to catch the rabbits and the squirrels and the hares, and a pot to cook them in.

W.M. Go away . I have other things to think of now than of giving you pennies.

FOOL. Give me a penny and I will bring you luck . Bresal the Fisherman lets me sleep among the nets in his loft in the winter time because he says I bring him luck: and in the summer time the wild creatures let me sleep near their nests and their holes. It is lucky even to look at me or to touch me, but it is much more lucky to give me a penny, (Holds out his hand) If I wasn't lucky I'd starve.

W.M. (Touching the shears which the FOOL has in his hand together with the hat) What have you got the shears for?

FOOL. I wont tell you. If I told you you would drive them away.

W.M. Who would I drive away ?

FOOL. I wont tell you.

W.M. Not if I give you a penny ?

FOOL. No,

W.M. Not if I give you two pennies?

FOOL You will be very lucky if you give me two pennies, but I wont tell you.

W.M. Three pennies?

FOOL. Four and I will tell you

W.M. Very well, four, But I will not call you Teigue the

---

36 Why, Fool? *comma and question mark inserted in pencil PCii, carbon PCi*

37 gone. *PC, PG*

40 that *inserted in ink after* squirrels *then smudged PCii*

45–6 wintertime . . . luck; *PC* luck; *PG*

49 penny. (holds *PC* penny. . . . hand.) *PG*

50/51 (touching . . . fool *PC* *stage direction del PF, omitted PG*

54 Who] Whom *PG*

57 No. *PC, PG*

60 won't *apostrophe inserted in ink PG*

62 you. *PC, PG*

63 four. *PC, PG*

Fool any longer.

FOOL. Let me come close to you where nobody will hear me. But first you must promise you will not drive them away. (Wise Man nods) Every day men go out dressed in black and spread great black nets over the Hills, great black nets.

W.M. Why do they do that?

FOOL. That they may catch the feet of the angels. But every morning just before the dawn, I go out and cut the nets with my shears, and the angels fly away.

W.M. Ah, now I know that you are Teigue the Fool . You have told me that I am wise, and I have never seen an angel.

FOOL. I have seen plenty of angels.

W.M. Do you bring luck to the angels too?

FOOL. Oh, no, no; no one could do that. But they are always there if one looks about one; they are like the blades of grass, I think I saw one coming after me a little time ago. It was of the colour of red embers, and there was something shining

its

about his head. Glory be to God!

W.M. You a fool say Glory be to God, but before I came the wise men said it. There are your four pennies. Run away now. I must ring the bell for my scholars.

FOOL. Four pennies. That means a great deal of luck. Great teacher, I have brought you plenty of luck! (He goes out shaking the bag).

---

67 man *PC* *ink mark aligns* Man *with left margin PG* nods.) *PG*

68 hills, *PC, PG*

72 shears, *comma then del in pencil PGii*

79 grass. *PC, PG*

79–81 I think . . . God! *del PF and rev in ink on separate sheet to*

W.M — When do you see them?

Fool — When one gets quiet, then something wakes up inside one, something happy & quiet like the stars — not like the seven that move, but like the fixed stars

(He points upward)

Wise Man And what happens then?

Fool — Then all in a minute one smells summer flowers, & tall people go by, happy & laughing, & their clothes are the colour of burning sods —.

Wise Man — Is it long since you have seen them, Teigue the Fool — ?

Fool — Not long, Glory be to God — I saw one coming behind me just now; it was not laughing, but it had clothes the colour of burning sods, & there was something shining about its head —

Rev adopted PG but caps for idents, periods for dashes except stars — not *(dash is in ink), and reads* gets quiet: . . . fixed stars. . . . upward.)*; in last line* colour] color

81 *ink rev not in PC*

82–83 There . . . pennies *moved to before* You *in l. 82, with* Well *inserted in ink in front of* There *PF; rev adopted as* Well, there . . . pennies. *PG* You, a fool, *PG*

85 pennies! *PG*

W.M. Though they call him Teigue the Fool he is not more foolish than everybody used to be, with their dreams and their preachings and their three worlds, but I have over-thrown their three worlds with the seven sciences. (He touches the books with his hands) With Philosophy that was made for the lonely star I have taught them to forget Theology; with Architecture I have hidden

M

the ramparts of their cloudy heaven; and with music, the fierce planets daughter whose hair is always upon fire; and with Grammer that is the moon's daughter, I have shut their ears to the imaginary harpings and speech of the angels; and I have made formations of battle with Arithmetic that have put the hosts of heaven to the rout. But Rhetoric and Dialectic that have been born out of the light star and out of the amorous star, you have been my spearman and my catapult. (He stands at his desk and turns over the pages of the book) "Dialectic is under Mercury for Mercury is the smallest of the planets". Oh! my swift horseman , Oh! my keen darting arguments, it is because of you that I have over-thrown the hosts of foolishness. (An Angel in a dress the colour of embers and carrying a blossoming apple bough in his hand and a gilded halo about his head stands upon the threshold) To-day I

---

89 overthrown *PC*
90 (he *PC*
91 hands.) *PG* philosophy *overwritten with ink* P *to* Philosophy *PC*
92 Theology *PC* Theology; *semicolon in ink PF* Theology; *PG*
93 heaven, . . . music, *PC* Music, *PG* *PF as PD*
94 planets' *PG* Grammer *PF, PG* Grammar *PC*
95 daughter, *comma inserted in ink PC*
98–99 that ~~were made by the light and by the amo~~ have been born *PCii del pencil, carbon PCi*
100 (he *PC*
102 planets.' *PC* *exclamation marks omitted PC* horseman *del to* horsemen *PGii*, horsemen *PC*
100–102 *stage direction and* "Dialectic . . . planets." *del PF, omitted PG*
103 overthrown *PC* over-thrown *dash inserted in ink PG*
104/105 and having a blossoming *PC*
105 threshold.) *PG* Today *PC*
105–123 To-day . . . that dress *del PF and rev in ink to:*

Before I came, men's minds were stuffed with folly about a heaven where birds sang the hours, & about angels that came & stood upon men's thresholds. But I have locked the visions into heaven & turned the key upon them — Well, I must consider this passage about the two countries — My mother used to say something of the kind — She would say that when our bodies sleep our souls awake, & that whatever withers here ripens yonder, & that harvests are ~~snatched~~ snatched from us that they may feed invisible people — But the meaning of the book must be different, for ~~only~~ only fools & women have thoughts like that; their thoughts were never written upon the walls of Babylon — (He sees the angel.) What are you ? Who are you ? I think I saw some that were like you in my dreams when I was a child; — that bright thing — that dress *Rev adopted PG but with periods for dashes except* child — *(dash reinforced in ink),* embers — But *(dash reinforced in ink) and* thing, that. men's] mens' *PGi* mens' *rev in ink to* men's *PGii*

---

92 The semi-colon following "Theology" in PD was inserted in ink.

am going to expound this great Saracen, and I must refute that passage in Ter tullian we spoke of yesterday. (He takes down another book) I cannot find it — Ah! Here it is — I will give them wholesome bread to eat that will be better than dreams and visions. I have locked the visions into heaven; I have turned the key upon them. But before I came men's hearts and minds and mouths were stuffed with folly. One would look up and tell another that the stars were holes in the floor of heaven, while others thought that Heaven waited for them somewhere with gates made out of precious stones, and there were some that dreamt of angels who walked about among golden and silver apple trees where the birds sang the hours; and sometimes the angels would come down and stand upon their thresholds, but I have overturned all that. I have over-thrown the hosts of foolishness, ~~an~~ my name shall be remem- always but they shall be forgotten. (He sees the angel) What are you? Who are you? I think I saw some that were like you in my dreams when I was a child,— that bright thing, that dress that is the colour of embers, but I have done with dreams, I have done with dreams.

ANGEL. I am the Angel of the Most High God .

W.M. Why have you come to me?

ANGEL. I have brought you a message.

W.M. What message have you got for me?

ANGEL. You will die within the hour. You will die when the last grains have fallen through this glass, (He turns the hour glass)

W.M. My time to die has not come. I have my pupils, I have a young wife and children that I cannot leave, why must I die?

ANGEL. You must die because no souls have passed over the threshold of Heaven since you came into this country. The threshold is grassy and the gates are rusty and the angels that keep watch there are lonely.

W.M. Where will death bring me to?

ANGEL. The doors of Heaven will not open to you, for you have denied the existence of Heaven ; and the doors of Purgatory

---

106 Saracen, but *PC*
107 Ter tullian *closed up in ink PD*
108 *no paren PC* — Ah here it is — *PC*
119 overthrown *PC* remembered *PC, PG*
122 *dash inserted in ink PC*
130 glass. PG hourglass). *PC* hour glass.) *PGi* hour-glass.) *hyphen inserted in ink PGii*
131 pupils. *PG*
132 leave. Why *PC, PG*

will not open to you for you have denied the existence of Purgatory.

W.M. But I have also denied the existence of Hell.

ANGEL. Hell is the place of those who deny.

W.M. (Kneels) I have indeed denied everything, and have taught others to deny. I have believed in nothing but what my senses told me. But, Oh, beautiful Angel, forgive me, forgive me!

ANGEL. You should have asked forgiveness long ago.

W.M. Had I seen your face as I see it now Oh, beautiful Angel, I would have believed, I would have asked forgiveness. Maybe you do not know how easy it is to doubt. Storm, death, the grass rotting , many sicknesses, those are the messengers that come to me. Oh, why are you silent! You carry the pardon of the Most High, give them to me! I would kiss your hands if I were not afraid. No, no, the hem of your dress.

ANGEL. You let go undying hands too long ago to take hold of them now .

W.M. You cannot understand. You live in that country people only see in their dreams. You live in a country that we can only dream about. Maybe it is as hard for you to understand why we disbelieve as it is for us to believe. Oh! what have I said! You know everything! Give me time to undo what I have done. Give me a year—a month—a day—an hour! Give me to this hours end that I may undo what I have done!

ANGEL. You cannot undo what you have done. Yet I have this power with my message. If you can find one that believes before the hour's end, you shall come to Heaven after the years of Purgatory. For from one fi {er / rey} seed, watched over by those that

---

140 to you, *comma inserted in ink PGii*

143 (kneels) *PC* (Kneels). *PG* *no comma PG*

144–145 taught *del to* told *PC* But Oh Beautiful *PC* Oh *PG*

148 now, *PG* *no comma after* Oh *PC, PG*

149–152, 157 *PCii gives alternative reading on a separate sheet as follows:*

W.M. Have pity upon me; you are not weak, you do not understand our weakness; you have never wandered here where beauty turns to ugliness and bread to a stone and sweetness in withered by the wind. You live, say, where there is neither frost nor cold where there is neither too great heat nor frost nor snow and where

152 came *PG* to men. Oh *PC* pardons *PC*

153 High; *PG*

154 no. no. the *PC*

160 Oh, *PC*

162 *dashes inserted in ink PG* hour's end *PG*

167 Purgatory. ~~But now~~ For from *PC* *PF as PD*

sent me, the harvest can come again to heap the golden threshing floor. But now farewell, for I am weary of the weight of time.

W.M. Blessed be the Father, blessed be the Son, blessed be the Spirit, blessed be the Messenger T} t hey have sent!

ANGEL. (At the door and pointing at the hour-glass) In a little while the uppermost glass will be empty. (goes out)
W.M. Everything will be well with me, I will call my pupils, they only say they doubt. (Pulls the bell) They will be here in a moment, I hear their feet outside on the path. They want to please me, they pretend that they disbelieve. Belief is too old to be overcome all in a minute. Besides I can prove what I once disproved. (Another pull at the bell). They are coming now, I will go to my desk, I will speak quietly as if nothing had happened. (He stands at the desk with a fixed look in his eyes)
(Enter pupils and the FOOL).

FOOL. Leave me alone. Leave me alone. Who is that pulling at my cloak. King's son, do not pull at my cloak.

A YOUNG MAN. Did your friends the angels give you that cloak? Why dont they give you a better cloak.

FOOL. Let go my coat and give me pennies.

A YOUNG MAN. Let go his cloak, it is coming to pieces. What do you want pennies for with that great bag at your waist?

---

169 farewell. I *rev with pencil insertion to* farewell for I *PCii, carbon PCi*
171 spirit, *comma inserted in ink PC* they *overtyped to* They *PC, PF*
172 (at . . . hourglass) *PC* hour-glass). *PG*
173 out). *PC* (Goes out.) *PG*
174 me. *PC, PG* pupils. *PC* pupils; *PG*
175 (pulls *PC* bell.) *PG* *stage direction underlined in ink PG*
176 moment. *PG* want] wanted *PC*
177 me; *PG*
179 bell.) *PG*
180 *periods for commas PG*
181 eyes. (Enter . . . Fool). *PC* 3 *inserted in ink after* Enter *PCii* eyes.) Enter Pupils . . . FOOL. *PG*
182 alone. leave *PC*
183 cloak . . . cloak *del in ink* to bag . . . bag *PF* my bag? . . . my bag. *PG*
184 1 *inserted in ink before* A *PCii then del in pencil* *all inserted in ink PFadd*
185 cloak . . . give you a better cloak *del in ink to* bag . . . fill your bag for you? *PF* bag? . . . they fill your bag for you? *PG, so PFadd (in ink)*
186 Let . . . and *del PF* give me pennies. *rev in ink to* Give me pennies, give me some pennies — *PF* FOOL. Give me pennies, give me some pennies. *PG, so PFadd (in ink)*
187 2 *inserted in ink before* A *PCii then del in pencil*
188 waist.? *PC*

FOOL. I want to buy bacon in the shops and nuts in the market, and strong drink for the time the sun is weak, and snares to catch rabbits and the squirrels that steal the nuts, and hares, and a great pot to cook them in.

A YOUNG MAN. Why dont your friends tell you where buried treasures are?

ANOTHER. Why dont they make you dream about treasures. If one dreams three times there is always treasure.

FOOL. (Holding out his hat). Give me pennies. Give me pennies!

(They throw pennies into his hat. He is standing close to the door that he may hold out his hat to each new comer.)

A YOUNG MAN. Master, will you have Teigue the Fool for a scholar?

ANOTHER. Teigue the Fool will not be a scholar, Teigue the Fool will teach. Master, will you become a pupil? What will you teach us Teigue?

W.M. Be silent all. (He has been standing silent looking away). Stand still in your places, for there is something I would have you tell me.

(A moments pause. They all stand round in their places. Teigue still stays at the door).

W.M. Is there any one amongst you who believes in God? In Heaven? Or in Purgatory? Or in Hell?

ALL THE YOUNG MEN. No one Master! no one!

---

190 market and *PG*

191 nuts, *comma inserted in ink PCii*

193 3 *inserted in ink before* A *PCii then del in pencil*   don't *apostrophe inserted in ink PG*

195 1 *inserted in ink before* ANOTHER *PCii then del in pencil*   don't *apostrophe inserted in ink PG*   treasures? *PG* treasures? *question mark inserted in ink PFadd*

197 FOOL. *period del PG*   (holding . . . pennies. give me *PC*

198 pennies.! *PC*

198/199 newcomer.) *PC* new-comer. *PG* new-comer.) *hyphen added in ink PFadd*   *no parens PG*

199 2 *inserted in ink before* A *PCii then del in pencil*

199–203 *del PF, rev in ink to:*

A Young Man — Master, will you have Teigue the Fool for a scholar ?

Another Young Man — Teigue, will you give us your pennies if we teach you lessons ? No, he goes to school for nothing on the mountains — Tell us what you learn on the mountains, Teigue — *Rev adopted PFadd and PG (typed) but with periods for dashes*   Teigue? *(PFadd)*

201 3 *inserted in ink before* ANOTHER *PCii then del in pencil*

205 away.) *PG*   Sit *del to* Stand *PC*

206/207 moment's pause, *PC, PG, PFadd (with apostrophe added in ink)*   still stands . . . door. *no parens PG*

207 If *del in ink to* Is *PFadd*   anyone *PC*

209 Master, no *PC*   one, Master! No *PG* one, Master! no *PFadd, comma added in ink*

[MS. PD; 250–283]

W.M. I knew you would all say that; but do not be afraid, I will not be angry. Tell me the truth. Do you not believe?

A YOUNG MAN. We once did, but you have taught us to know better.

W.M. Oh, teaching, teaching does not go very deep. The heart remains unchanged under it all. You believe just as you always did, and you are afraid to tell me.

A YOUNG MAN. No, no Master.

W.M. If you tell me that you believe I shall be glad and not angry.

A YOUNG MAN. (To his neighbour) He wants somebody to dispute with.

HIS NEIGHBOUR. I knew that from the beginning.

W.M. If there is one amongst you that believes he will be my best friend. Surely there is one amongst you (They are all silent)

W.M. Surely what you learned at your mother's knees has not been so soon forgotten.

A YOUNG MAN. Master, till you came, no teacher in this land was able to get rid of foolishness and ignorance. But everyone has listened to you, every one has learned the truth. You have had your last disputation.

ANOTHER. What a fool you made of that monk in the market place! He had not a word to say.

W.M. (Comes from his desk, and stands among them in the middle of the room). Pupils, dear friends I have deceived you all this time. It was I myself who was ignorant. There is a God. There is a Heaven. There is fire that passes and there is fire

---

210 afraid. *PG*

212 1 *inserted in ink before* A YOUNG *PCii then del in pencil*

214 teaching,] *comma added in ink PF*

215 You] We *del to* You *PC*

217 2 *inserted in ink before* A YOUNG *PCii then del in pencil* No, no, *PG*

220 2 *inserted in ink before* A YOUNG *then rev to* 3 *PCii then del in pencil* neighbor). *PG*

222 1 *inserted in ink before* HIS *PCii then del in pencil* NEIGHBOR. *PG* *PF inserts in ink after l. 222:* A Young Man —That is not the subject for today; you were going to talk about the words the beggar wrote upon the walls of Babylon — *Rev adopted PG, but with periods for dashes*

223 believes, *PG*

224 you. . . . silent.) *PC, PG*

227 2 *inserted in ink before* A YOUNG *PCii then del in pencil*

229 everyone . . . everyone *PC, PG*

231 3 *inserted in ink before* ANOTHER. *PCii then del in pencil*

232 place? *PC*

232/233 WISE MAN. *period del in ink PG* *no comma PC, PG*

233 friends, *PC, PG*

---

214 The comma after the first "teaching" was added in ink.

that lasts for ever.

(Teigue through all this is sitting on a stool by the door reckoning on his fingers what he will buy with his money).

A YOUNG MAN. (To another). He will not be satisfied till we dispute with him. (To the WISE MAN) Prove it, Master. Have you seen them?

W.M. (In a low solemn voice) Just now, before you came in, someone came to the door, and when I looked up I saw an angel standing there.

A YOUNG MAN. You were in a dream. Anybody can see an angel in his dreams.

W.M. Oh, my God! It was not a dream! I was awake, waking as I am now. I tell you I was awake as I am now.

A YOUNG MAN. Some dream when they are awake, but they are the crazy and who would believe what they say? Forgive me Master, but that is what you taught me to say. That is what you said to the monk when he spoke of the visions of the saints and the martyrs.

ANOTHER YOUNG MAN. You see how well we remember your teaching.

W.M. Out, out from my sight! I want a believer, a believer, that I may save my soul from the fire, and you answer me with argument. Out with you or I will beat you with my stick! (The young men laugh)

A YOUNG MAN. How well he plays at faith! He is like the monk when he had nothing more to say.

W.M. Out, out, or I will lay this stick about your shoulders. Out with you though you are a King's son. (They begin to hurry out)

236/237 *no parens PG*

237 1 *inserted in ink before* A YOUNG *PCii then del in pencil* another.) *PC* not *omitted then inserted in ink after* will *PGi, erroneously after* be *PGii*

238 wise man) *PC*

240 W.M. In *PC* voice). *PG*

241 *comma del PG*

243 2 *inserted in ink before* A YOUNG *PCii then del in pencil*

247 2 *inserted in ink before* A YOUNG *then rev to* 3 *PCii then del in pencil*

248 say. *period rev in ink to* ? *PC* me, *PG*

252 1 *added in ink before* ANOTHER *then del in pencil PCii*

253 teaching. You *(typing error?) PC*

254–256 I want . . . argument *del PF and replaced in ink on a separate sheet with*: I want someone with belief, I must find that grain the angel spoke of before I die — I tell you I must find it, & you answer me with arguments — *rev adopted PG (typed) but with periods for dashes and reads* some one . . . belief. . . . Angel . . . it and

256/257 laugh.) *PC, PG*

257 2 *(in ink then del in pencil) PCii* W. *(del in pencil)* A YOUNG *PCii, carbon PCi*

259 out or *PC*

260 with you, . . . out.) *PG* kings *PC*

[MS. PD; 312–335]

A YOUNG MAN. Come, come, he wants us to find someone who will dispute with him. (All go out)

W.M. (Alone .he goes to the door at the side) I will call my wife, she will believe; women always believe. (He opens the door and calls) Bridget! Bridget! (Bridget comes in wearing her apron, her sleeves turned up from her floury arms)

W.M. Bridget, tell me the truth; do not say what you think will please me. Do you sometimes say your prayers?

BRIDGET. Prayers, no, you taught me to leave them off long ago. At first I was sorry, but I am glad now for I am sleepy in the evenings.

W.M. But do you not believe in God?

BRIDGET. Oh, a good wife only believes what her husband tells her.

W.M. But sometimes when you are alone, when I am in the school and the children asleep, do you not think about the saints, about the things you used to believe in? What do you think of when you are alone?

BRIDGET. (Considering) I think about nothing. Sometimes I wonder if the pig is fattening well, or I go out to see if the crows are picking up the chicken's food.

W.M. Oh, what can I do! Is there nobody that believes?

---

261 3 *inserted in ink before* A YOUNG *PCii then del in pencil*

262 out.) *PG*

263 (Alone). He *then second paren del in pencil PCii, carbon PCi* He *PG* the d side) *PC* side). *PGi* side). *rev in ink to* side.) *PGii*

264 wife. She *PG*

265/266 arms.) *PC, PG*

268 ~~Bridget.~~ BRIDGET . . . no. you *PC* Prayers? No, *PG*

271 W%M% *PC*

278 (considering) *PC* (Considering). *underlined in ink PG*

280 chickens *PC*

281–286 *PCii inserts in ink after* believes?:

I must go out & find somebody, I have no time to talk (goes towards door — but no no, (pointing to the hour glass) I cannot go away from that — I must battle the grains, I must see how fast they go — *PF adds, typed on the verso of previous sheet, evidently to replace ll. 281–286, although they are not canceled:*

WISE MAN O what can I do! Is there nobody who believes! I must go and find somebody, (He goes towards the door but stops with his eyes fixed on the hourglass) I cannot go out, I cannot leave that.

BRIDGET. you want somebody to get up an argument with.

WISE MAN. O look out of the door and tell me if there is anybody [there *inserted in ink*] in the street. I cannot leave this glass, somebody might shake it ! Then the sand would fall more quickly.

BRIDGET. I dont understand what you are saying. (Looks out) There is a great crowd of people talking to your pupils. *Rev adopted PG but reads* Oh, . . . somebody! . . . hour-glass.) . . . that! . . . You . . . glass; . . . I don't . . . out.) *PFadd. follows PF unthinkingly, incorporating Slip A without realizing that its insertion requires the omission of the lines it revises in PF. WBY canceled* O, . . . believes! *wrote* stet, *then canceled it and the subsequent lines from PF that should have been omitted.*

BRIDGET. You want somebody to get up an argument with?

W.M. Look out at the door and tell me if there is anybody there in the street.

BRIDGET. There is a great crowd of people talking to your pupils.

W.M. Oh, run out Bridget and see if they have found somebody that believes!

BRIDGET. (Wiping her arms in her apron and pulling down her sleeves) Its a hard thing to be married to a man of learning that must be always having arguments. (Goes out, and shouts through the kitchen door) If you two children put your fingers on the dough, I'll give you !—

W.M. (Kneels down. Begins a Latin prayer, breaks off). I have forgotten it all. It is thirty years since I have said a prayer. I must pray in the common tongue like a clown begging in the market, like Teigue the Fool! (He prays) Help me Father, Son and Spirit!

(Bridget enters followed by the FOOL who is holding out his hat to her)

FOOL. Give me something , give me a penny to buy bacon in the winter and nuts in the market and strong drink for the time when the sun grows weak.

BRIDGET. I have no pennies. (To the WISE MAN) Your pupils cannot find anybody to argue with you. There is nobody in the whole country who had enough belief to fill a pipe with since you put down the monk. Cant you be quiet now and not always be wanting to have arguments. It must be terrible to have a mind

---

283–284 (He stands looking. *added in ink after* street. *Then both lines del though cancellation misses ink addition PCii*

285 BRIDGET. *del in ink to* W.M. *PC* your *del and rev in ink to* my *PC*

287 W.M. *intended cancellation of ident misses it PCii* Oh run *PC* out, Bridget, *PG*

289 sleeves). *PG* It's *apostrophe inserted in ink PGii*

290 out and *PG*

291–292 *PF cancels from* If *and inserts in ink:*

Dont be meddling with the bread children while I'm out

Rev adopted PG but Don't . . . bread, children, . . . out.

292 *comma and dash inserted in ink PC*

293–294 Begins . . . off), *del and replaced in ink with*) Salvum me fac, deus — Salvum — Salvum — *PF* down) Salvum me fac, Deus — salvum — salvum . . . . I have *dashes reinforced in ink PG* off.) *PC*

296 me, *PG* Father *PC*

297/298 Fool . . . ~~for~~ to her) *PC* *no parens PG* her. *PG*

298 FOOL Give *PC* something; *PG*

301 wise man) *PC*

303 who has *PC*

304 Can't *PG*

305 arguments? *PG*

like that!

W.M. I am lost! I am lost!

BRIDGET Leave me alone now, I have to make the bread for you and the children.

W.M. Out of this woman, out of this I say (BRIDGET goes through kitchen door) Will nobody find a way to help me! But she spoke of my children, I had forgotten them, they will believe. It is only those who have reason that doubt, the young are full of faith. Bridget, Bridget, send my children to me!

BRIDGET. (Inside) Your father wants you, run to him now. (The two children come in, they stand together a little way from the threshold of the kitchen door, looking timidly at their father)

W.M. Children, what do you believe? Is there a Heaven? Is there a Hell, Is there a Purgatory?

First **~~ONE~~ CHILD. We haven't forgotten, father.**

Second **~~THE OTHER~~ CHILD. Oh, no father. (~~They both speak together as if in school~~) There is no Heaven , there is no Hell: there is**

First Child —

nothing we cannot see.^**Foolish people used to think that there were, but you are very learned and you have taught us better.**

W.M. You are just as bad as the others! just as bad as the others. Out of the room with you, out of the room! (The children begin to cry and run away) Go away, go away, I will teach you better—no, I will never teach you again, go to your mother, no, she will not be able to teach them...help them Oh God! (Alone) The

---

306 that. *PG*

307 lost. I *period overwritten in ink to* ! *PG*

308 now; *PG*

309 and] are *PC*

310 W.M. Out of this woman! Out *del to* ~~W.M~~. Out of this, woman, out *PC* this, . . . say! *PG* (Bridget *PC*

311 door.) *PG*

312 children. . . . them. They *PG*

313 doubt; *PG*

315–316 (inside) *PC* threshold] door *del in pencil to* threshold *PCii, carbon PCi* (Inside). . . . The . . . father. *PG* come in, they *overwritten in ink to* come in. They *PG*

317 Hell? *PC, PG*

318 First *omitted, no del PC* ONE *del in ink to* 1st *PF* FIRST CHILD. *PG* havnt *PC*

319 Second *omitted PC* *no del PC, PF* THE OTHER CHILD. Oh no, *PC, PG*

319–320 *stage direction not del PC, PF, PG*

320 Heaven; *PG* Hell; *PC, PG*

321 First Child — *omitted PC* 1st child *inserted in ink before* Foolish *PF* FIRST CHILD. Foolish *PG*

325 away.) *PG* away, *comma rev in ink to period PGii*

326 no I *PC* *dash reinforced in ink PG* No, . . . again. Go . . . mother; *PG*

327 Help *PC* (alone) *del in pencil PCii, registers as underline PCi* teach them. . . . them, *PG*

grains are going very quickly . There is very little sand in the uppermost glass. Somebody will come for me in a moment, perhaps he is at the door now! All creatures that have reason doubt. Oh, that the grass and the clouds would speak to me and I might be saved, for they know where they are rooted and whither they go. I dare not know the moment the messenger will come for me, I will cover the glass. (He covers it and brings it to the desk and The Fool is sitting by the door fiddling with some flowers which he has stuck in his hat. He has begun to blow a dandelion head).

W.M. What are you doing?

FOOL. Wait a moment. (He blows) four, five six.

W.M. What are you doing that for?

FOOL. I am blowing at the dandelion to find out what time it is.

W.M. You have heard everything! That is why you want to find out what hour it is! You are waiting to see them coming through the door to carry me away. (FOOL goes on blowing)

W.M. Out through the door with you! I will have no one here when they come. (He seizes the FOOL by the shoulders, and begins to force him out through the door, then suddenly changes his mind) No, I have something to ask you! (He drags him back into the room) Is there a Heaven? Is there a Hell ? Is there a Purgatory?

FOOL. So you ask me now. I thought when you were asking your pupils, I said to myself, if he would ask Teigue the Fool, Teigue could tell him all about it, for Teigue has learned all about it when he has been cutting the nets.

W.M. Tell me! Tell me!

---

328 quickly ~~now~~. *PCii del in pencil, carbon PCi*

331 *no comma PC*

331–333 Oh, . . . go. *del in PF and replaced in ink on additional slip of paper by*: O that the grass & the planets could speak! Somebody has said that they would wither if they doubted — O speak to me, O grass blades, O fingers of God's certainty, speak to me — You are millions & you will not speak — *Rev adopted PG (typed) but periods for dashes*

333 me. *PG*

334/335 brings it to the desk & *inserted in ink after* He *PC* *PF as PD* covers it) The Fool *paren del in pencil PCii, carbon PCi*

336 four] one, two three. four, *del in pencil to* four, *PCii, carbon PCi* Four, five, *PG*

341 coming] come in *PC*

342 (Fool *PC* blowing.) *PG*

344/345 Fool . . . shoulders and *PC* mind.) *PG*

345 room.) *PG*

348 pupils, *comma inserted in pencil PCii, carbon PCi*

349 learned all] learned about *then* all *inserted (typed) after* learned *PC*

FOOL. I said, Teigue knows everything. Not even the owls and the hares that milk the cows have Teigue's wisdom. But Teigue will not speak he says nothing.

W.M. Tell me, Tell me. For under the cover the grains are falling and when they are all fallen I shall die; and my soul will be lost if I have not found somebody that believes! Speak, speak!

FOOL. (Looking wise) No, no, I wont tell you what is in my mind, and I wont tell you what is in my bag. You might steal away my thoughts. I met a bodach on the road yesterday, and he said, Teigue, tell me how many pennies are in your bag, I will wager three pennies that there are not twenty pennies in your bag; let me put in my hand and count them. But I pulled the strings tighter, like this; and when I go to sleep every night I hide the bag where no one knows.

W.M. (Goes towards the hour glass as if to uncover it) No, no, I have not the courage! (He kneels) Have pity upon me Fool and tell me!

FOOL. Ah! Now that is different. I am not afraid of you now. But I must come near you, somebody in there might hear what the angel said.

W.M. Oh, what did the angel tell you?

FOOL. Once I was alone on the hills and an angel came by and he said "Teigue the Fool, do not forget the Three Fires; The Fire that punishes, the Fire that purifies, and the Fire wherein the soul rejoices for ever!

W.M. He believes! I am saved! Help me, the sand has run out, I am dying...(FOOL helps him to his chair) I am going from

---

353 Teigues *rev in ink to* Teigue's *PC*
354 speak; *PG*
355 me, tell *PC* me! For *PG*
359 wise). . . . won't *PG*
360 won't *PG*
362 "Teigue, *PG*
364 them." *PG*
367 MAN. *period then del* . . . it). *PG* (goes towards hourglass *PC* hour-glass *hyphen inserted in ink PGii*
368 *no comma PC* kneels.) . . . me, Fool, *PG*
370 Ah now *PC*
373 you! *PC*
375 Fires; the *PC, PG*
377 forever!" *PG*
378 me. The *PG*
379 out. . . . chair.) *PG* Fool *PC*

[MS. PD; 486–500]

380 **the country of the seven wandering wandering stars, and I am**
381 **going to the country of the fixed stars! Ring the bell (FOOL rings**
382 **the bell) Are they coming? Ah! Now I hear their feet... I will**
383 **pray.. I am too weak to pray... Pray Fool, that they may be given**
384 **a sign and save their souls alive. Your prayers are better than**
385 **mine. (FOOL bows his head. WISE MAN'S head sinks on his arm**
on the books. PUPILS enter).
386 **A YOUNG MAN. Look at the bell-ringer!**
387 **ANOTHER. He has turned teacher, I told you the Fool would**
388 **be our teacher!**
389 **ANOTHER. No wonder the Master has had dreams, see he**
390 **is asleep now. (He goes over and touches him) Oh, he is dead!**
391 **FOOL. Do not stir! He asked for a sign that you might be**
392 **saved. (All are silent for a moment)..Look at the butterfly!)**
393 **A YOUNG MAN. It is his soul! (They all kneel. The butterfly**
goes up. The FOOL points upward)

---

380 seven wandering stars, *PG* *no comma PC*

381 bell. *PG* (Fool *PC*

382 bell.) *PG* Ah now *PC*

382–383 I will . . . to pray *del PF and rev in ink on separate slip of paper to*: I will speak to them, I understand it all now, one sinks in on God, we do not see the truth, God sees the truth in us — I cannot speak, I am too weak — Tell them Fool that when the life & the mind are broken the truth comes through them like the peas through a broken peascod — But no, I will pray — yet I cannot pray —

382–385 *PG reads:* I will speak to them. I understand it all now. One sinks in on God; we do not see the truth; God sees the truth in us. I cannot speak, I am too weak. Tell them, Fool, that when the life and the mind are broken the truth comes through them like peas through a broken peascod. But no, I will pray — Yet I cannot pray. Pray, Fool, that they may be given a sign and save their souls alive. Your prayers are better than mine. *dash in ink,parens round stage direction on ll. 385–386 omitted*

383 *no comma PC*

385/386 'Fool . . . Wise Man's . . . Pupils *PC*

386 2 *inserted in ink before* A YOUNG *PF, so then del PCii* bellringer! *PC* fool turned *inserted in ink before* bell-ringer! *PF rev adopted PG*

387–8 3 *inserted in ink before* ANOTHER *PF, so then del PCii* He . . . teacher!, *del in ink to* What have you called us in for Teigue, what are you going to tell us? *PF* ANOTHER. What have you called us in for, Teigue? What are you going to tell us? *PG*

389 1 *inserted in ink before* ANOTHER *PF, so then del PCii* the Master *del in ink to* he *PF* wonder he has had dreams. See *PG*

390 fast *inserted in ink before* asleep *PF* is fast asleep . . . him.) *PG* 'He goes *PC*

392 *opening paren only PC* moment.) . . . butterfly! *PG* *PF as PD*

393 1 *inserted in ink before* A YOUNG *PF, so then del PCii* Fool *PC* upwards) *del to* upward) *PC* upward.) CURTAIN *PG*

---

392 The parenthesis after "moment" was added, and the parenthesis after "butterfly!" canceled, in ink.

North American Review (1903)

Transcriptions, with apparatus criticus *of variants in MSS. PE, PH, PI, PJ, PK, PL, PM, PN, PO (i, ii, and iii), PP, PR, and PS*

[*North American Review*]

THE HOUR-GLASS.

A MORALITY.

BY W. B. YEATS.

DRAMATIS PERSONAE:
A WISE MAN. SOME PUPILS.
A FOOL. AN ANGEL.
THE WISE MAN'S WIFE AND TWO CHILDREN.

SCENE.

A large room with a door at the back and another at the side opening to an inner room. A desk and a chair in the middle. An hour-glass on a bracket near the door. A creepy stool near it. Some benches. An astronomical globe. A blackboard. A large ancient map of the world on the wall. Some musical instruments. Floor strewed with rushes. A wise man sitting at his desk.

Wise Man (turning over the pages of a book). **Where is that passage I am to explain to my pupils to-day? Here it is, and the book says that it was written by a beggar on the walls of Babylon:**

---

title "THE HOURGLASS" *PE* THE HOUR-GLASS: A MORALITY. *PK, PL, PM, PN, PO, PP, so PI, PJ but on two lines, and lack colon and period. PR deletes colon* By W. B. Yeats *PE omitted PI, PJ, PK, PL, PM, PN, PO, PP, PR, replaced with signature PH*

dramatis personae DRAMATIS PERSONAE *PJ, so PI but* (Q[uer]y. Persons/See p. 2) *omitted PE, PM, PN, PO, PP replaced by* PERSONS IN THE PLAY *PR no periods after characters PI, PJ periods after* A WISE MAN, A FOOL & AN ANGEL, *then del ink PR Cancelled note reads:* Type old arrangement as in first two plays. *then del and* stet *written beside list PR*

scene Scene. . . . side (R) *(ink)* . . . and chair . . . Astronomical Globe *PE* An astronomical . . . rushes. *del PI, omitted PJ* globe perhaps. Perhaps a large ancient . . . wall or some . . . Floor may be strewed *PR* A Wise *del in ink to* The Wise *PI* WISE MAN *PE, PR* Wise Man *PK, PL, PM, PN, PO, so PP but marked caps*

character idents in caps, indented, not abbreviated PI, PJ, PR in caps with periods after the names sometimes omitted PE WISE MAN *is one word for his first two speeches but reverts to two words thereafter PE* Man *usually abbreviated as* M. *PM, PN, PO, PP*

stage directions in square brackets, italicised PI, PJ, PK, PL, PM, PN, PO, PP, PR closing bracket omitted where the end of the stage direction coincides with the end of a line PK, PL, PM, PN, PO, PP, PR underlined up to l. 399 PE character idents in caps throughout unless otherwise noted PE, PI, PJ, PK, PL, PR in Roman, not caps PM, PN, PO, PP

single quotes throughout PR

1–9 (turning . . . hand.] (Turning . . . book). Ah, this is the passage. "There was a time when men thought that the truth could be found through dreams and visions. They imagined that it was quiet and unchanging like the fixed stars and that the mind had to become quiet and unchanging too, as it is when sleeping and in trances before it could look on truth." (The FOOL comes in. LD *(ink)* He is dressed in skins. He stands holding out his hat but the WISEMAN does not see him). *PE* (Turning *PK, PL, PM, PN, PO, PP*

"There are two living countries, the one visible and the one invisible; and when it is winter with us it is summer in that country, and when the November winds are up among us it is lambing-time there." I wish that my pupils had asked me to explain any other passage, for this is a hard passage. (*The Fool comes in and stands at the door holding out his hat. He has a pair of shears in the other hand.)* It sounds to me like foolishness; and yet that cannot be, for the writer of this book, where I have found so much knowledge, would not have set it by itself on this page, and surrounded it with so many images and so many deep colors and so much fine gilding, if it had been foolishness.

***Fool.* Give me a penny.**

***Wise Man (turns to another page).* Here he has written: "The learned in old times forgot the visible country." That I understand, but I have taught my learners better.**

***Fool.* Won't you give me a penny?**

***Wise Man.* What do you want? The words of the wise Saracen will not teach you much.**

***Fool.* Such a great wise teacher as you are will not refuse a penny to a Fool.**

***Wise Man.* What do you know about wisdom?**

***Fool.* Oh, I know! I know what I have seen.**

***Wise Man.* What is it you have seen?**

***Fool.* When I went by Kilcluan where the bells used to be ringing at the break of every day, I could hear nothing but the peo-**

---

5 us, *comma del PI*

5–6 country; *PI, PJ* us, *comma del PI*

8 *PM, PN, PO, PP, PR omit* for this is a hard passage FOOL *PE, PI, PK, PL, PM, PN, PO, PP, PR*

8/9 door, *PI, PJ*

9–13 *replaced by* But now we have learned that we come to truth. . . . *dots in text PE*

10 be *underlined in pencil PK*

13 colours *PI, PJ, PK, PL, PM, PO, PP, PR*

14 At door *added in pencil after* penny. *PE*

15 (Turns . . . page.) *PK, PL, PM, PN, PO, PP*

15–17 WISEMAN (goes on reading) By the activity of the mind. This activity is called Dialectic. . . . *(sic)*
FOOL Give me a penny.
WISE MAN (Goes on reading) "and is under the government of the lightest and all but the swiftest of the planets." *PE*

17 my *underlined in pencil PK*

18 FOOL Wont *PE*

19 Saracen] Sa *and* ce *underlined in pencil PK*

21 a wise *rev in ink to a* great wise *PE*

24 Oh I know, I *PE* Oh, *del to* O, *PR*

26 Down to C *written in pencil above* When I went by *PE* looking down the house *written in pencil above* used to be ringing *PE* Kilcluan, *then comma del PI* Kilcluan, *comma inserted in ink, marginal note reads:* comma as below *with circle round* Carrigoras, *PR*

27 break of every Sunday and every holiday, I *PE*

ple snoring in their houses. When I went by Tubbervanach where the young men used to be climbing the hill to the blessed well, they were sitting at the crossroads playing cards. When I went by Carrigoras where the friars used to be fasting and serving the poor, I saw them drinking wine and obeying their wives. And when I asked what misfortune had brought all these changes, they said it was no misfortune, but it was the wisdom they had learned from your teaching.

***Wise Man.* Run round to the kitchen, and my wife will give you something to eat.**

***Fool.* That is foolish advice for a wise man to give.**

***Wise Man.* Why, Fool?**

***Fool.* What is eaten is gone. I want pennies for my bag. I must buy bacon in the shops, and nuts in the market, and strong drink for the time when the sun is weak. And I want snares to catch the rabbits and the squirrels and the hares, and a pot to cook them in.**

***Wise Man.* Go away. I have other things to think of now than giving you pennies.**

***Fool.* Give me a penny and I will bring you luck. Bresal the Fisherman lets me sleep among the nets in his loft in the winter-time because he says I bring him luck; and in the summer-time the wild creatures let me sleep near their nests and their holes. It is lucky even to look at me or to touch me, but it is much more lucky to give me a penny. *(Holds out his hand.)* If I wasn't lucky, I'd starve.**

***Wise Man.* What have you got the shears for?**

---

28 Tubbervanach, *then comma del PI* Tubbervanach, *comma inserted in ink, marginal note suggesting word be split* [*Tubber-vanach*]*:* hyphen as on p. 5? *WBY inserts hyphen PR*

29 the young men] they *overwritten in ink to* there *PE* climbing . . . well,] a Station for Confession, *PE*

30 they] the young men *PE* cross road *PE* cross-roads *PM, PN, PO, PP, PR*

31 Carrigoras, *PK, PL, PM, PN, PO, PP so PI but comma del, so PR but comma circled*

34 turns to Wise Man *written in pencil above* they said it was no *PE* *no comma PE*

36 Run *underlined PK*

39 *no comma PE*

40 eaten, *then comma del PI*

41 shops and *PE*

42 drinks *PE*

46 of giving *PE*

47–48 Bresal . . . sleep] The fishermen give me leave to sleep *PR* his loft] their lofts *PR*

48–49 winter time *PE*

49 winter-time, *then comma del PI* he says . . . him] they say . . . them *PR* summer time *PE*

51 it is lucky *PE*

53 *no comma PE*

54 MAN (Touching the sheares which the fool has in his hand together with the hat) What *PE*

Fool. I won't tell you. If I told you, you would drive them away.

Wise Man. Whom would I drive away?

Fool. I won't tell you.

Wise Man. Not if I give you a penny?

Fool. No.

Wise Man. Not if I give you two pennies?

Fool. You will be very lucky if you give me two pennies, but I won't tell you.

Wise Man. Three pennies?

Fool. Four, and I will tell you!

Wise Man. Very well, four. But I will not call you Teigue the Fool any longer.

Fool. Let me come close to you where nobody will hear me. But first you must promise you will not drive them away. *(Wise Man nods.)* Every day men go out dressed in black and spread great black nets over the hills, great black nets.

Wise Man. Why do they do that?

Fool. That they may catch the feet of the angels. But every morning, just before the dawn, I go out and cut the nets with my shears, and the angels fly away.

Wise Man. Ah, now I know that you are Teigue the Fool. You have told me that I am wise, and I have never seen an angel.

Fool. I have seen plenty of angels.

Wise Man. Do you bring luck to the angels too?

Fool. Oh, no, no! No one could do that. But they are always there if one looks about one; they are like the blades of grass.

Wise Man. When do you see them?

Fool. When one gets quiet; then something wakes up inside one, something happy and quiet like the stars—not like the seven that move, but like the fixed stars. *(He points upward.)*

55, 58, 63 wont *PE*
57 Whom] Who *PE*
63 you! *PM, PP, PR*
65 *no comma PE* you. *PE*
66 Teigue *circled, marginal note in ink reads:* Teig as in Countess Cathleen? *del in ink by WBY PR*
68 nobody will hear *underlined in pencil PK*
69 *no period PE*
70 nods *underlined in pencil, no period PE*
71 Hills, *PE*
74 morning just *PE*
76 *marginal note in ink reads:* Teig? *del in ink by WBY PR* now I know *underlined in pencil PK*
79 (sarcastic) *added in pencil after* too? *PE*
80 Oh no, no. *PE* Oh, *del to* O, *PR*
82–91 *omitted PE*
83 quiet, *PK, PL, PM, PN, PO, PP, PR*
85 *stage direction omitted PR*

Wise Man. And what happens then?

Fool. Then all in a minute one smells summer flowers, and tall people go by, happy and laughing, and their clothes are the color of burning sods.

Wise Man. Is it long since you have seen them, Teigue the Fool?

Fool. Not long, glory be to God! I saw one coming behind me just now. It was not laughing, but it had clothes the color of burning sods, and there was something shining about its head.

Wise Man. Well, there are your four pennies. You, a fool, say "glory be to God," but before I came the wise men said it. Run away now. I must ring the bell for my scholars.

Fool. Four pennies! That means a great deal of luck. Great teacher, I have brought you plenty of luck! _(He goes out shaking the bag.)_

Wise Man. Though they call him Teigue the Fool, he is not more foolish than everybody used to be, with their dreams and their preachings and their three worlds; but I have overthrown their three worlds with the seven sciences. _(He touches the books with his hands.)_ With Philosophy that was made for the lonely star, I have taught them to forget Theology; with Architecture, I have hidden the ramparts of their cloudy heaven; with Music, the fierce planets' daughter whose hair is always on fire, and with Grammar that is the moon's daughter, I have shut their ears to the imaginary harpings and speech of the angels; and I have made formations of battle with Arithmetic that have put

---

86 And *underlined in pencil PK*

88 their clothes *underlined in pencil PK*

89 colour *PI, PJ, PK, PL, PM, PN, PO, PP, PR*

90 Teigue *circled PR*

92 *replaced by* I think I saw one coming after me *PE*

93 *replaced by* a little time ago! It was the colour of *PE*   colour *PI, PJ, PK, PL, PM, PN, PO, PP, PR*

94 burning sods] red embers, *PE*   head. Glory be to God! *PE*

95 WISE MAN You are a fool *(are del in ink) PE*   Well, there are your *underlined in pencil PK*   fool, *ink note in margin reads:* F *PR*

96 *no quotes PE*   Glory *PE, PJ, PR*

97 There are your four pennies. Run *PE*   Run away . . . my scholars. *del PK*

98 pennies. . . . luck, *PE*   That means *del to* Thats *PR*

99 Teacher. I *PE*

99/100 LD *(inserted in ink)* shaking the bag) *PE*

100 *no comma PE*   Teigue *circled PR with pencil note* This is right

102 worlds, . . . over-thrown *PE*

104 for *del in pencil to* from *PE, PK, rev adopted PR*

105 *no commas PE*

106 heaven; and with *PE*   heaven *(ink note in margin reads:* H, as on p. 140, *referring to ll. 145ff.) PR*

107 planet's . . . always upon fire; *PE*

111 **the hosts of heaven to the rout. But, Rhetoric and Dialectic,**
112 **that have been born out of the light star and out of the amorous**
113 **star, you have been my spearman and my catapult! Oh! my**
114 **swift horsemen! Oh! my keen darting arguments, it is because**
115 **of you that I have overthrown the hosts of foolishness!** ***(An***
116 ***Angel, in a dress the color of embers, and carrying a blossoming***
apple bough in his hand and a gilded halo about his head, stands
upon the threshold.) **Before I came, men's minds were stuffed**
117 **with folly about a heaven where birds sang the hours, and about**
118 **angels that came and stood upon men's thresholds. But I have**
119 **locked the visions into heaven and turned the key upon them.**
120 **Well, I must consider this passage about the two countries. My**
121 **mother used to say something of the kind. She would say that**
122 **when our bodies sleep our souls awake, and that whatever withers**
123 **here ripens yonder, and that harvests are snatched from us that**
124 **they may feed invisible people. But the meaning of the book**
125 **must be different, for only fools and women have thoughts like**
126 **that; their thoughts were never written upon the walls of Baby-**
127 **lon.** ***(He sees the Angel.)*** **What are you? Who are you? I**
128 **think I saw some that were like you in my dreams when I was**
129 **a child— that bright thing, that dress that is the color of em-**

---

111 heaven *note reads:* Qy. cap or l.c.? See following page. *PI* heaven *with note in margin:* H *PR* *no commas PE*

112 light *underlined in pencil PK*

113 catapult. (He stands at his desk and turns over the pages of the book). "Dialectic is under Mercury for Mercury is the smallest of the planets." Oh! my *PE* and my *underlined in pencil PK* Oh! *del to* O! *PR*

114 horseman *PE* Oh! *del to* O! *PR*

115 over-thrown . . . foolishness. (AN *PE*

116/117 *no commas in stage directions PE* ANDEL *rev in ink to* ANGEL *PI* colour *PE, PI, PJ, PK, PL, PM, PN, PO, PP, PR* her hand . . . her head, *PK, PL, PM, PN, PO, PP, PR* with a gilded *PJ* upon the threshold LD [*ink*]) To-day I am going to expound this great Saracen, and I must refute that passage in Tertullian we spoke of yesterday. (He takes down another book) I cannot find it. Ah! Here it is. I will give them wholesome bread to eat that will be better than dreams and visions. I have locked the visions into heaven; I have turned the key upon them. But before I came men's hearts and minds and mouths were stuffed *PE*

117 with folly *underlined in pencil PK* with folly. One would look up and tell another that the stars were holes in the floor of heaven, while others thought that Heaven waited for them somewhere with gates made out of precious stones, and there were some that dreamt of angels who walked about among golden and silver apple trees where the birds sang the hours; and sometimes *PE* *ink note in margin opposite* heaven *reads:* H *PR*

118 the angels would come down and stand upon their thresholds, but I have *PE* thresholds] thre *underlined in pencil PK*

119 overturned all that. I have over-thrown the hosts of foolishness. rises [rises *inserted purple carbon*] My name shall be remembered always but they shall be forgotten. *PE* l.c. *at foot of page which may refer to* heaven *(see l. 141) PI* *ink note in margin opposite* heaven *reads:* H *PR*

120–126 *omitted PE*

125 must] may *PM, PN, PO, PP, PR*

127 I must ring the bell for my scholars. *added purple carbon above* (He sees the angel) *PE* ANGEL *PJ* I must ring the bell for my pupils *added in pencil after* Babylon. *PK*

129 *dots replace dash PE* colour *PE, PI, PJ, PK, PL, PM, PN, PO, PP, PR*

bers! But I have done with dreams, I have done with dreams.

Angel. I am the Angel of the Most High God.

Wise Man. Why have you come to me?

Angel. I have brought you a message.

Wise Man. What message have you got for me?

Angel. You will die within the hour. You will die when the last grains have fallen in this glass. *(He turns the hour-glass.)*

Wise Man. My time to die has not come. I have my pupils. I have a young wife and children that I cannot leave. Why must I die?

Angel. You must die because no souls have passed over the threshold of Heaven since you came into this country. The threshold is grassy, and the gates are rusty, and the angels that keep watch there are lonely.

Wise Man. Where will death bring me to?

Angel. The doors of Heaven will not open to you, for you have denied the existence of Heaven; and the doors of Purgatory will not open to you, for you have denied the existence of Purgatory.

Wise Man. But I have also denied the existence of Hell!

Angel. Hell is the place of those who deny.

Wise Man. (kneels). I have, indeed, denied everything and have taught others to deny. I have believed in nothing but what my senses told me. But, oh! beautiful Angel, forgive me, forgive me!

Angel. You should have asked forgiveness long ago.

Wise Man. Had I seen your face as I see it now, Oh! beautiful Angel, I would have believed, I would have asked forgiveness. Maybe you do not know how easy it is to doubt. Storm, death, the grass rotting, many sicknesses, those are the messengers that came to me. Oh! why are you silent? You carry the pardon of

---

129–130 embers, but I have *PE*

136 in] through *PE* in this *underlined in pencil PK* hour glass) *PE* (He] (She *PK, PL, PM, PN, PO, PP, PR*

137–138 I have a *underlined in pencil PK*

141, 145, 146 Heaven (*ink note in margin beside each reads:* l c*) PI* heaven *PJ*

142 *no commas PE*

146–148 Purgatory . . . Hell (*ink note in margin beside each reads:* l c*) PI* purgatory . . . hell *PJ*

147 *no comma PE*

148 *no exclamation mark PE*

150 (Kneels) I have indeed denied everything, and *PE* I have, indeed, . . . *then commas del PI* *no commas PJ* (Kneels.) *PK, PL, PM, PN, PO, PP* everything, *PM, PN, PO, PP, PR*

152 O beautiful angel, *PE* A *of Angel in ll. 152 and 155 underlined in pencil with crosses in left margin, pointing to inconsistency in capitalisation PP* But, oh! *del in ink to* But O *accepted by WBY PR* angel, *PR*

154 Oh!] O *PE* oh! *PI, PJ, PK, PL, PM, PO, PP* oh! *del in ink to* O *accepted by WBY PR*

155 angel, *PE, PM, PN, PO, PO, PR*

157 sicknesses; these *PE*

157–158 *pencil cross in left margin PK*

158 come to men. O! . . . silent! *PE* Oh! *del to* O! *PR*

the Most High; give it to me! I would kiss your hands if I were not afraid—no, no, the hem of your dress!

***Angel.* You let go undying hands too long ago to take hold of them now.**

***Wise Man.* You cannot understand. You live in that country people only see in their dreams. You live in a country that we can only dream about. Maybe it is as hard for you to understand why we disbelieve as it is for us to believe. Oh! what have I said! You know everything! Give me time to undo what I have done. Give me a year—a month—a day—an hour! Give me to this hour's end, that I may undo what I have done!**

***Angel.* You cannot undo what you have done. Yet I have this power with my message. If you can find one that believes before the hour's end, you shall come to Heaven after the years of Purgatory. For, from one fiery seed, watched over by those that sent me, the harvest can come again to heap the golden threshing floor. But now farewell, for I am weary of the weight of time.**

***Wise Man.* Blessed be the Father, blessed be the Son, blessed be the Spirit, blessed be the Messenger They have sent!**

Angel (at the door and pointing at the hour-glass).* In a little while the uppermost glass will be empty. *(Goes out.)

***Wise Man.* Everything will be well with me. I will call my pupils; they only say they doubt. *(Pulls the bell.)* They will be here in a moment. I hear their feet outside on the path.**

---

159 High, give them to *PE*

160 not afraid. No, . . . dress. *PE*

163 You live in that country *underlined in pencil PE*

163–164 You live . . . dreams *del in ink PM, PN, PO, PP, omitted PR* that country people only . . . dreams *all underlined in pencil PK*

164–165 You live . . . dream about. *del PK*

165 May be *PE* understand *underlined in pencil PK*

166 Oh! *del to* O! *PR* said! *del by WBY to* said? *PR*

167 Give me *underlined in pencil PK*

168 *dots for dashes PE*

169 *no comma PE*

172 Heaven *marginal note in ink reads:* l.c. *PI* heaven *PJ*

173 Purgatory *marginal note in ink reads:* l.c. *PI* purgatory *PJ* For from *PE*

174–175 threshing-floor *PI, PJ hyphen inserted in ink PR*

175 weary with the *PR*

178 (At . . . hour glass) *PE* (At the *PK, PL, PM, PN, PO, PP* door, and *PR*

179 empty (Goes out) *PE*

181 pupils, they . . . (PUlls bell) *PE* *pencil line under* they doubt *indicates bell is pulled at this point PE* (Pulls the bell) *underlined in pencil PK*

182 I hear . . . the path. *del PK*

They want to please me; they pretend that they disbelieve. Belief is too old to be overcome all in a minute. Besides I can prove what I once disproved. *(Another pull at the bell.)* They are coming now. I will go to my desk. I will speak quietly, as if nothing had happened. *(He stands at the desk with a fixed look in his eyes.)*

Enter Pupils and the Fool.

***Fool.* Leave me alone. Leave me alone. Who is that pulling at my bag? King's son, do not pull at my bag.**

***A Young Man.* Did your friends the angels give you that bag? Why don't they fill your bag for you?**

***Fool.* Give me pennies! Give me some pennies!**

***A Young Man.* Let go his cloak, it is coming to pieces. What do you want pennies for, with that great bag at your waist?**

***Fool.* I want to buy bacon in the shops, and nuts in the market, and strong drink for the time when the sun is weak, and snares to catch rabbits and the squirrels that steal the nuts, and hares, and a great pot to cook them in.**

***A Young Man.* Why don't your friends tell you where buried treasures are?**

***Another.* Why don't they make you dream about treasures? If one dreams three times there is always treasure.**

***Fool (holding out his hat).* Give me pennies! Give me pen-**

---

183 me, *PE* *pencil stroke in margin alerting WBY to* believe . . . belief, *words which he modified elsewhere in this edition PP*

184 Besides, *PI, PJ*

185 prove what I once disproved. *underlined in pencil, suggesting the bell is pulled during these words. PE* bell) *PE*

186 *no comma PE*

187/188 & FOOL *PE* FOOL *PR*

189 my bag? . . . my bag.] my cloak. . . . my cloak. *PE*

190 bag?] cloak? *PE*

191 Why dont they give you a better cloak. *PE*

192 Give me . . . some pennies!] Let go my coat and give me pennies. *PE*

193 cloak,] coat; *PE* Let . . . pieces *omitted PK, PL, PM, PN, PO, PP, PR*

194 *no comma PE* for, that great bag at you waist is heavy? *PK, PL, PM, PN, PO, PP, so PR but* for, that *overwritten to* for? That *accepted by WBY*

195 shops and *PE*

196 when *omitted PE*

197 & hares *inserted in ink after* rabbits, *PE* and hares *then del, then reinstated (pencil) PE*

199 dont *PE*

201 Another. *del PK* dont . . . treasures. *PE*

202 times, *PI, PJ*

203 (Holding *PE, PK, PL, PM, PN, PO, PP* hat) *PE* pennies. *PE*

203–204 pennies. *PE*

nies!

They throw pennies into his hat. He is standing close to the door, that he may hold out his hat to each newcomer.

A Young Man. **Master, will you have Teigue the Fool for a scholar?**

Another Young Man. **Teigue, will you give us your pennies if we teach you lessons? No, he goes to school for nothing on the mountains. Tell us what you learn on the mountains, Teigue?**

Wise Man. **Be silent all. *(He has been standing silent, looking away.)* Stand still in your places, for there is something I would have you tell me.**

A moment's pause. They all stand round in their places. Teigue still stands at the door.

Wise Man. **Is there any one amongst you who believes in God? In Heaven? Or in Purgatory? Or in Hell?**

All the Young Men. **No one, Master! No one!**

Wise Man. **I knew you would all say that; but do not be afraid. I will not be angry. Tell me the truth. Do you not believe?**

A Young Man. **We once did, but you have taught us to know better.**

Wise Man. **Oh! teaching, teaching does not go very deep! The heart remains unchanged under it all. You believe just as you always did, and you are afraid to tell me.**

A Young Man. **No, no, Master!**

Wise Man. **If you tell me that you believe I shall be glad and**

204/205 (They . . . door that . . . new comer) *PE* (They *PK, PL, PM, PN, PO, PP, PR*

205, 207, 210 Teigue *circled PR*

207–210 *replaced by* ANOTHER. Teigue the Fool will not be a scholar. Teigue the Fool will teach. Master, will you become a pupil? What will you teach us Teigue. *PE*

211 all! *PK, PL, PM, PN, PO, PP, PR* *no comma PE*

212 Stand . . . places, *del in pencil PE*

213/214 (A . . . stays at the door) *PE* (A *PK, PL, PM, PN, PO, PP, PR*

214 any one *rev to* anyone *ink note in margin reads:* <Qy: anyone in first play> *PI* anyone *PJ*

214–215 in God? . . . in Hell? *del to* that there is something in us that can never pass away. *PK del to* in God Who believes that we have imperisible souls [we have . . . souls *del*] something within us that can never pass away. *PL*

215 Or in Purgatory? *with* Or *del in pencil PE* heaven? . . . purgatory? . . . hell? *PJ*

216 *no comma PE*

221 Oh teaching, . . . deep. The *PE* Oh! *del in ink to* O! *accepted by WBY PR*

222 under it all. *del in ink to* It only pretends to listen. It knows all the time. *PL*

222–223 You . . . did, *del in ink to* You have the faith that you always had, *PM, PN, PP rev adopted PR* You . . . did, *del in ink to* have faith just as you have always had *PK so POi and POii but* always did, *POiii also del* just as

224 MASTER *del in ink to* MAN *accepted by WBY PR* no, Master!] no Master. *PE* no, Master. *PI, PJ*

225 that you believe *del in ink to* I have not been able to change you *PL* believe *del in ink to* have not changed *PM, PN, PO, PP rev adopted PR but with ink comma inserted after* changed that you believe *del in ink to* have kept your faith *then del to* have not changed *PK* glad, *comma del PI*

not angry.

A Young Man (to his neighbor). **He wants somebody to dispute with.**

His Neighbor. **I knew that from the beginning.**

A Young Man. **That is not the subject for to-day; you were going to talk about the words the beggar wrote upon the walls of Babylon.**

Wise Man. **If there is one amongst you that believes, he will be my best friend. Surely there is one amongst you. *(They are all silent.)* Surely what you learned at your mother's knees has not been so soon forgotten.**

A Young Man. **Master, till you came, no teacher in this land was able to get rid of foolishness and ignorance. But every one has listened to you, every one has learned the truth. You have had your last disputation.**

Another. **What a fool you made of that monk in the market-place! He had not a word to say.**

Wise Man (comes from his desk and stands among them in the middle of the room). **Pupils, dear friends, I have deceived you all this time. It was I myself who was ignorant. There is a God. There is a Heaven. There is fire that passes and there is fire that lasts forever.**

Teigue, through all this, is sitting on a stool by the door, reckoning on his fingers what he will buy with his money.

A Young Man (to another). **He will not be satisfied till we dis-**

---

227 (To *PE, PK, PL, PM, PN, PO, PP* neighbour) *PE*, so *PI, PJ but with period* Neighbour.) *PK, PL, PM, PN, PO, PP*

227, 229 Neighbour *PE, PI, PJ, PK, PL, PM, PN, PO, PP, PR*

230–232 *omitted. PE*

233 *no comma PE* believes, *del in ink to* has not changed, *PM, PN, PO, PP, rev adopted PR*

233–234 that believes, . . . best friend. *del to* who has said to himself, 'let him say what he pleases I think [think *del*] know' — If there is one who has said that he will be my best friend. *PL*

235 silent) *PE* (WISE MAN *typed before* Surely what, *which begins line, then del in pencil PE* mother's *rev to* mothers' *PR*

238 everyone *PE*

241–242 market place. *PE*

242/243 (Comes . . . room. *PE* (Comes . . . room.) *PK, PL, PM, PN, PO, PP*

244–246 There is a God . . . for ever. *del (ink) in margin to* It is my belief that we become undying — that was what the angel said. It is my belief that we come to understanding. It is hard but if you are patient. *Then rewrites at top of page:* It is hard to understand. If you will be patient I will explain it all. *these last two sentences then del PL*

245 heaven *PJ* passes, *PI, PJ*

246 for ever *PE, PJ, PK, PL, PM, PN, PO, PP, PR* forever *underlined in ink then del, ink note in margin reads:* <Qy: see page 30> *then del PI*

246/247 (TEIGUE . . . money) *with no commas PE* (Teigue, *PK, PL, PM, PN, PO, PP, so PR but* TEIGUE *circled and ticked by editor*

247 (To another) *PE* (To Another.) *PK, PL, PM, PN, PO, PP* ANOTHER). *PR circled with note in margin:* lc ital *(editor)*

pute with him. ***(To the Wise Man.)*** **Prove it, Master. Have you seen them?**

Wise Man (in a low, solemn voice). **Just now, before you came in, some one came to the door, and when I looked up I saw an angel standing there.**

A Young Man. **You were in a dream. Anybody can see an angel in his dreams.**

Wise Man. **Oh, my God! It was not a dream! I was awake, waking as I am now. I tell you I was awake as I am now.**

A Young Man. **Some dream when they are awake, but they are the crazy and who would believe what they say? Forgive me, Master, but that is what you taught me to say. That is what you said to the monk when he spoke of the visions of the saints and the martyrs.**

Another Young Man. **You see how well we remember your teaching.**

Wise Man. **Out, out from my sight! I want some one with belief. I must find that grain the Angel spoke of before I die. I tell you I must find it, and you answer me with arguments. Out with you, or I will beat you with my stick!** ***(The young men laugh.)***

A Young Man. **How well he plays at faith! He is like the monk when he had nothing more to say.**

Wise Man. **Out, out, or I will lay this stick about your shoulders! Out with you, though you are a King's son!** ***(They begin to hurry out.)***

---

248 MAN) *PE, PJ* MAN.) *PI but period then del*

249 seen *underlined in pencil PK*

250 (In a low solemn voice) *PE* (In . . . voice.) *PK, PL, PM, PN, PO, PP*

251 someone *PE, PK, PL, PM, PN, PO, PP*

255 Oh, *del to* O, *PR* dream. *PI, PJ*

258 *no comma PE* crazy, *PI, PJ, PK, PL, PM, PN, PO, PP, PR*

264–266 I want . . . arguments.] I want a believer, a believer that I may save my soul from the fire, and you answer me with argument. *PE*

264–267 I want . . . stick! *del in ink to* I want somebody who has not changed. That is the grain the angel spoke of—I must find it before I die. *PM, PN, PO, PP rev adopted PR*
PM continues in margin: The sands are falling through [through *then del to* there] and you answer me with arguments. Out of my sight [Out . . . sight *then del to* out with you], out of my sight! or I will . . . stick! *del to* out of my sight *PK*; *PN, PO continue in ink in margin:* I tell you I must find it. The sands are falling there & you answer me with arguments. *POi, POiii read* falling through, *PN adds* Out with you, out of my sight! *so PP but* sight. *PO reads* Out of my sight, out of my sight! *PR follows revs to PN*

267 *no comma PE*

267/268 (The Young Men *PK, PL, PM, PN, PO, PP* young men *PE* laugh) *PE*

270 out, or . . . shoulders! *del in ink to* out. ~~This~~ This is no time for laughter *PM* or . . .shoulders!] *del in ink to* This is no time for laughter. *PK, PO, PP rev adopted but* this *PR*

270–271 shoulders. . . . you though . . . son. . . . out) *PE* Out with . . . son! *del in ink to* This is no time for laughter. *PN* king's *PK, PL, PM, PN, PO, PP, PR*

A Young Man. Come, come; he wants us to find some one who will dispute with him. _(All go out.)_

Wise Man (alone; he goes to the door at the side). I will call my wife. She will believe; women always believe. _(He opens the door and calls.)_ Bridget! Bridget! _(Bridget comes in wearing her apron, her sleeves turned up from her floury arms.)_ Bridget, tell me the truth; do not say what you think will please me. Do you sometimes say your prayers?

Bridget. Prayers! No, you taught me to leave them off long ago. At first I was sorry, but I am glad now for I am sleepy in the evenings.

Wise Man. But do you not believe in God?

Bridget. Oh, a good wife only believes what her husband tells her!

Wise Man. But sometimes when you are alone, when I am in the school and the children asleep, do you not think about the saints, about the things you used to believe in? What do you think of when you are alone?

Bridget (considering). I think about nothing. Sometimes I wonder if the pig is fattening well, or I go out to see if the crows are picking up the chicken's food.

---

272 come. He . . . someone *PE*

273 him (All go out) *PE*

274 (Alone. He . . . side) *PE* (Alone; he *PK, PL, PM, PN, PO, PP* (alone; he *overwritten in ink to* Alone. He *PI, rev adopted PJ*

275 believe. Women *PE* She will . . . always believe] *del to* Why did I not speak to her first. She is lost if I cannot save her but no I am sure she believes as she always did. My pupils have nothing in there minds but what I put there but when I speak she sits thinking of something else, smiling as if she listened — but only pretending to listen Besides women always believe. *PL*

276 calls) . . . apron; . . . arms) *PE*

277 WISE MAN. Bridget; tell *PE*

278 you *underlined in pencil PK*

279 Prayers, no. You *PE*

280 sorry,] sorry; *PE* sorry, *comma then del PI* now, *PI, PJ* now, *comma inserted in ink, accepted by WBY PR*

283 Oh, *del to* O, *accepted by WBY PR*

284 her. *PE*

287 about the things . . . in? *del to* about angels, about the soul. *PL*

289 (Considering) *PE* (Considering.) *PK, PL, PM, PN, PO, PP*

290 if . . . well, *circled, and on the previous verso is a handwritten ink note in Lady Gregory's hand:* if the cloths are bleaching white/ (may be changed if desired). *PE* pig . . . is well, *del to* linen is bleaching white *PJ* wonder if the linen is bleaching white, or *PK, PL, PM, PN, PO, PP, PR*

291 chickens' *PE, PJ, PK, PL, PM, PN, PO, PP, PR* chicken's *with ink note in margin* <Qy: s'> Yes. plural s' *PI*

292 ***Wise Man.* Oh, what can I do! Is there nobody who believes?**
293 **I must go and find somebody! *(He goes towards the door, but***
294 ***stops with his eyes fixed on the hour-glass.)* I cannot go out; I**
295 **cannot leave that!**
296 ***Bridget.* You want somebody to get up an argument with.**
297 ***Wise Man.* Oh, look out of the door and tell me if there is any-**
298 **body there in the street. I cannot leave this glass; somebody**
299 **might shake it! Then the sand would fall more quickly.**
300 ***Bridget.* I don't understand what you are saying. *(Looks out.)***
301 **There is a great crowd of people talking to your pupils.**
302 ***Wise Man.* Oh, run out, Bridget, and see if they have found**
303 **somebody that believes!**
Bridget (wiping her arms in her apron and pulling down her
304 ***sleeves).* It's a hard thing to be married to a man of learning that**
305 **must be always having arguments. *(Goes out and shouts through***
306 ***the kitchen door.)* Don't be meddling with the bread, children,**
307 **while I'm out.**

---

292 Oh, *del to* O, *WBY accepts PR* can *underlined in pencil PK* who believes? *del to* who has faith in things invisible *then del to* who believes he can never die. *PK* believes? *rev to* believes he can never die? *PM, PO, so PN, PP but* die *PR adopts revs to PM*

292–301 WISE MAN Oh! what can I do! Is there nobody that believes?
BRIDGET. You want somebody to get up an argument with?
WISE MAN Look out at the door and tell me if there is anybody there in the street.
BRIDGET. There is a great crowd of people talking to your pupils.
These lines then del in ink with note insert slip A *written in right margin. Slip A, which is badly typed, reads:*
WISE MAN. O What can I do! Is there nobody who believes! I must go and find somebody! (He goes towards the door but stops with his eyes fixed on the hourglass) I cannot go out, I cannot leave that!
BRIDGET. You want somebody to get up an argument with.
WISE MAN. O look out of the door and tekk [*del pencil and* tell me *inserted*] if there is anybody there in the street! I cannot leave this glass, somebody might shake it! [Then the sand would fall more quickly *inserted in ink*]
BRIDGET. I dont understand what you are saying. There is a great crowd of people talking to your pupils. *PE*

293 door, *then comma del PI* *no comma PJ*

295 that!] that. *PO then inserts in ink in margin* Go and call my pupils again. I will make them understand. I will say to them that only amid spiritual terror or only when all that can [*? del to* laid] hold on life is shaken, can we see truth. There is something in Plato, but — No, do not call them. They would answer as I have bid. *so PN but* terror, *so PM but* can *del to* laid [*POii replaces* have bid *with* have done.] *PP, PR follow revised PM but omits comma after* shaken *PP omits commas*

297 Oh, *del to* O, *accepted by WBY PR*

302–3 Oh, *del to* O, *PR* out Bridget and *PE*

303 believes!] believes! in God *added in ink (not WBY) then canceled by WBY to* believes he can never die *PK PM, PN, POi and iii, PP print revised PK but del in ink* that believes he can never die *to* all the time I was teaching understood nothing, or did not listen! *so POii but* teaching, that, all the time I was teaching, understood nothing or did not listen! *PR*

303–304 (Wiping . . . sleeves) *PE* (Wiping . . . sleeves.) *PK, PL, PM, PN, PO, PP*

305 *This is the last line extant in PI; it ends at* shouts

306–307 door) *PE* If you two children put your fingers on the dough, I'll give you . . . [*dots in text*] *all del, replaced on previous verso in ink, in Lady Gregory's hand, with* Dont be meddling with the bread children while I'm out *PE*

***Wise Man (kneels down). "Salvum me fac, Deus—salvum—salvum . . ."* I have forgotten it all. It is thirty years since I have said a prayer. I must pray in the common tongue, like a clown begging in the market, like Teigue the Fool! *(He prays.)* Help me, Father, Son and Spirit!**

Bridget enters, followed by the Fool, who is holding out his hat to her.

***Fool.* Give me something; give me a penny to buy bacon in the shops, and nuts in the market, and strong drink for the time when the sun grows weak.**

***Bridget.* I have no pennies. *(To the Wise Man.)* Your pupils cannot find anybody to argue with you. There is nobody in the whole country who had enough belief to fill a pipe with since you put down the monk. Can't you be quiet now and not always be wanting to have arguments? It must be terrible to have a mind like that.**

***Wise Man.* I am lost! I am lost!**

***Bridget.* Leave me alone now; I have to make the bread for you and the children.**

***Wise Man.* Out of this, woman, out of this, I say! *(Bridget goes through the kitchen door.)* Will nobody find a way to help me! But she spoke of my children. I had forgotten them. They will believe. It is only those who have reason that doubt; the**

308–309 (Kneels down Begins a Latin prayer, breaks off) *PE* (Kneels down.) *PK, PL, PM, PN, PO, PP* "Salvum me fac, Deus—salvum—salvum" *omitted PE, del in ink to* Confiteor Deo Omnipotenti, beata Maria *PM, PN, PO but POii, POiii omit comma, so PP but* beatae Mariae, *and del ends at* D *of* Deus. *No deletion and* Confiteor Deo omnipotenti beatae Mariae *written at foot of page (not by WBY) PK* 'Confiteor Deo Omnipotenti, beatae Mariae—salvum—salvum . . . ' *(dots in text) PR*

310 *no comma PE*

311 prays) Help *PE* Teigue *circled and ticked by editor PR*

312 me Father, *PE*

312/313 (BRIDGET enters followed . . . FOOL who . . . her) *PE* (BRIDGET *PK, PL, PM, PN, PO, PP, PR*

313 something, *PE*

314 shops] winter *PE* *no commas PE*

316 MAN) *PE*

318 had] has *PK, PM, PN, PO, PP, PR* had *del to* has *PJ* *PR omits* with

319 always be] always *PM, PN, PO, PP, PR*

320 arguments. *PE*

321 that! *PE*

322 I am . . . am lost! *del to* There is no hope. She is lost. My child & my pupils & myself. *PL*

323 now. I have come to *(come then del in ink) PE*

324 children. *Added in pencil:* (Exit L [*L then erased*] RD followed by Fool) *PE*

325 this I say (BRIDGET *PE*

326 goes through kitchen door). *PE*

327 children. *del in ink to* child *PL* them; they *PE*

327–328 I had . . . will believe. *del in ink to* I must call my child my child will believe *PL*

328 doubt, the *PE* believe. *del in ink to* not have changed. *PM, PN, PO, PP, PR*

young are full of faith. Bridget, Bridget, send my children to me!

Bridget (inside). **Your father wants you; run to him now.**

The two children come in. They stand together a little way from the threshold of the kitchen door, looking timidly at their father.

Wise Man. **Children, what do you believe? Is there a Heaven? Is there a Hell? Is there a Purgatory?**

First Child. **We haven't forgotten, father.**

The Other Child. **O no, father.** ***(They both speak together as if in school.)*** **There is no Heaven; there is no Hell; there is nothing we cannot see.**

First Child. **Foolish people used to think that there were, but you are very learned and you have taught us better.**

Wise Man. **You are just as bad as the others, just as bad as the others! Out of the room with you, out of the room!** ***(The children begin to cry and run away.)*** **Go away, go away! I will teach you better—no, I will never teach you again. Go to your**

---

329 Bridget! Bridget, *PE* my children to me. *del in ink to* me my child. *PL* me. *PM, PN, PO, PP, PR*

330 (Inside) *PE* (Inside.) *PK, PL, PM, PN, PO, PP*

330/331 (The *PE, PK, PL, PM, PN, PO, PP, PR* Children *PK, PL, PM, PN, PO, PP* CHILDREN *PR* in they . . . door; . . . father) *PE*

331–332 heaven? . . . hell? . . . purgatory? *PJ*

331–333 Children . . . forgotten, father. *del in ink to* Speak quickly there is very little time and do not be afraid. You believe that there is something eternal — no you will not understand that. When children laugh in their sleep we say that they can see the angels Do you ever see the angels child. Do you believe that they are always about us that there is a world we cannot see. *PL*

334 The Other *del in ink PL* Oh no *PE no comma* O *rev in ink to* Oh *PP* Oh *del to* O *accepted by WBY PR*

335 school) *PE* There is no Heaven; there is no Hell; *del PE, PJ but* heaven . . . hell; *omitted PK, PL, PM, PN, PO, PP, PR* Hell; there *rev (ink) to* There *PE, PJ, rev adopted PK, PL, PM, PN, PO, PP, PR*

335–336 There is . . . see; there is nothing we cannot touch. *PK, PL, PM, PN, PO, PP, PR, so PL but then del in ink to* all that is imagination and fancy there . . . nothing we cannot see. *del pencil, del erased, underlined with broken lines in yellowed ink over pencil with* stet *inserted above.* there] There *rev ink and* there is nothing we cannot touch — *added in pencil to right PE, added in ink with semi-colon in place of period after* see *PJ*

337 First Child. *del PL* were, *del in pencil to* is *PE, del (ink) to* is *PR* there was, *PK, PL, PM, PN, PO, PP, PR*

339 others! just *PE*

339–343 Wise Man. You are . . . teach them . . . *del in ink to* Wise Man (taking child by the hand) Come to your mother (going to door) Bridget teach this child all that you believed once about angels — teach her that belief is the mother of truth, not its child. run to your mother she will teach you — but no Bridget will not listen. She is baking a cake & she could not understand *PL*

340 others. *PE* others! *PR* Out . . . room! *del in ink to* Do not run away. Come back to me! *PM, PN, PO, so PK in pencil but omits* to me *so PP with exclamation omitted in second canceled rev at foot of page, rev adopted PR but* away!

341 Children *PE, PM, PN, PO, PP CHILDREN PR* go away. I *PE* Go away, go away! *del in pencil PK, del in ink to* Why are you afraid? *PM, PN, PO, so PP but omits question mark above l. 341 but not in the canceled revision at foot of page, rev adopted PR*

342 *dots replace dash PE* no; *PE* no, teach you again. *all marked to be emphasized PK*

mother; no, she will not be able to teach them . . . Help them, O God! *(Alone.)* The grains are going very quickly. There is very little sand in the uppermost glass. Somebody will come for me in a moment; perhaps he is at the door now! All creatures that have reason doubt. O that the grass and the planets could speak! Somebody has said that they would wither if they doubted. O speak to me, O grass blades! O fingers of God's certainty, speak to me. You are millions and you will not speak. I dare not know the moment the messenger will come for me. I will cover the glass. *(He covers it and brings it to the desk, and the Fool is sitting by the door fiddling with some flowers which he has stuck in his hat. He has begun to blow a dandelion head.)* What are you doing?

***Fool.* Wait a moment. *(He blows.)* Four, five, six.**

***Wise Man.* What are you doing that for?**

***Fool.* I am blowing at the dandelion to find out what time it is.**

Wise Man.* You have heard everything! That is why you want to find out what hour it is! You are waiting to see them coming through the door to carry me away. *(Fool goes on blowing.)* Out through the door with you! I will have no one here when they come. *(He seizes the Fool by the shoulders, and begins to force him out through the door, then suddenly changes his mind.)* No, I have something to ask you. *(He drags him back into the

---

343 mother. No; *PE* mother! *PK, PL, PM, PN, PO, PP, PR* help them, Oh *PE* *dash replaces semi-colon PJ*

344 (Alone) *PE, PJ replaced by three dots PK, PL, PM, PN, PO, PP, PR*

346 moment, . . . now. *PE* Going to the door *added in pencil in margin PK*

347 Oh, *PE* O *rev in ink to* Oh *PP* Oh *del to* O *accepted by WBY PR* planets could] clouds would *PE* planets] plants *PK, PL, PM, PN, PO, PP, PR*

348 speak to me and I might be saved, for they know where they are rooted and whither they go. *PE* said that that *PM, PN, PO, so PP with second, erroneous* that *circled in pencil*

348–350 Somebody . . . not speak *omitted PE*

349 O [*rev in ink to* Oh] speak *PP* Oh [*del to* O] speak *accepted by WBY PR* grass-blades! *hyphen inserted in ink by WBY PR*

350 me! *PK, PL, PM, PN, PO, PP, PR*

352–353 glass (. . . desk and . . . head) *PE* and brings it to the desk. *del in ink to* with a cloth. *PM, PN, PO, PP, rev adopted PR* and the Fool . . . head.)] Sees the Fool, who is . . . door playing . . . head.) *PK, PL, PM, PN, PO, PP, so PR but* dandelion-head.)

355 (He blows) four, *PE* Four,] Four *PK, PL*

358 You have *underlined in pencil PK*

360 *no periods PE*

361 Out through the door with you! *del in ink to* I will not have you sitting there. *PM, PN, PO, so PP but omits period, rev to PM adopted PR*

362 Going up *written in pencil in margin beside* they come. *PK*

362/363 *no commas in stage directions PE*

363 No] N; *PE* you! *PE*

363–364 *underline in pencil at beginning and end of stage directions PK*

room.) Is there a Heaven? Is there a Hell? Is there a Purgatory?

***Fool.* So you ask me now. I thought when you were asking your pupils, I said to myself, if he would ask Teigue the Fool, Teigue could tell him all about it, for Teigue has learned all about it when he has been cutting the nets.**

***Wise Man.* Tell me; tell me!**

***Fool.* I said, Teigue knows everything. Not even the owls and the hares that milk the cows have Teigue's wisdom. But Teigue will not speak; he says nothing.**

***Wise Man.* Tell me, tell me! For under the cover the grains are falling and when they are all fallen I shall die; and my soul will be lost if I have not found somebody that believes! Speak, speak!**

***Fool (looking wise).* No, no, I won't tell you what is in my mind, and I won't tell you what is in my bag. You might steal away my thoughts. I met a bodach on the road yesterday, and he said, "Teigue, tell me how many pennies are in your bag. I will wager three pennies that there are not twenty pennies in your bag; let me put in my hand and count them." But I pulled the strings tighter, like this; and when I go to sleep every night I hide the bag where no one knows.**

***Wise Man. (goes towards the hour-glass as if to uncover it).* No, no, I have not the courage! *(He kneels.)* Have pity upon**

---

364 room) *PE*

364–365 Is there . . . a Purgatory? *del in ink to* You believe in the soul and in heaven *PL* Heaven? . . . Hell? . . . Purgatory?] heaven? . . . hell? . . . purgatory? *PJ*

367–368 Teigue *circled in ink each time and marked* stet *(by editor?) PR*

370 me! tell *PE* ; tell me! *del in ink to* quickly *PM, so PN, PO, PP but* quickly. me; tell me!] me quickly! *PR*

371–372 owls and] cats or *PK, PL, PM, PN, PO, PP, PR, del to* cats and *PJ* Teigue *circled each time PR* Coming down *written in pencil after* wisdom. *PK*

374 me. For *PE*

375 falling, *PJ, PK, PL, PM, PN, PO, PP, PR* all *omitted PE*

376 believes. *PE* knows and *inserted in ink before* believes! *PM, PO, PP, rev adopted PR* believes! *del erroneously in ink to* believes knows and *PN*

377 *pencil mark under* speak! *PK*

378 (Looking wise) *PE* (Looking wise.) *PK, PL, PM, PN, PO, PP* No, no. I wont *PE* No, no, I won't *del in ink to* I will not speak. I will not *PM, PN, PO, POiii erroneously del* tell, *PP, rev adopted but* speak! *PR*

379 wont *PE*

381 *no quotes PE* bag; *PE, PK, PL, PM, PN, PO, PP, PR* Teigue *circled, with tick in margin (by editor?) PR*

383 *no quotes PE*

385/386 (Goes . . . hour glass . . . it) *PE* (Goes . . . it.) *PK, PL, PM, PN, PO, PP* towards] toward *PJ*

386 No, no; . . . kneels) *PE* courage. *PK, PL, PM, PN, PO, PP, PR*

me, Fool, and tell me!

Fool. **Ah! Now, that is different. I am not afraid of you now. But I must come near you; somebody in there might hear what the Angel said.**

Wise Man. **Oh, what did the Angel tell you?**

Fool. **Once I was alone on the hills, and an angel came by and he said, "Teigue the Fool, do not forget the Three Fires; the Fire that punishes, the Fire that purifies, and the Fire wherein the soul rejoices forever!"**

Wise Man. **He believes! I am saved! Help me. The sand has run out. I am dying . . .** ***(Fool helps him to his chair.)*** **I am going from the country of the seven wandering stars, and I am**

387–388 *no commas PE*

389 you, somebody *PE* come near *with marginal note in ink:* ?slip *PH* near] nearer to *PK, PL, PM, PN, PO, PP* now. What is that I am to tell you? But . . . near, somebody *then rev in ink to* near; somebody *PR*

390 *omitted* PL angel *PE, PR* Angel *(with* A *then del and annotation* l.c. *added in pale grey ink) PP*

391 Oh! what . . . angel *PE* Angel *(with* A *then del and annotation* l.c. *added in pale grey ink) PP* oh, what . . . you?] But speak and I am saved. What did the angel say to you? *PR*

392 *no comma PE* Angel *PJ*

392–395 Once I . . . rejoices forever!" *del in ink to* Once I was alone on the hills and an angel came by and said 'Teig if your body were to wither as your wits are withered your soul would shake off the little fistful of dust. If the world were broken like an egg your soul would not be broken but go shouting and laughing through the country [?by/of] the summer stars' & that wise man is why I am always happy cracking my nuts. *PL*

392–396 *replaced by:* FOOL. On no, no, no. How could poor Teigue see angels? O, [*comma inserted in ink*] Teigue tells one tale here, another tale there, and everybody gives him pennies. If Teigue had not his tales he would starve. (He backs away and goes out.

WISE MAN. My last hope is gone and now that it is too late I can see it all. Those words about winter and summer, about our November being the lambing — *[ink note in margin:* as on p. 135 *i.e. ll. 6-7*] time in that other country—all, all is plain now. We sink in on God, we find him [*ink note in margin:* H] in becoming nothing—we perish into reality. (The FOOL comes back.

FOOL. There was one there—there by the threshold stone, writing there; and she said, 'Go in, Teigue, and tell him everything that he asks you. He will give you a penny if you tell him.'

WISE MAN. We perish into reality—strange that I never saw it until now.

FOOL. Will you give me a penny if I tell you?

WISE MAN. O no, do not tell me anything. I am content to know that God's will prevails whatever that be.

FOOL. Waiting till the moment had come—that is what the one out there was saying, but I might tell you what you asked. That is what he was saying.

WISE MAN. Be silent. May God's will prevail though that be my damnation. [*ink note in margin:* !] What was I born for but that I might cry that His will be fulfilled upon the instant, though that be my damnation. [*ink note in margin ? WBY rev to* !] I am dying. The sand has *PR,* Teigue *circled each time*

393 said "Teigue *PE* Three Fires: *PJ*

394 punishes; . . . purifies; *PE*

395 for ever! *closing quotes omitted PE* for ever!' *PJ*

396 me, the *PE* Help me. *del in ink PK*

397 dying (FOOL *PE* I am dying . . . *del in ink PK*

397–399 run out. Ring the bell, ring for my pupils. (FOOL rings.) For I am *PR*

398 I *omitted PR*

going to the country of the fixed stars! Ring the bell. ***(Fool rings the bell.)*** **Are they coming? Ah! now I hear their feet. . . . I will speak to them. I understand it all now. One sinks in on God; we do not see the truth; God sees the truth in us. I cannot speak, I am too weak. Tell them, Fool, that when the life and the mind are broken the truth comes through them like peas through a broken peascod. But no, I will pray— Yet I cannot pray. Pray, Fool, that they may be given a sign and save their souls alive. Your prayers are better than mine.**

Fool bows his head. Wise Man's head sinks on his arm on the books. Pupils enter.

A Young Man. **Look at the Fool turned bell-ringer!**

Another. **What have you called us in for, Teigue? What are you going to tell us?**

Another. **No wonder he has had dreams! See, he is fast asleep now.** ***(Goes over and touches him.)*** **Oh, he is dead!**

---

399 stars. *PE, PR* bell (FOOL *PE* *stage directions from here to end not underlined PE*

399–401 Ring the bell . . . speak to them. *del in ink PM, PN, PO, PP, so PK but does not delete* (Fool rings the bell.) *all omitted PR*

399–407 stars!] stars. (Voices of PUPILS singing.) They are coming. I must make all plain to them, that they may wish His will be fulfilled though that be our damnation. There is no other truth. (Dies. PUPILS enter *PR*

400 bell) Are. . . Ah! Now *PE*

401–405 I will speak . . . But no, *omitted PE*

402–403 I cannot speak, I am too weak. *then del in ink to* Ring the bell. They are coming. *PM, PN, PO, PP* *del to* Ring the bell are they coming [*not WBY*] *PK*

404 broken] broken, *PJ*

405 Yet] yet *PJ*

405–406 . . . I will pray . . . I am too weak to pray [*dots in text*] *PE* But no, I will pray — Yet I cannot pray. *del PK, PN, PP, del to* Ring the *which rev then also del PM*

406 *no commas PE*

406–407 Your prayers are better then mine. *moved to after* Pray, Fool, *then* Pray fool *inserted before* that they may . . . *PK* save their souls alive. *del in ink to* carry their souls alive out of a dying world. *PM, so PN, PO, PP but* of the *and in POi, POiii, PP WBY cancels* Your *and rewrites it at beginning of next sentence*

407–408 mine (FOOL . . . enter) *PE* (Fool *PK, PL, PM, PN, PO, PP*

408 Look at the bell-ringer! *PE* bell-ringer. *PR*

409–410 Another . . . tell us?] ANOTHER. [*cross penciled beside ident*] He has turned teacher. I told you the Fool would be our teacher. *PE* What are . . . us? *omitted PR, which then inserts:* FOOL. There was something he wanted to say, but you must wake him, he has fallen asleep. [Teigue *circled with tick in margin*]

411 wonder the Master has had dreams. See he is asleep *PE*

411–412 has dreams. He is so fast asleep that I cannot wake him. O, he is dead. . . . [*dots in text*] PUPILS gather round *PR*

412 now. (He goes . . . him) Oh! he *PE* He is fast asleep. I cannot wake him. *inserted in ink after* him.) *PM, PN, POi and iii (POii places it erroneously after l. 414 again.), so PP but* so fast *and insertion is first placed after* now. *then erroneously placed between* him. *and closing parenthesis* him.] the WISE MAN *PJ*

413 ***Fool.* Do not stir! He asked for a sign that you might be**
414 **saved. (*All are silent for a moment.*) . . . Look at the butterfly!**
415 ***A Young Man.* It is his soul! *(They all kneel. The butterfly***
goes up. The Fool points upward.)

CURTAIN.

413–414 *replaced by* Look, look, what has come from his mouth . . . a little winged thing . . . a little shining thing . . . it has gone to the door. . . . O, [*comma inserted in ink accepted by WBY*] look, there in the door. . . . [*dots in text*] (The ANGEL appears at the door, she opens her hands and closes them again.) The Angel has taken it in her hands. *PR*

414 moment) *no dots PE* butterfly. *del in pencil to* white flame *PE* Look at the butterfly! *omitted PJ, PK, PL, PM, PN, PO, PP, replaced by:* Look what has come from his mouth . . . a little winged thing . . . a little shining thing . . . It is gone to the door. (The Angel appears in the doorway, stretches out her hands and closes them again.) The Angel has taken it in her hands . . . She will open her hands in the Garden of Paradise. [*dots in text*] *PK, PL, PM, PN, PO, PP, so PJ but* has gone to . . . she will . . . (They all kneel.)

413–415 *PH has poorly typed slip with text identical to PM and PP, except* again) The angel has . . . she will

415 soul. *PE* *omitted except for* (They all kneel. *PM, PN, PO, PP, so PH except* kneel)

415 replaced by A YOUNG MAN. What are you pointing at?
FOOL. The Angel has taken it in her hands. She will open her hands in the Garden of Paradise.
A YOUNG MAN. There is nobody there—there is nobody in the door. *PR* (CURTAIN) *PE* CURTAIN. *PH, PK, PL, PM, PN, PO, PP* THE END *added in ink PR* *After* CURTAIN. *PK adds in ink (not WBY):* Students song

I was going the road one day
O the brown and the yellow Beer
And I met with a man that was no right man
O my dear my dear
Give me your wife said he
O the brown & the yellow beer
till the sun goes down & an hour by the clock
O my dear my dear
Good bye Good bye my husband
Oh the brown & yellow beer
For a year & a day by the clock of the sun
O my dear my dear

MS. PQ

Transcriptions, with facing photographs

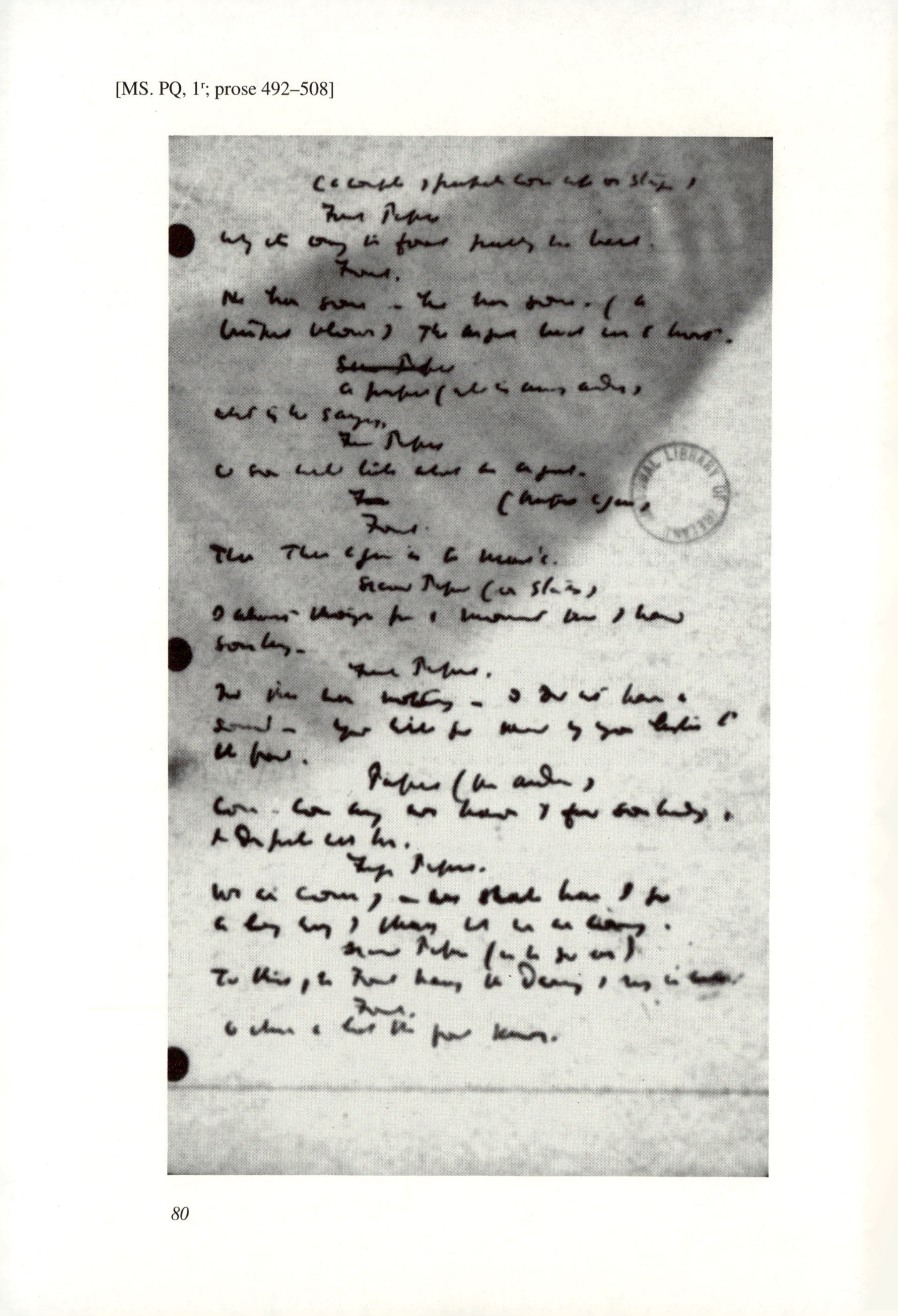

[MS. PQ, 1^{r}; prose 492–508]

[MS. PQ, 1^{r}; prose 492–508]

(a couple of pupils come up on stage)

First Pupil
Why its only the fool pulling the bell.

Fool.
He has gone — he has gone. (a
trumpet blows) The angel back in the host.

~~Second Pupil~~
A pupil (who is among audience)
What is he saying.

First Pupil
O some wild talk about an angel.

~~Foo~~ (trumpet again)
Fool.
There There again is the music.

Second Pupil (on stairs)
I almost thought for a moment that I heard
Something —

First Pupil.
No there was nothing — I do not hear a
Sound — You will go mad if you listen to
the fool.

Pupils (from audience)
Come — Come away we have to find somebody
to dispute with him.

Fifth Pupil.
We are coming — we shall have to go
A long way I [?think] but we are coming.

Second Pupil (as he goes out)
To think of the Fool having the daring to ring the bell.

Fool.
O what a lot the fool knows.

---

3 "'s" omitted after "angel"?

The Mixed Version

In the process of putting parts of *The Hour-Glass* into verse, Yeats turned it into "practically a different work of art." He had wanted to use poetry for it even before the prose version had been performed, but did not do so until 1910. A letter Yeats sent Gordon Craig in 1910 suggests that he had made fairly extensive revisions in the first half of that year. There are extant nine groups of manuscripts that probably belong to the period between 1910 and 1912. Only two of these are of the whole play. The main difficulties in arranging them stem from the fact that very few pages are numbered and it is impossible to tell how much material has been lost. There are, for example, very few leaves from the middle sections of the play.

It is, nonetheless, possible to work out a rough sequence of the manuscript groups and to suggest dates for some of them. There are four groups of manuscripts of the play's opening. The first of these, VA 1–7, is an early redrafting of the prose opening, written on wide paper. It is titled but has no stage directions and shows the pupils discussing among themselves the choosing of a subject for the lesson. The Wise Man is not present but the Fool is. Yeats retained the basic structure of this new opening throughout the poetic versions, although he experimented with the quantity of information and the atmosphere that he used it to establish. There is a page missing after VA 4 which would have contained the description of the passage about the two countries and the Fool's understanding of it. One of the main differences in tone occurs in the Wise Man's speeches, which are much more fanciful and poetic with more emphasis on figurative expression of feeling than in the prose version. The two leaves VB 1 and 2 revise the speeches on VA 1.

Whereas the opening dialogue of VA and VB concentrates on the description of the book from which the enigmatic passage is chosen and the pupils' inability to judge whether it is wise or foolish, VC's initial discussion among the pupils is devoted to establishing the Wise Man's reputation and his triumph over Christianity in closing churches and driving out the monks. Some doubt over the complete dismissal of God is expressed by the Fourth Pupil, and the resultant quarrel among the pupils is expanded to cover four pages. The first five pages (VCi) are numbered and are written on narrow paper similar to that used for VB, and indeed for the majority of the drafts of the play. Page 5 contains only three lines. There is then a hiatus that covers the Wise Man's initial reaction to the description of the two countries, and then a further four unnumbered pages (VCii). These contribute such fragments to this section of the play as the introduction of the Fool into the argument about the two countries. The draft breaks off just before that description and resumes with the Wise Man's interpretation of its meaning. It ends, with a page only partially filled, at the point at which the pupils leave while the Wise Man and the Fool remain, the Wise Man musing to himself. The final sheet contains the first part of the dialogue between the Wise Man and the Fool over what constitutes wisdom.

The final group of pages relating to the play's opening (VD) has few cancellations, almost all immediately followed by their revisions. It is unusually neatly written, is titled, and has stage directions. Narrow paper was used, inverted, and the pages have been numbered in pencil, probably not by Yeats. The draft ends at the bottom of a page in mid-sentence, indicating that sheets have been lost.

There is a single sheet (VE) housed in the NLI (30,385) which contains part of the dialogue between the Wise Man and his pupils. It is slightly different from other versions of the passage. Since, like VA, it uses Master as the character identification for the Wise Man—a styling Yeats subsequently abandoned—it may belong to much the same period as VA.

The ending of the play clearly gave Yeats a great deal of trouble. There are two groups of approximately half a dozen pages and four pages respectively that are not clearly related to either draft. The first group, VF, consists of five sheets with two additional ones that may relate to it. It was written hurriedly on narrow paper and begins partway through the Wise Man's last speech to his children, "but yes yes go . . ." There is a hiatus, marked with a long dash, between the Fool's explanation that he is blowing the dandelion to find out what the time is and the Wise Man's cry to Teigue, "[I] Kneel to you. / If you on who my hands rest have / faith I am saved if you have wit." There are clearly no pages missing here, and the very fragmentary nature of the revisions Yeats was making shows that he was modifying a text in front of him rather than drafting anew. He made careful revisions to the Wise Man's two speeches in which he accepts God's Will and sets out the relation of dream and reality. These, which carry the bulk of the play's metaphysical schema, were modified time and again, as was the Fool's final speech, which ends the play. The final six lines, on a page by themselves, make an abbreviated finish in which, because the Angel does not speak, the Fool has to explain what the Angel is doing. This page (VF 5) and VF 4 may not in fact belong to this draft.

Some of the pages of VG are inverted. VH 1^r is written on the inverted verso of VG 4A^r. VH seems to have been written at much the same time as VG but is in pencil and explores a metaphor not found elsewhere in the play—of the bird of truth that will not sing until the leaves of summer have withered away. A letter from Yeats may date these related drafts. On 23 May 1910 he wrote to Gordon Craig: "I am myself busy with 'The Hour-Glass' again. . . . I have just done the Wise Man's dying speech in rhyme, and the Fool rings the bell for the pupils and the strokes of the bell come at certain arranged moments of his speech like a Dirge." Yeats's description might apply to leaves VG 2–3 and VH, which show this use of a bell. They contain some rhymes, although not every line is rhymed. Leaf VG 1 appears to belong to the group, and VG 4A^r, which is clearly a revision, may have been intended to modify leaf VG 3^r. VG and VH may be part of the same draft as VD, but are in a much less finished state.

The first nine pages of the complete copy (VI) were written on wide ruled paper. These pages take the dialogue as far as the exchange between the Fool and the Wise Man over the cutting of the nets. The middle section is written on a combination of wide and narrow ruled sheets and there is much partial revision on separate leaves. The last eighteen pages are on narrow paper. None of the pages are numbered. Although VI is titled and has a brief "scene," it is still very much a working copy. There are pages missing after VI 6, 14, and 38. These would have covered the first part of the dialogue between the Fool and the Wise Man, the central part of the latter's dialogue with the Angel, and his dying speech and death. There is also an additional sheet after VI 22 containing seven lines in which the Wise Man expresses his inability to cope with the new ideas with which he is faced. Frequent ink blotting shows that Yeats worked quickly both in the initial writing and when revising, but there is no evidence to enable us to tell whether the revisions on versos were made immediately after the writing of the pages they modify. It may be to this "complete" copy that Yeats was referring in a letter to his father in March 1912 in which he said that he was revising the play extensively.

VJ, a holograph of thirty-seven pages, housed in the Humanities Research Center of the University of Texas, appears to predate the prompt copy, which often incorporates its revisions. The prompt copy (VK) of the mixed version is twenty-seven pages long and is owned by the National Library of Ireland. VK is marked "Corrected by W. B. Yeats," and most of the alterations it contains appear to be in his hand. These not only amend the text but mark the points at which characters are to enter or carry out significant acts. The cover and edges of the paper were singed by the 1951 fire in the Abbey Theatre.

Of the copies marked up for later editions, the most extensively altered was VQ, NLI (14), of 1922, into which Yeats wrote the translations into Latin that he used to decrease the repetition of phrases in the play. He noted that he was helped with the translations by Alan Porter. Of the corrections to proofs for intermediate editions, the majority of the alterations were slight; the most significant changes were concentrated at the end of the play. Of these the most important was the change inserted into VP, Emory (2), probably in preparation for the London edition of *Responsibilities* (1916), where Yeats cancelled the Wise Man's suggestion that he kneel to Teigue in the hope that his belief will save him. In this copy the Wise Man simply remembers the Fool's stories of angels, and is convinced that he is saved. Teigue's denial of the truth of the stories he has told leaves the Wise Man declaring that all is lost. The four holograph pages, constituting VO, housed with MS. 8763 (2) at NLI, modify final speeches in *Responsibilities* (1914), but some of the changes do not appear in any of the printed editions. Yeats was evidently satisfied with the 1922 text of the mixed version, for he made no further substantive changes to it when checking the proofs of his Macmillan Collected Edition (VR) in 1931–1932.

MSS. VA–VD

Transcriptions of the play's opening, with facing photographs

[MS. VA, 1r; 1–26]

[MS. VA, 1r; 1–26]

Hour Glass.

First Pupil.
Where is the Master
2 Talking to his children.
3 He s left the big book there, the book
That holds he says, the knowledge of the world
~~Let s find a passage~~
Let find a passage in it for our lesson
He said that we ourselves might choose the subject
For the days lesson

Fool. Give me a penny sir.

1. How can we choose a passage. We do not know enough
Has he not told us that to question rightly
Is the first half of knowledge.

F Is there nobody
To give a penny to poor Teig the Fool.

First Pupil.
Teig knows what he wants & yet he is a fool
I d choose a [?finely] gilt & coloured page
For that would mean that he who made the book
~~Thought it a wise one~~.

{~~Second.~~
{F Thought it a wise one, ~~& I [?hear] that if theres purple~~ on it
~~I should~~
~~I should be certain, we that he loved the page~~
~~Because~~ they
~~Because they ground pure gold into~~ their purple
I ~~should be certain that he loved the page~~.

1}
3} Find a purple page

[MS. VA, 2r; 27–35]

[MS. VA, 2^{r}; 27–35]

1 I have heard they mix pure gold into their purple.
(one takes up book)
2 3. Come spread it out.
1 It s such a weight
3 It ought to hold the wisdom of the world
{2
4 {1 We can all see it if we spread it out
5 On the fool s back. Make him spread out his arms
6 ~~Down on your knees fool~~
2 ——————— ~~And Hunch up your~~ back.
7 Down down on your knees.
Hunch up your back.
8 And look like a gold eagle in a church
9 Fool. Give me a penny.
1 Give me a penny. ~~Silence, Fool~~
hush
10 Is that a right cry for an eagle cock
11 That s a fine passage with the birds & beasts.
3.
12 But surely there d be men not beasts upon it
13 If it were wise.
1. My mother used to say
14 ~~Had more of nature in them, than had~~
15 That birds & beasts had more of nature in them
16 Than men & women, & for that saw more
17 2 But how can they lack reason and know more.
18 3. ~~John there has got some story in his head~~

---

9 "me" written in error for "you"? "Silence" canceled twice.

14–18 On the facing recto, 1^{v}, WBY wrote a comment:

> Make the choice depend on 'angel
> or beast' take out emphasis on
> guilding—use ordinary blank verse or
> prose.

[MS. VA, 3r, 36–43]

[MS. VA, 3[r], 36–43]

Jack
1 ~~John~~ there has got some story in his head
~~Of~~
2 Of how his man [?] learned the talk of beasts
3 And married the kings daughter.
Fool.
Give me a penny.
3 pupil.
4 I close my eyes & pick a passage out
1 Pupil
5 ~~Thats the best way.~~
~~1 Now put~~ your finger on it.
~~2 Pupil~~
1 pupil
6 ~~Thats the best way I Ill turn the pages~~ over
7 That s the best way—You down your finger on it
8 Ill turn the pages slowly.
Third.
There I ve chosen
First Pupil.
9 So many beasts that it is hard to read it
10 What s that first letter thats a sort of band
11 Twisted & [?strained] into a love knot
12 Keep still, keep still—grip him & keep him still
13 Now I have got it—initial letter & all
14 And if as I have heard what s wise is strange
15 And sounds like nonsense till you are used to it
16 This is pure wisdom.
~~Fool.~~ 3. Here s Master coming.

7 "put" omitted after "You".

[MS. VA, 4r; 44, 50–59]

[MS. VA, 4r; 44, 50–59]

Takes book from fools back.
Fool
1 Will no one give me pennies.
1 Pupil.
2 We have chosen it Master
3 ~~This book was~~
4 This book was lying open on your desk
found
5 ~~And we have chosen a su~~
6 And we have picked a subject for the lesson
7 ~~There by the twisted beast.~~
8 This passage by the beast that s knotted up
9 ~~As [? ? ?] fury.~~
10 As though it would devour itself in fury
Master.
11 That passage what right had you to choose that passage.
Pupil.
12 ~~Master~~ —
13 ~~You said that you might choose the subject of the lesson~~
14 Master — You were to choose the lesson.
Master
15 That is a foolish passage.
Pupil.
We would know
16 ~~The meaning not the truth of it —~~
17 ~~The~~ Its meaning though there be no truth in it
18 ~~For you have taught us these are all untrue~~

13,14 In both lines the expected subject of "choose" is "we," but the shape of the word is more characteristic of "you."

[MS. VA, 7r, 101–103]

[MS. VA, 7^{r}, 101–103]

  unto
Aye
~~Aye to~~ some frenzy of the mind
And all we have done would be undone
And all our speculation wind.

~~Pupil.~~

~~That must be why — its written~~
~~That must be why its set down that~~ a beggar
~~Wrote it upon the walls of Babylon.~~
Twas written on the wall of Babylon
This passage has it — by a wandering beggar

Wise Man.

Dream as they please that world is a sollid thing
And shall be to the end & the rest is nothing.
And know you know why it has made angry
That you should choose that passage. Since yesterday
~~It~~
~~It came upon it it~~
~~It~~ But let them dream — the world is underfoot
~~Dream as they will earth s sollid underfoot~~
  That much is sollid &
~~And shall be to the end~~ — the rest is nothing.
And know you know why you have made me angry
That you should choose that passage. Since yesterday
It has been in my head by a strange change
And even now though I can see its mischief
I am not certain that I understand
~~To him that wrote it~~
All that it meant

Several manuscript pages appear to be missing ahead of this page.
11 "me" probably omitted after "made".
11, 18 "know you know" written instead of "now you know."
20 "change" written for "chance"?

[MS. VA, 8^r; 105]

Pupil.
~~Lets leave him to himself~~
~~Lets~~
be gone
Come lets ~~away be off~~
The Master is not like himself to day.
~~S~~ 2 Pupil
~~Master shall you till you ve thought it out~~
Master we ll leave till you think it out.
Master.
~~Yes life~~
Life were [?true would/two worlds] the clashing of sources
~~Streaming against the stream~~, ~~& vanishing~~ away
~~In [?swiftly] giddy frenzies, &~~
Streaming against the stream, and shooting up
Till all was [?be~~as~~ts] & ~~ag~~ angels
1 Pupil.
He is troubled
~~When you are ready Master—ring the bell.~~
Ring the bell Master & we ll come again

[MS. VA, 9^{r}, 106–114]

Wise Man

Strange & out of all imagining strange
That when I have been followed by this thought
~~Beyond all~~
~~Against all reason~~
Though all my reason mocks it —

~~Twice~~
Twice have have I dreamt it in a morning dream
~~And~~ ~~and now my pupils come~~
~~Now nothing serves my pupils but they~~ come stet
With a like thought — Reason is growing dim
~~And Frenzy beats upon his drum~~
~~And And Frenzy has begun to beat his~~ drum
And ~~I must dance to it~~ —
And Frenzy beats upon his drum
And I must dance in follies dream
But now its like a hawk a hawk a hawk
Twice has it come, & this time makes the third
And I must tremble like a bird

A moment more Frenzy will beat his ~~drum~~ drum,
And laught aloud And scream.
And I must dance in the dream
No no but it is
~~But now its~~ like a hawk, a hawk a hawk,
~~That has swooped~~ twice, and this
~~Twice has it come & this time makes the third~~
~~And And what can I but tremble like a bi~~ bird .
has
He ^ swooped ~~over~~ down, & this swoop makes the third
And what can I but tremble like a bird

This speech caused Yeats great difficulty. On this page alone he made three separate attempts at it.

[MS. VB, 1r; 1–20]

[MS. VB, 1^{r}; 1–20]

can the Master be
1. Where ~~is the Master~~

2 He Talking to his children.

3. Hes left the big book there
The book that holds he says
~~The folly & the~~
The wisdom of the word
And all the follies men
~~All~~
& All that has come down
~~From~~ the old days he says.

1. Yes thats the very book
Lets pick a passage out
~~For the days lesson~~
To ask him queries on.
He said that we might choose
~~The lesson for ourselves.~~
The subject for today.

Fool. Give me a penny Sir.

1. How can we choose a passage.
We are too ignorant
that of
He said^the half ~~all~~ knowledge
but the
Was^questioning rightly.
me
Fool. Will no one give^a penny

---

6 "world" seems to have been intended.

[MS. VB, 2^r]

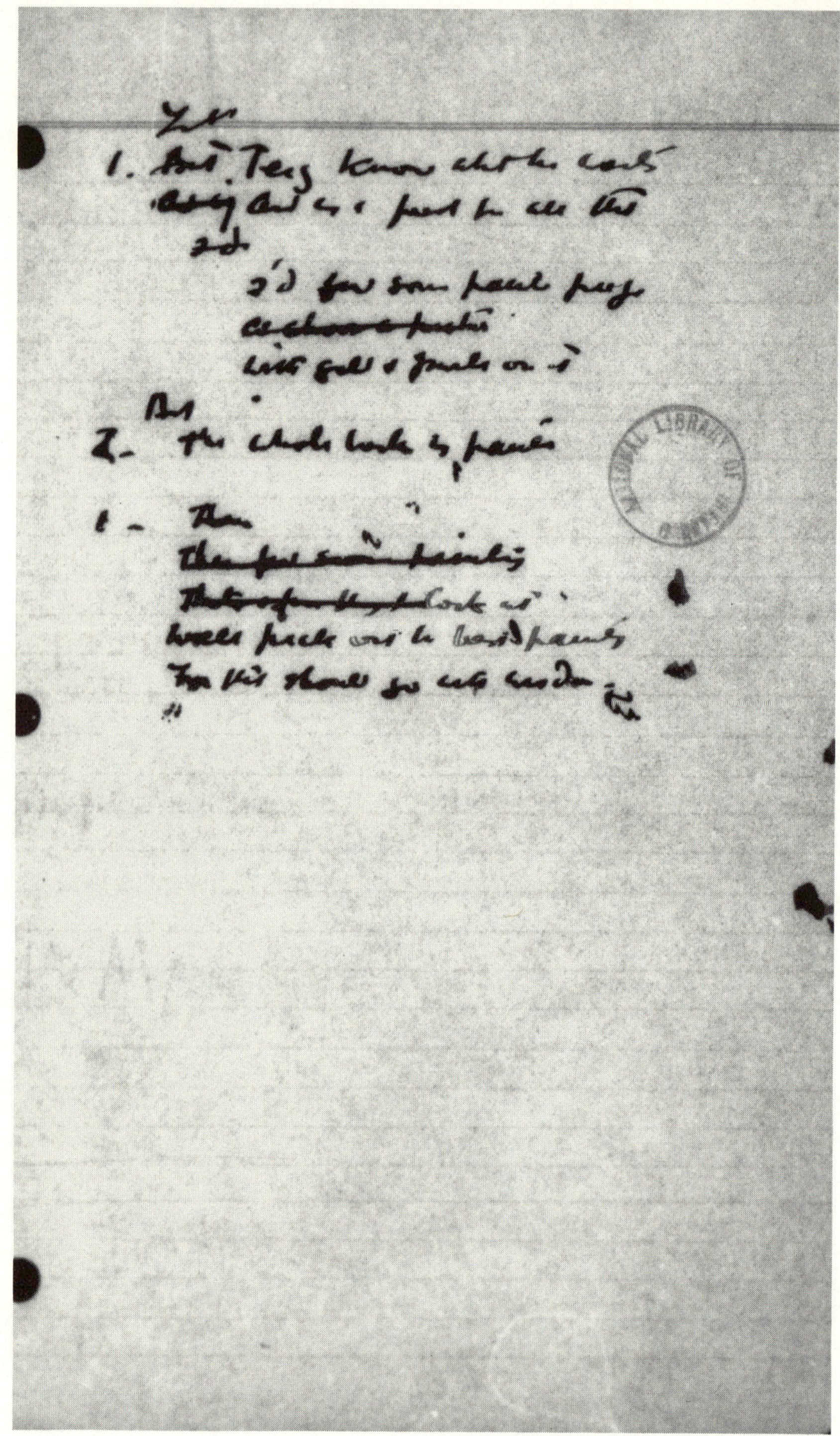

[MS. VB, 2^{r}]

Yet
1 1. ~~But~~ Teig knows what he wants
2 ~~And if~~ And is a fool for all that
~~Id~~
3 I'd find some painted page
4 ~~And choose a picture~~
5 With gold and paints on it

{2 But
6 {1. The whole book is painted

1. ~~Then~~
7 ~~Then find some painting~~
8 ~~Thats a fine thing to~~ look at
9 Well pick out the best painting
10 For that should go with wisdom.

[MS. VCi, 1^{r}; 1–17]

[MS. VCi, 1r; 1–17]

(1

First Pupil

He s in the kitchen talking to his children.

Second Pupil

They seem afraid of him

Third Pupil.

No wonder in that

And he the greatest teacher in the world.
~~When are older, & become his pupils~~
~~As we are~~
When they are older & their minds have grown
And they become his pupils as we are
’ll
They love as well as fear him

Fourth Pupil.

You are right

He is the greatest teacher in the world
Yet may be not so wise in everything
He s closed the churches—driven out the monks
Good riddance too—& yet when all is said
~~They had some~~
They may have had some rags & tags of the truth

First Pupil.

They were half crazed.

Fourth Pupil.

~~there s~~ course
~~It may be that there is some middle~~.
| They said there was a god
He says there is no god & it may be
~~And~~ That as there is a thought twixt mind & body
~~That we call poetry & art & music~~
That we call music poetry and art.
~~So theres a~~ middle course.

~~Second Pupil~~

~~[?Twixt] God &~~ none

This and the following 4 pages are numbered by WBY.
4 “they” omitted after “When”?

[MS. VCi, 2^{r}; 18–25]

[MS. VCi, 2^{r}; 18–25]

(2

Fourth Pupil

1 Whole crazed for all I know
2 And yet if you but give me time I ll prove

First Pupil

3 You ve nothing but a bladder for a head
4 Rattles your thoughts as though they were dried peas
5 But we ll not listen.

Fourth Pupil.

~~If you but give~~ me time.

Second Pupil

6 ~~He s left his big book here~~
7 ~~Stop quarrelling—He said that we might choose~~
show
8 If I'd but time I d ~~prove~~

Second Pupil

9 Stop quarrelling—He said that we might choose
10 ~~A subject for the lesson for our selves~~
11 The subject of the lesson by ourselves
12 And there is that big book of his & in it
13 The wisdom and the folly of the world
14 Let choose a passage.

First Pupil

We have not the wit
15 I ve heard him that but to know our wants
16 ~~Is to be w~~
17 Is the first of wisdom—we are but pupils.

Second Pupil

18 That s true, & if our choice were folly
19 He'd make a mock of us

Teigue

Give me a penny
20 Who ll give a penny to poor Teigue the fool

---

15 "say" omitted after "him".
17 "half" omitted after "first".

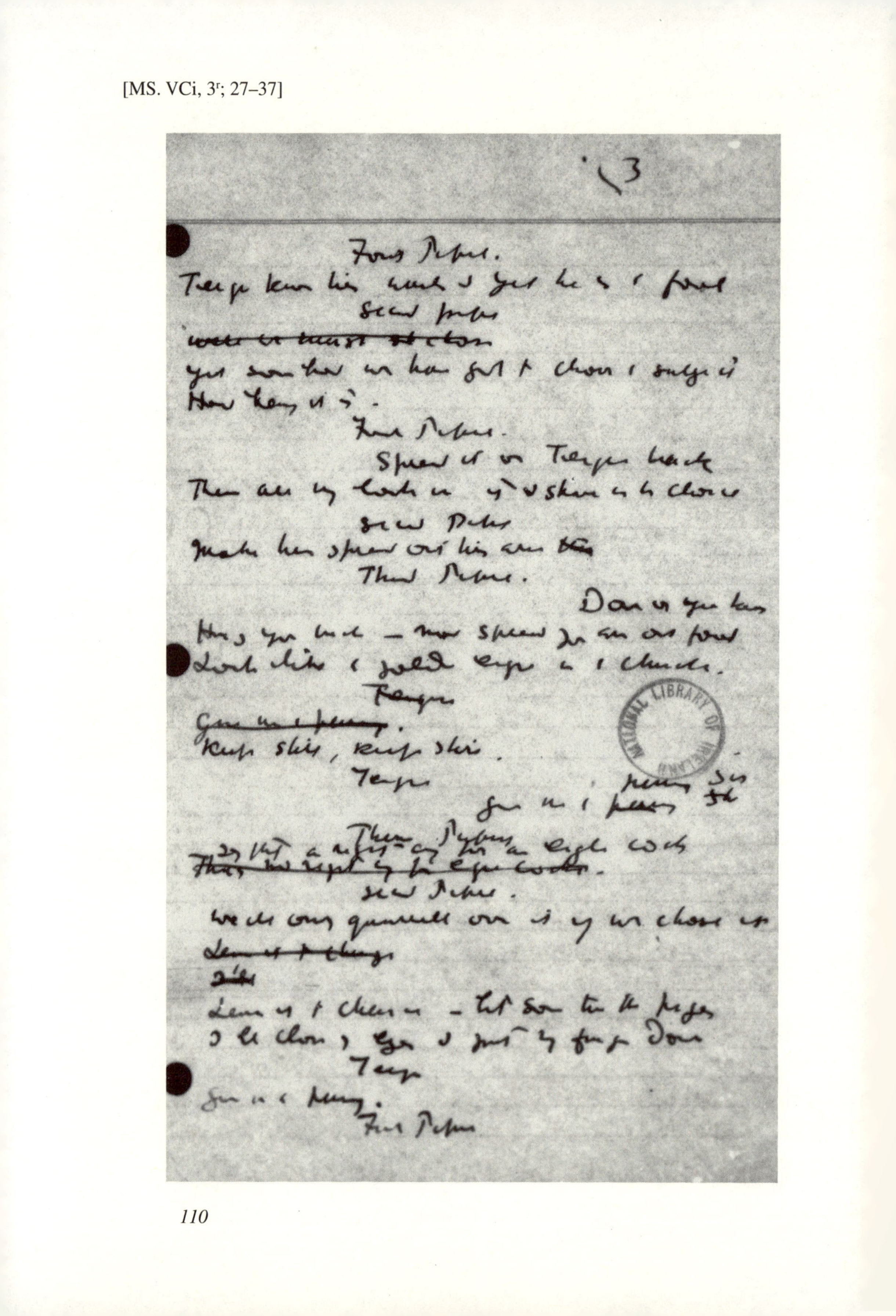

[MS. VCi, 3^r; 27–37]

[MS. VCi, 3r; 27–37]

(3

Fourth Pupil.

Teigue knows his wants & yet he is a fool

Second pupil

~~Well we must st choose~~
Yet somehow we have got to choose a subject
How heavy it is.

First Pupil.

Spread it on Teigues back
Then all may look in it & share in the choice

Second Pupil

Make him spread out his arms ~~there~~

Third Pupil.

Down on your knees
Hug your back—now spread your arms out fool
Look like a golden eagle in a church.

~~Teigue~~

~~Give me a penny~~.
Keep still, keep still.

Teigue

penny Sir
Give me a ~~penny Sir~~

Third Pupil

Is that a right cry for an eagle cock
~~That s no right cry for eagle cocks.~~

Second Pupil.

We ll only quarrell over it if we chose it
~~Leave it to change~~
~~I'll~~
Leave it to chance—let some turn the pages
I ll close my eyes & put my finger down

Teigue

Give me a penny.

First Pupil

---

15 "someone" intended rather than "some"?

[MS. VCi, 4r; 38–48]

[MS. VCi, 4^{r}; 38–48]

4

That is the best way
For then we are not to blame what ever happens.

Fourth Pupil.

No let me choose the subject—~~for~~ I know things
Things by the score and by the hundred, things
You could not reckon over in a life time
I'd argue with him

First Pupil.

~~No well~~
Keep your mouth shut there

Second Pupil

I have chosen now—but its hard to read
For the first letter is a sort of dragon
All twisted up into a lovers knot
~~Keep still—keep still—ah now I ve got that right~~
And the whole page is painted—Fool keep still
Ah now I ve got it—~~Init~~ initial letter and all
And if what s wise is strange & sounds like nonsense
This must be wisdom.

First Pupil.

Here is the Master coming.

Fool.

body
Will no ~~one~~ give a penny to a fool
(enter Wise Man)

Second Pupil

We ve chosen the subject for the lesson Master
~~We ve chosen it from the book—this is the~~ passage
"~~There are~~
~~that~~ says
This passage ~~here~~ 'there are two living countries
One visible & one invisible
And when its summer here its winter there

[MS. VCi, 5^{r}; 48–49]

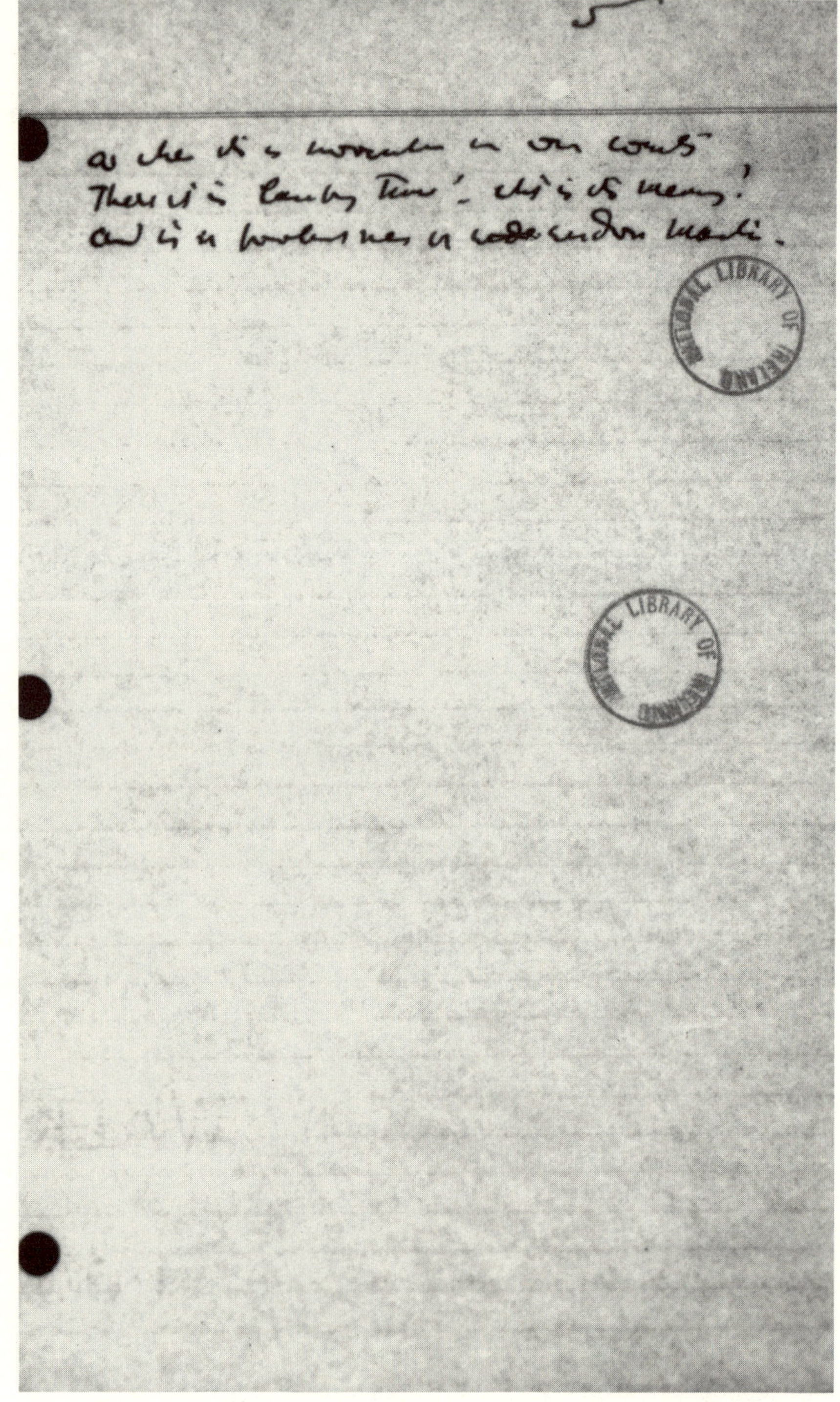

[MS. VCi, 5^{r}; 48–49]

5

And when it is November in our country
There it is lambing time'—what is its meaning?
And is it foolishness or ~~wide~~ wisdom Master.

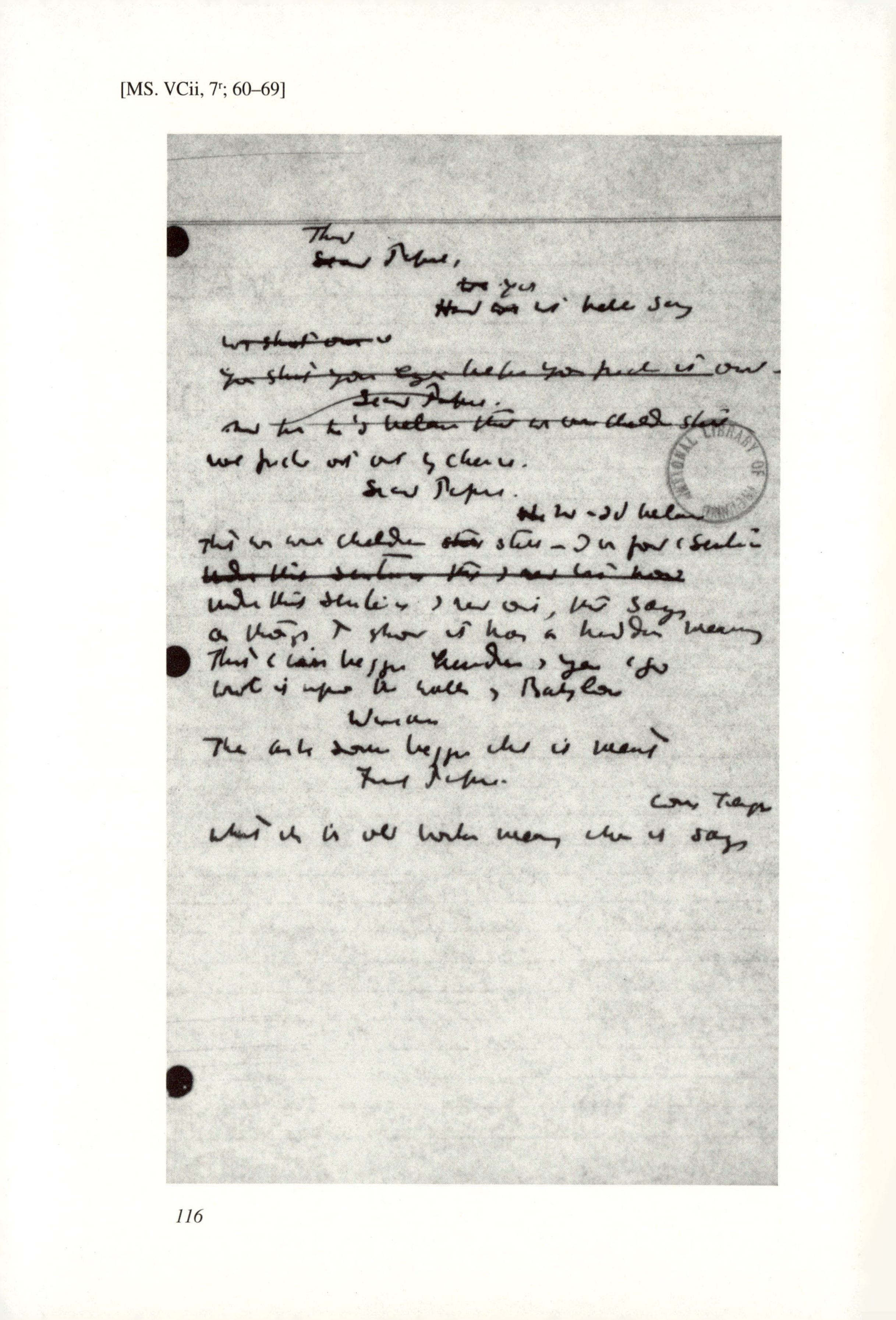

[MS. VCii, 7r; 60–69]

[MS. VCii, 7^r; 60–69]

Third
~~Second~~ Pupil.
~~We~~ you
Had ~~we~~ not better say
~~We shut our~~ e
~~You shut your eyes before you picked it~~ out.

~~Second Pupil~~.
No ~~for he'd believe that we were children still~~
We picked out out by chance.

Second Pupil.
~~He~~ would believe
That we were children ~~still~~ still — I ve found a sentence
~~Under this sentence that I read but now~~
Under this sentence I read out, that says
As though to show it has a hidden meaning
That a wise beggar hundreds of years ago
Wrote it upon the walls of Babylon

Wise man
Then ask some beggar what it meant

First Pupil.
Come Teigue
What the the old books meaning when it says

One MS page probably missing ahead of this page.
5 "out out" in error for "it out"?
13 "the the" in error for "is the"?

[MS. VCii, 9r; 80–105]

[MS. VCii, 9r; 80–105]

Wise man
Who wrote that on the walls of Babylon
Meant that there is a spiritual state
That can alone be touched & known & [?tastes]
When all the faculties where by our minds
Are masters of their state, when all the life
~~We know, or ever can know~~
We know or ever shall know is burnt out
Withers, as though in Autumns wind
And that we mount into reality
Not by laborious, cold deliberate thought
But in a frenzy.

First Pupil.
If he meant all that
I ll take an oath that he was spindle shanked
Cross eyed & had a lousy [?hitching] shoulder
heart
And that his ~~eyes~~ being crosser than his eyes
He wrote it out of malice

Second Pupil.
Lets come away
Well find a better subject for the lesson

Fourth
~~Third~~ Pupil
~~Yes come away~~
subject
And maybe now you ll let me choose the ~~sub~~

First Pupil
Yes come away.

Fourth Pupil
Well make a better
But toll the bell if were too long about it

One MS page probably missing ahead of this page.

[MS. VCii, 10r; 106–107, 115–117]

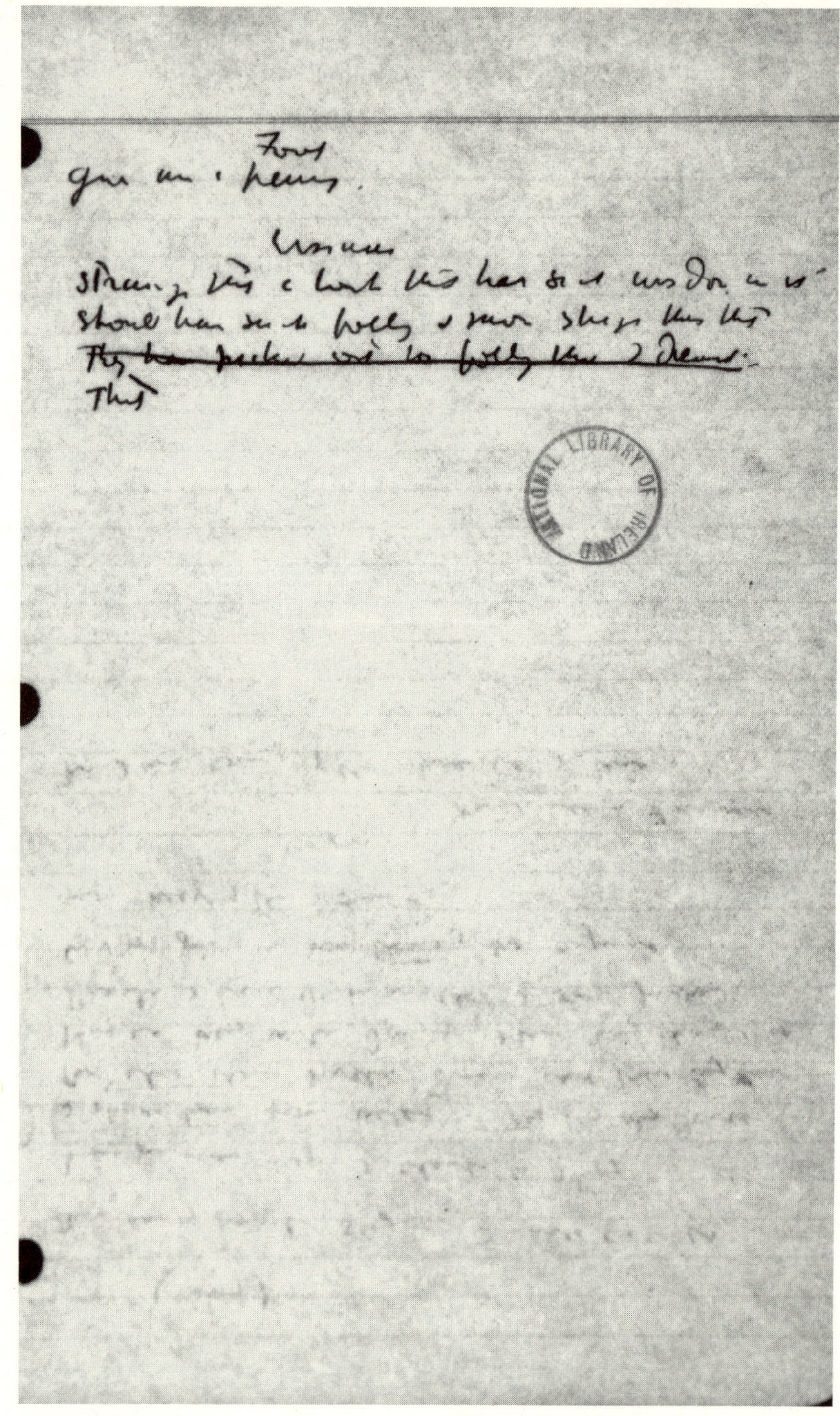

[MS. VCii, 10[r]; 106–107, 115–117]

Fool

Give me a penny.

Wise man

Strange that a book that has such wisdom in it
Should have such folly & more strange than that
~~They have picked out the folly there I dreamt~~
That

[MS. VCii, 11r; 115–128]

[MS. VCii, 11^{r}; 115–128]

Fool
Give me a penny.

Wise man.
That I should dream it twice & after that
That they should pick it out.

Fool.
Wont you give me a penny.

Wise man.
What can it be to you
What do you want — ~~What can it be to you~~
~~Whether the words that I am reading~~
Whether the words I m reading
~~Are wisdom or or mere folly.~~
~~Are sense or nonsense~~
Be
~~Are~~ wisdom or sheer folly

Fool.
Such a great wise teacher as you are will not
Refuse a penny to a fool.

Wise man
~~Why do you call me wise~~
~~Seeing that every body in the world~~
Seeing that every body is a fool
When he s a sleep and dreaming
What do you call me wise?

Fool.
O I know, I know, I know what I have seen

Wise man.
Well to see rightly is the half of wisdom
What ever dreams do with us.

---

5 Cancellation and "What can it be to you" written in same ink as VD.
17 "What" written in error for "Why"?

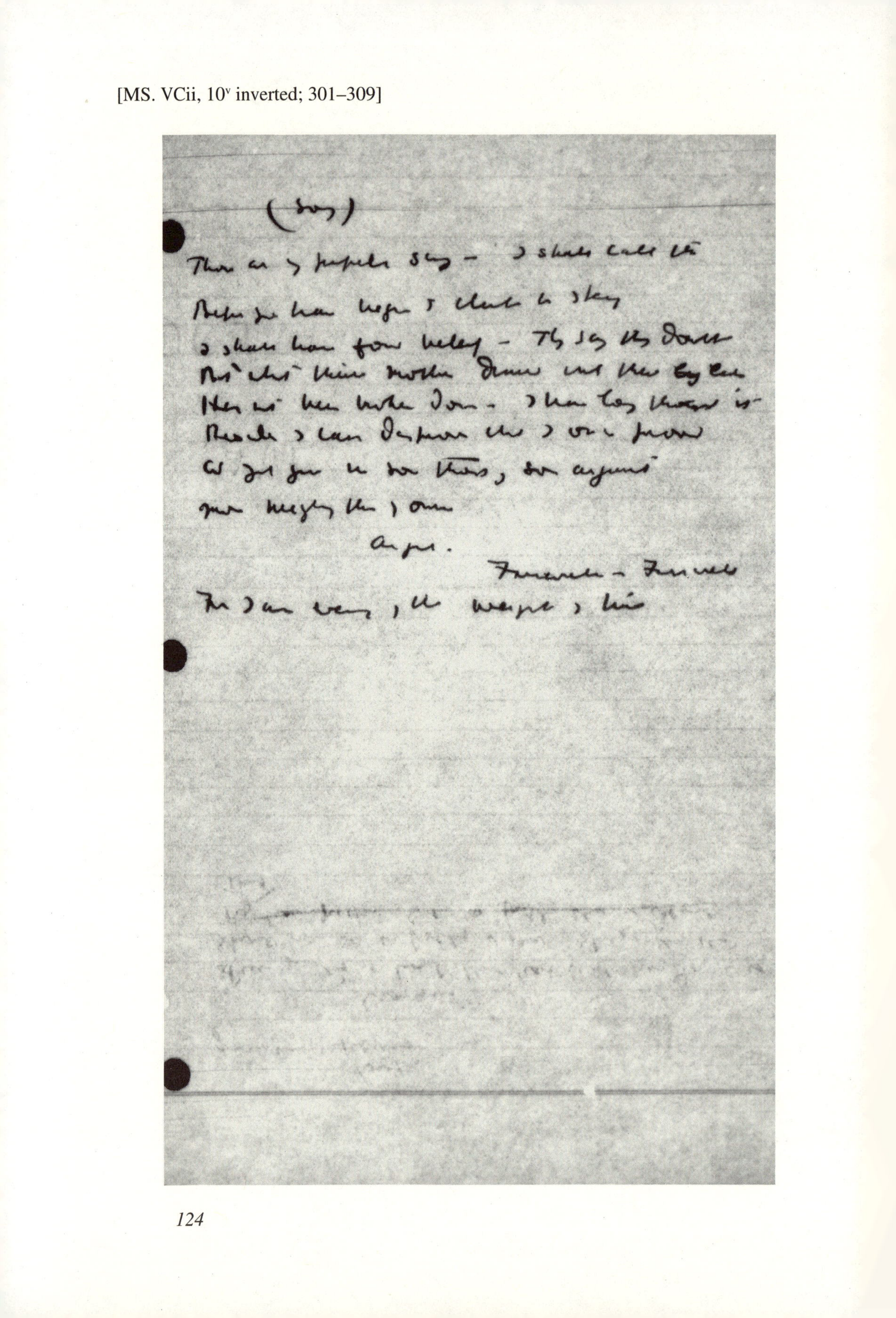

[MS. VCii, 10v inverted; 301–309]

[MS. VCii, 10v inverted; 301–309]

(Song)

There are my pupils singing — I shall call them

Before you have begun to climb the sky
I shall have found belief — They say they doubt
But what their mothers dinned into their ~~ey~~ ears
Has not been broken down — I have long thought it
Besides I can disprove what I once proved
And yet give me some thought, some argument
More mighty than my own

Angel.
Farewell — Farewell
For I am weary of the weight of time

[MS. VD, 1r]

[MS. VD, 1^{r}]

1.

The Hour Glass.

~~Be~~
The wise mans house — an Hour glass on a
stand & a big chair with a great
book upon a desk in front of it.
Before the rise of the curtain there have been
several deep strokes upon a bell. A crowd
pupils of the Wise man
of young men ^ of various ages come in.

First Pupil.

Where is he —

Second Pupil

Not here.

First Pupil

He rang his bell for us

Fourth ~~Second~~ Pupil

And a queer melancholy sound it had.
~~It did not sound so yes yesterday~~
~~Has a bell moods~~
~~No wonder at all if~~ it is
No wonder at all now if it were half human
Being his bell & had its moods like a man.

~~Fo~~ Third Pupil

He s in the kitchen talking to his children

Fourth Pupil

They are afraid of him

First Pupil

No wonder in that
And he the greatest teacher in the world
When they are older & their minds have grown
And they become his pupils as we are

This and the following 6 pages are neatly numbered in pencil in top right-hand corner, perhaps by NLI staff.

[MS. VD, 2^{r}; 1–6, 12–19]

[MS. VD, 2^{r}; 1–6, 12–19]

2.

They ll love as well as fear him

Fourth Pupil.

You are in the right

He is the greatest teacher in the world

~~Fourth Pupil~~

Yet maybe not so wise in everything
He s closed the churches — driven out the monks
Good riddance to — & yet when all is said
They ~~h~~ may have had some rags & tags of truth

First Pupil

They were half crazed.

Fourth Pupil

Whole crazed for all I know

And yet if you but give me time I'll prove

T}
F} hird Pupil

You ve nothing but a bladder for a head
Rattles your thoughts as if they were dried peas
But we ll not listen

Fourth Pupil

If I but time I ll show

Second Pupil

Stop quarrelling — he said that we might choose
The subject of the lesson for ourselves
And here is that big book of his, & in it
The wisdom and the folly of the world
Let s choose a passage

(The Fool comes in & goes
about among them begging)

First Pupil

We have not the wit

For but to find out what one likes & wants
Is a great wisdom — I heard him say that once.

Second Pupil

~~And if when we had found it out it were folly~~
That s true enough & if ~~what we had choosen~~
our choice were folly

---

11 "'ve" omitted after "I".

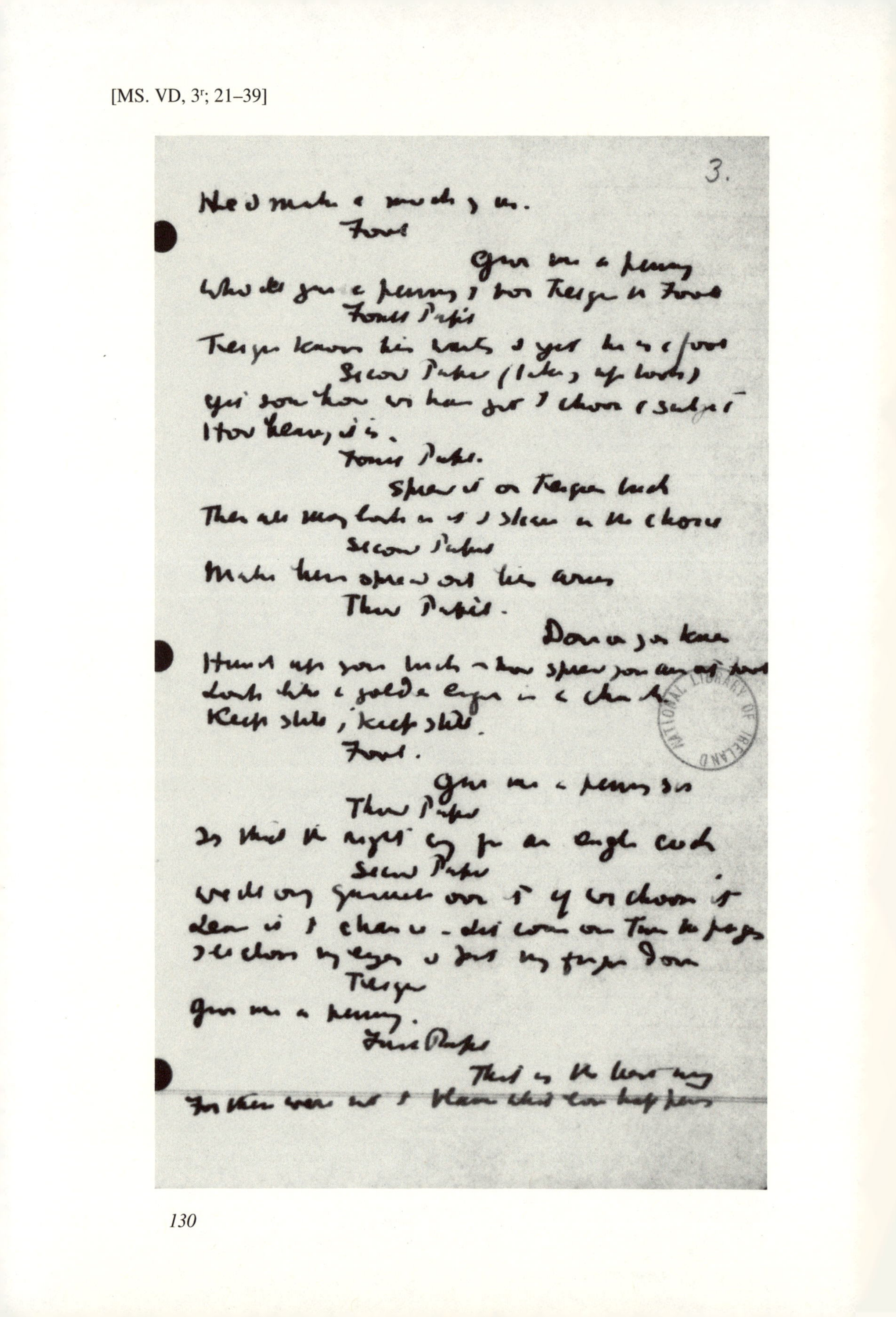

[MS. VD, 3r; 21–39]

[MS. VD, 3^{r}; 21–39]

3.

He d make a mock of us.

Fool

Give me a penny
Who ll give a penny to poor Teigue the Fool

Fourth Pupil

Teigue knows his wants & yet he is a fool

Second Pupil (taking up book)

Yet somehow we have got to choose a subject
How heavy it is.

Fourth Pupil.

Spread it on Teigues back
Then all may look in it & share in the choice

Second Pupil

Make him spread out his arms

Third Pupil.

Down on your knees
Hunch up your back — now spread your arms out fool
Look like a golden eagle in a church.
Keep still, keep still.

Fool.

Give me a penny sir

Third Pupil

Is that the right cry for an eagle cock

Second Pupil

We ll only quarrel over it if we choose it
Leave it to chance — Let some one turn the pages
I ll close my eyes & put my finger down

Teigue

Give me a penny.

First Pupil

That is the best way
For then were not to blame what ever happens

[MS. VD, 4r; 40–51]

4.

[MS. VD, 4^{r}; 40–51]

4.

Fourth Pupil

~~No I~~ No let me choose the subject — I know things
Things by the score & by the hundred things
You could not reckon up in a life time
Ill argue with him

First Pupil

Keep your mouth shut there

Second Pupil

I have chosen now — but it is hard to read
For the first letter is a sort of dragon
All twisted up into a lovers knot
And the whole page is painted — Fool keep still
Ah now I have got it. Initial letter and all
is
And if whats wise ~~&~~ strange & sounds like nonsense
This must be wisdom.

First Pupil

Here is the Master ~~now~~ coming.

Fool.

Will nobody give a penny to a fool

(Enter Wise man)

Second Pupil

We ve chosen the passage for the lesson Master
This passage 'There are two living countries
One visible and one invisible
And when its summer here its winter there
And then it is November in our country
There it is lambing time.' What is its meaning
And is it foolishness or wisdom Master

Wise man

What mischief has there been since yesterday.

First Pupil

None sir

[MS. VD, 5r; 53–64]

[MS. VD, 5^{r}; 53–64]

5.

~~Fourth Pupil~~
Wise man

O yes there s been great mischief
Has queen Maeve tumbled the grey cairn about
And holloed to that dizzy troup of hers
The wanton flesh still light about her bones
That you — all that I ve said or done forgotten
Should pick that passage

First Pupil

The cairn is as it was
She cannot throw it off — you have made it heavy
Before you came she thought it but a feather

Wise man

For all that had you kept it in memory
That we have plucked the angels from the clouds
Wrung miracles from the worlds lips and scooped
Crazed ghosts out of the river bed
You had not followed some night rambling folly
Until you found this party coloured rag
Stuck on a thorn

(He [?] sits at desk)

Third Pupil

Had you not better say
We picked out by choice

~~First Pupil~~
Second Pupil

No — he d believe
That we were children still, ~~I ve~~

(to Wise man)

I have found a sentence
Under that sentence I read out that says

---

16 "it" omitted after "picked".

[MS. VD, 6^{r}; 64–84]

[MS. VD, 6^{r}; 64–84]

6.

As though to show it has a hidden meaning
That a wise beggar ~~a~~ hundreds of years ago
Wrote it upon the walls of Babylon

Wise man
Then ask some beggar what it meant

First Pupil
Come Teigue
What is the old books meaning when it says
That there are sheep, that drop their lambs somewhere
When our Novembers howling.

Fool.
To be sure — everybody knows, everybody in
The world knows when its spring with us
a
There trees are withering when its summer with
Us there snow is a falling, & havent I
Myself their lambs a bleating on a
Cold November day — to be sure does
Not everybody with an intellect know
That & maybe when its night with us
It is broad day there for many a night
I have seen the roads lighted before me.

Wise man
Who wrote that on the walls of Babylon
Meant that there is a spiritual state
That can be touched tasted and understood
~~Only~~ when all the faculties where by our minds
~~Wh~~ Our intellects are masters of this
When we must know our lives are perishing
~~As though they shivered~~
As they were leaves fallen & withered in Autumn
And that we mount into reality

12 "heard" omitted before "their"?

[MS. VD, 7r; 80–95]

[MS. VD, 7[r]; 80–95]

7.

~~Not by laborious cold deliberate thought~~
~~But in a frenzy. That is why I called~~ it

Wise man
Who wrote that on the walls of Babylon
Meant that there is a spiritual state
That can alone be touched, or known or tasted
every
When ~~all the~~ faculties whereby our minds
Are masters of their state, when all the life
We know or ever shall know is burnt out
Withers, as though in Autumns wind
And that we mount into reality
Not by laborious cold deliberate thought
But in a frenzy.

First Pupil
If he meant all that
{Ill
{C take an oath that he was spindle shanked
Cross-eyed and had a lousy [?~~&~~] itching shoulder
And that his heart being crosser than his eyes
He wrote it out of malice

Second Pupil
Let s come away
We ll find a better subject for the lesson

~~First Pupil~~
Fourth Pupil
And maybe now you will let me choose the subject

First Pupil
No
~~Yes~~ come away.

Second Pupil
We ll find a better
But toll the bell if we are too long about it

19 "subject" omitted after "better"?

MSS. VE–VH

Transcriptions of the play's middle and ending, with facing photographs

[MS VE, 1; *c*. 389–398]

THE HOUR GLASS

[MS VE, 1; *c.* 389–398]

[?Have] [?you] [?seen] this.

Our knowledge is but a [?gust it] all [?turns]
~~It changes drifts from us [?floats] away~~
To know what is truth — there is a door we open.
Thoughts come — sightless under stars — all is changed —
One is not quite awake perhaps
1 Pupil — You but say all that to confuse us —
Wise Man — we get a new sight ~~get one sight~~
~~M~~ Pupil — ~~Perhaps one is not quite away~~
so ~~it was but a dream~~
so ~~it is [?but] a dream~~ That is it master — one
is not awake — heaven is a dream.
Master
No — no — no — ~~one sees but it is hard to~~ remember
~~afterwards — even now~~ (draws hand over his eyes)
~~though it were a moment ago~~, it is like a dream
~~I had to believe~~ But I tell you it was no dream
But had I seen an angel ~~staning~~ standing there.

Pupil - You were in a dream — any body can see
an angel in his dreams.
Sec Pupil. Prove that it was not a dream & we will believe
Master O my God how can I prove that, how can I prove

~~Things vanish & come again~~ —
~~Our~~ I thought I knowledge was the same always
I did not know~~, that it would com~~e & go
~~and vanish away~~. that it would vanish
as though lifted away & then come again
[?one] reasons & while we reason
all is changed in the blink of an eye
& we do not know all we believed
I was [?yes] I was awake as
I am now —

4–6 A line in the left margin transposes these lines to after l. 21.
9 "away"' written in mistake for "awake"?
23 Second "I" a mistake for "our"?

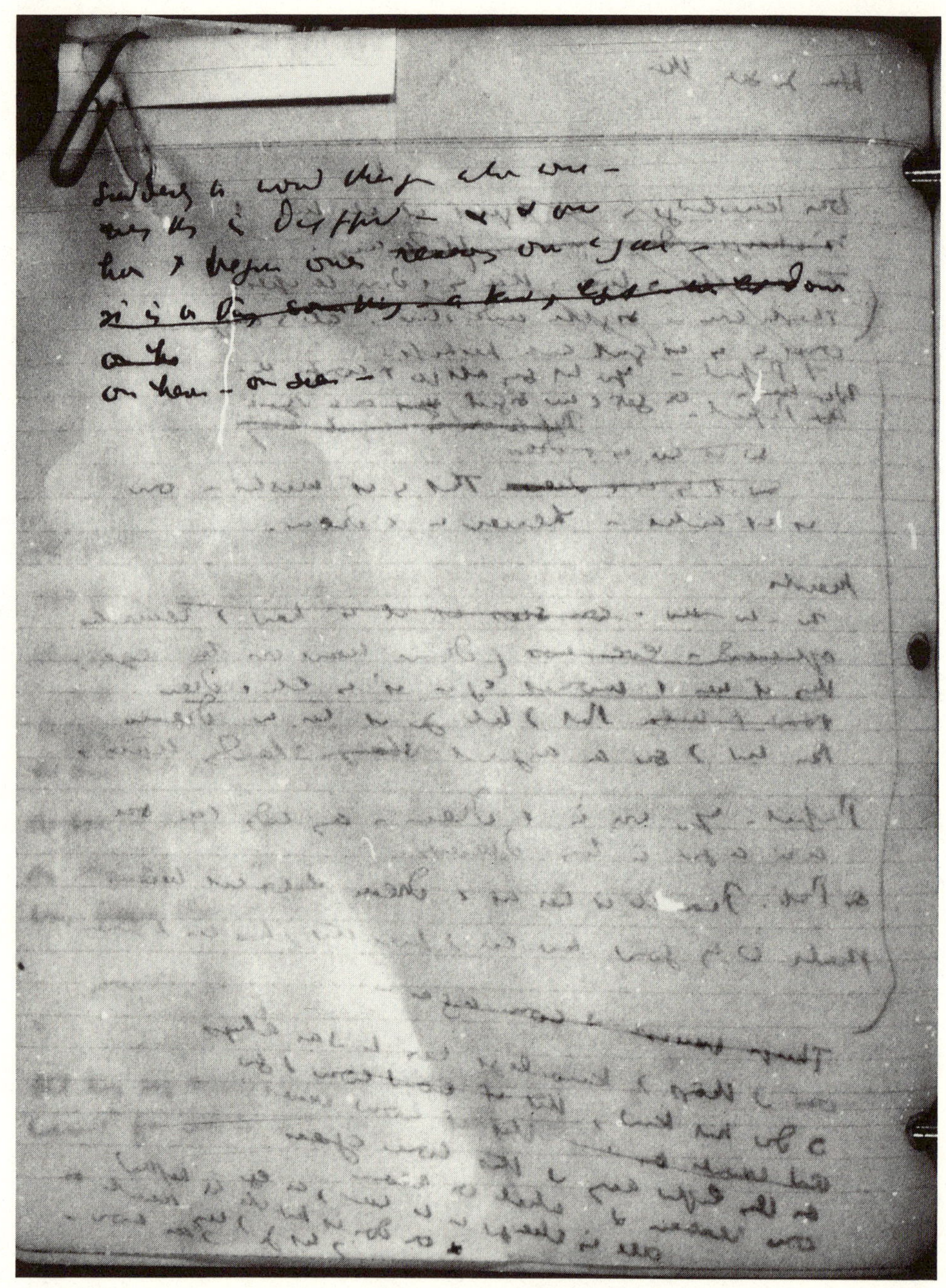

[MS. VE, 2]

Suddenly the world changes about one
everything is different — & so one
has to begin ones reasoning over again —
~~It is as though something — a kind of light — were let down~~
~~one he~~
one hears — one sees —

[MS. VF, 1r; 533–553]

1 but yes yes go — there is little glass
2 in the upper glass I have not the time
3 to teach you. (He lets them go then follows)
4 children if the blades of grass could doubt
{And
5 They d dry away, {F [? ?then ?they] speak to me
6 They all are the fingers of Gods certainty.
(He lets go the children who go out
unnoticed by him)
7 [?~~A~~]
8 ~~I need but one, they are a multitude & will not speak~~
9 ~~And will not speak~~ -
10 I need but one, & yet they will not speak
11 Although a multitude. They have gone away (Fool enters)
12 Can there have come into my face already
13 ~~Some sign~~
14 ~~Some thing~~
15 Some noch of the fiends nail that shows I am his.
(To the fool)
Look at me now fool ~~tell~~ & say if am changing
16 ~~Fool look into my face~~
17 ~~Look in my face & tell me if its changed~~.
(Fool takes no notice)
18 I dare not know the moment when they ll come
19 To carry me away — I ll cover this
20 What are you doing

Fool.
Four, five, six

Wise man.
21 What are you counting.

Fool.
Hush till I am finished

1 WBY evidently wrote "glass" for "sand."
16 "I" omitted after "if"?

[MS. VF, 2r; 553–555, 590–599]

[MS. VF, 2^{r}; 553–555, 590–599]

~~Fo~~ Wise man
What are you doing —

Fool
Hush.

Wise man
What do you count.

Fool
Hush I am blowing at the dandelion
To know what time it is.

Wise man

———————

Kneel to you.
If you on whom my hands rest have
faith I am saved if you have wit.

Fool.
O what a lot Teig knows but Teig
will say nothing.

~~Wise man~~.
To ~~late — to late~~ —

Wise man
Yes — Yes — You are the man that I have sought.

Fool
No No I do not say it.

Wise man.
The last hopes gone
And now that it is too late I can see all,
~~God do~~
Man —

1–3 Modify ll. 20–21 of VF, 1^{r}.

3/4 Long dash marks the omission of a passage that Yeats evidently decided against modifying.

[MS. VF, 2v; 609–624]

The sands have fallen — Goodbye fool goodbye
And I have found the secret of the world
    that
Now ~~I am~~ leaving it — I know what fixed their station
                                                            c
For [?glimpses] of stars & the disordered s} loud
~~For~~
~~I know that to grow simple is to die~~
And knowing all I cry
            ~~so~~
~~May what^ [?] God has willed~~
That what so God has willed
On the instant be fullfilled
Though that is my damnation
The world has changed its course
And every stream ha has run
Into some cloudy thundrous spring
~~Aye climbed its [?their] sourse~~
~~Its~~ Away to ~~som~~ own mountain sourse
Even into some frenzy of the mind
For all that we ve ~~undon~~ done s undone
Our speculation wind.

The lines above are possibly a later revision of ll. 8–28 of VF, 3r; ink blots show that 3r was initially placed on this page while still wet.

15 "into" intended instead of "its"?

16 "its" omitted after "to"?

[MS. VF, 3r; 599–600, 641–643, 611–617]

[MS. VF, 3^{r}; 599–600, 641–643, 611–617]

We perish into God & sink away
Into reality — the rests a dream,
Man dreams the truth, for it is God
man
Who sees the truth in ~~man~~.

Fool. begins to sing

I hear the ~~grow~~ grass grow
And the wind a blow
And all that they know I know

Wise Man.

The sands have fallen — I am growing weak
~~& now at last I know~~
I have found the secret of the world at ~~last~~ length
And found that its so simple that I laugh
~~I am lost — We~~
~~Away. Perishing away is~~
Perishing is but an exaltation
And all grows simple round me
~~All~~
And all grows simple round me —
And though I perish laugh
Finding that perishing is exaltation

And I have found the secret of the world
Now that I leave — I know
their
What gave the stars ~~the~~ station
And the disordered cloud its way
And find it so simple that I laugh.
God I accept your will
Although your will is my damnation
~~The world has changed its course~~
The stream of the world has changed its course

(etc a little altered)

[MS. VF, 3A^{r}; 597–600]

[MS. VF, 3A^{r}; 597–600]

I am growing weaker & now it is too late
I ~~understand~~
~~I understand it all, & & [?wonder]~~
I understand what truth is & have found
For Man does not perceive the truth but God
Perceives the truth in man
~~The world becomes a~~ vision
~~It slips away~~
~~It trembles & slips~~ away
~~The soul trembles be~~
~~And seeing that it slips~~ away
The world becomes a vision.
~~The~~
The strange thing slips away
And all that was held [?or doubted]
Becomes one story.
Go to the door there is one coming for me
Fool — come in & tell me if he is there

Possibly an alternative to the Wise Man's speech on VF, 3^{r}, and VF, 4^{r}, top.

[MS. VF, 4r; 548, 625–633]

[MS. VF, 4^{r}; 548, 625–633]

(He falls.)

~~Fool there is one that should be at the door~~
Fool there is a footstep at the door
It maybe he is terrible to look at
So cover up your face.

There is a footstep cover up your face
For he thats coming will be terrible
~~And if you do but look upon his face~~
I would not have you look upon his face.

(Fool looks out)
~~M~~ Returns to Wise man.
Master — Master —

Wise man.
For
Cover your face —^ There is one
Coming who will be terrible to look at
Put your hands over your face. (dies)

Fool
Master — Master ~~if you will~~ give me
~~a penny I will tell~~ There is something I
will tell you if you will give me a
penny — O Teig knows everything.
Teigue will tell if you give him a penny.
Why will you not answer Master.
(Angel comes in)
~~He is dead~~
Look look what has come out his mouth
There I have caught it my hand
The white butterfly — He is dead & he
Never knew that I am the one who believes

---

21 "of" omitted after "out"?
22 "in" intended, not "it"?

[MS. VF, 4A^{r}; 618–633]

The world has changed its course
And every stream has run
Into some cloudy thundrous spring
~~Even to i its mountain sourse~~
Aye to its own mountain sourse
Even its some frenzy of the mind
For all we have dones undone
Our speculation wind.

(dies)

Fool

Master — Master — There is something I will tell
You if you will give me a penny
Teigue knows everything & Teigue ~~will tell~~
~~What~~ shall tell all that you want if
You will give him a penny. Why
Will you not answer Master.

(Angel enters)

O look what has come out of his
Mouth — the white butterfly — I have
Caught it in my hands. He is dead
& his soul has come from his
Mouth & he never knew that I was the
one who believed, ~~& that he had found me~~.

Another version of VF, 3^{r}, & VF, 4^{r}.

1–8 probably canceled by diagonal pencil stroke that runs off the top of the page.

6 "into" intended, not "its"?

[MS. VF, 5r; 631–637]

[MS. VF, 5^{r}; 631–637]

I that am a fool — you will not
Speak to me angel because I am a fool
but there is the butterfly. Ah you
have taken it in your hands now
You will open your hands in the Garden
of Paradise.

[MS. VG, 1^r; 587–600, 641–643]

[MS. VG, 1r; 587–600, 641–643]

~~If you~~

Teigue

O what a lot the fool knows but he says nothing

Wise man

Yes ~~Yes You are the man I looked for~~ that I have saut

~~Fool Teig~~

No ~~no I do not say~~ it.

I kneel to you — you are the man I have saught
You alone can save me.

Teig

~~No no no I will not~~ speak
No no what should poor Teigue
Teigue that is out in all ~~weigh~~ wethers,
Teigue that sleeps in the fishermans ~~loft, po~~
Loft, poor Teigue the fool. (he breaks away & goes out

Wise man

The last hope is gone
And now that its too late I see it all
We perish into God & sink away
Into reality — the rests a dream
Man does not know the truth for it is God
Who sees the truth in man

Fool (~~looking at hour glass & lifting~~ cloth
(peering in again)

+

I hear the wind blow
And the grass a grow
And all that they know I know

Wise man.

The sands have fallen — I ~~understand the word wor~~ds
~~Thine are the [?shining] lights above~~
~~Even to the changeless [?shining] lights above~~

[MS. VG, 2r; 597–600]

[MS. VG, 2[r]; 597–600]

Wise man
~~Then I am lost. Teigue~~
Then I am lost, for the last grains are falling
And my life ebbs out — Teigue pull [?at] bell
And call my pupils, for it may be at my death
Some sign although it be most terrible
May show the truth, & showing it undo
What I have taught a miss —
(Teigue looks under cloth
at Hour glass & goes to bell)
~~And now too~~ late
~~I see it all — God sees the truth in our~~ us
~~We can see nothing~~
~~We can know nothing — God knows the truth~~ in us,
~~We know it when the world is like a dream~~
~~That at the break of day~~
~~That when the [? first ? ?] at the break of~~ day
I ~~know that~~

And now I know
God
We have no truth but what ^ knows in us
~~Being nothing in our selves~~
~~I was in dreams, & now I must desolve~~
now it is break of day
And Gods great cock begins to crow
And all my
~~And all my~~ dreams desolve away
(start of bell
~~And I begin to know~~
And now that tis too late I know
God sees the truth in man, not man
Whose ~~who~~ who is ignorant do all he can
Until he withers out of time

---

3 "at" written in error for "the"?

[MS. VG, 3r; 597–600, 609–624]

[MS. VG, 3^r; 597–600, 609–624]

And ~~not~~ now that its too late I know
~~God~~ That man is ignorant do what he can
~~Until~~
Until his life is fallen in decay (bell
God sees the truth in man, not man
For man is ignorant — ~~now all is done~~
world change your course
or
~~Now all things being [?] or done~~ (bell
~~And but the~~
~~So Do what it will the stream must~~ run
~~Into that thundrous cloudy~~ spring
Aye to that ~~mountain sourse~~
The world has changed its
course
~~And every stream has~~ r
What can its stream but run
~~Into that mountain sourse~~
Into some cloudy thundrous spring (bell)
Aye to that mountain sourse
Even to some frenzy of the mind
For all that we have dones undone
Our speculation wind. (bell)

Though he that gave their station
In the [?blue] sky
To ~~sun~~ moon & sun & conlation
Fool though he has [?decided] on my damnation
I cry aloud may that which he has ~~f~~ willed
On the instant come to pass (angel comes in.)

In left margin:

critical maxim — vigour is from
metaphor
Might [~~?~~] turn all on a metaphor
'the truths a bird that does not sing in the ~~br~~ tree
till all the leaves decay/

1–6 Revise ll. 24–27 of VG, 2^r.
24 "constellation" was evidently intended.

[MS. VG, 4A^{r}; 611–619]

[MS. VG, 4A^{r}; 611–619]

I understand the world [~~?~~] now that I leave it
I know what fixed the stations
Of star & cloud
And knowing all I cry
That what so God has willed
On the instant be fullfilled
Though that be my damnation
The world has changed its course
~~And every stream has run~~

Another version, perhaps a revision, of VG, 3^{r}.

[MS. VH, 1[r] [verso of VG 4A[r]]; 606–624]

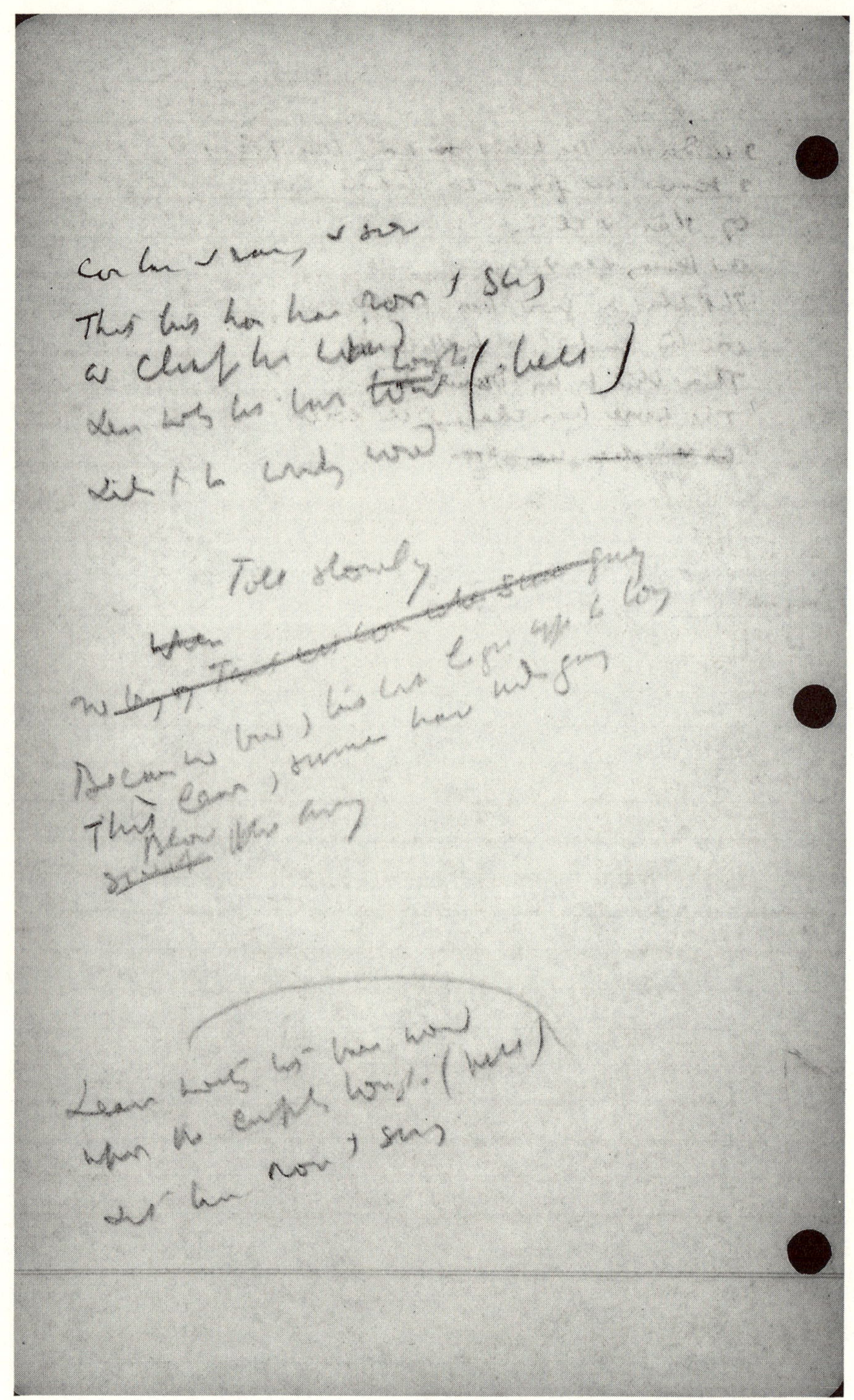

[MS. VH, 1[r] [verso of VG 4A[r]]; 606–624]

1 *Come* [?*hail*] *& rain & snow*
2 *That bird has his* [?*room*] *to sing*
3 *And* [?*clap his wings*]
boughs
4 *Leaves nothing but bare ~~wood~~ (bell)*
5 [?*Like*] *to the wintry wood*

Toll slowly
6 *~~When~~*
7 *No ~~bird of Truth will come when summers gay~~*
8 *Because no bird of truth will light upon the bough*
9 *That leaves of summer have made gay*
Blow
10 *~~Sweep~~ them away*

11 *Leave nothing but bare wood*
12 *upon the empty bough. (bell)*
13 *But has* [?*room*] *to sing*

[MS. VH, 2r; 609–624]

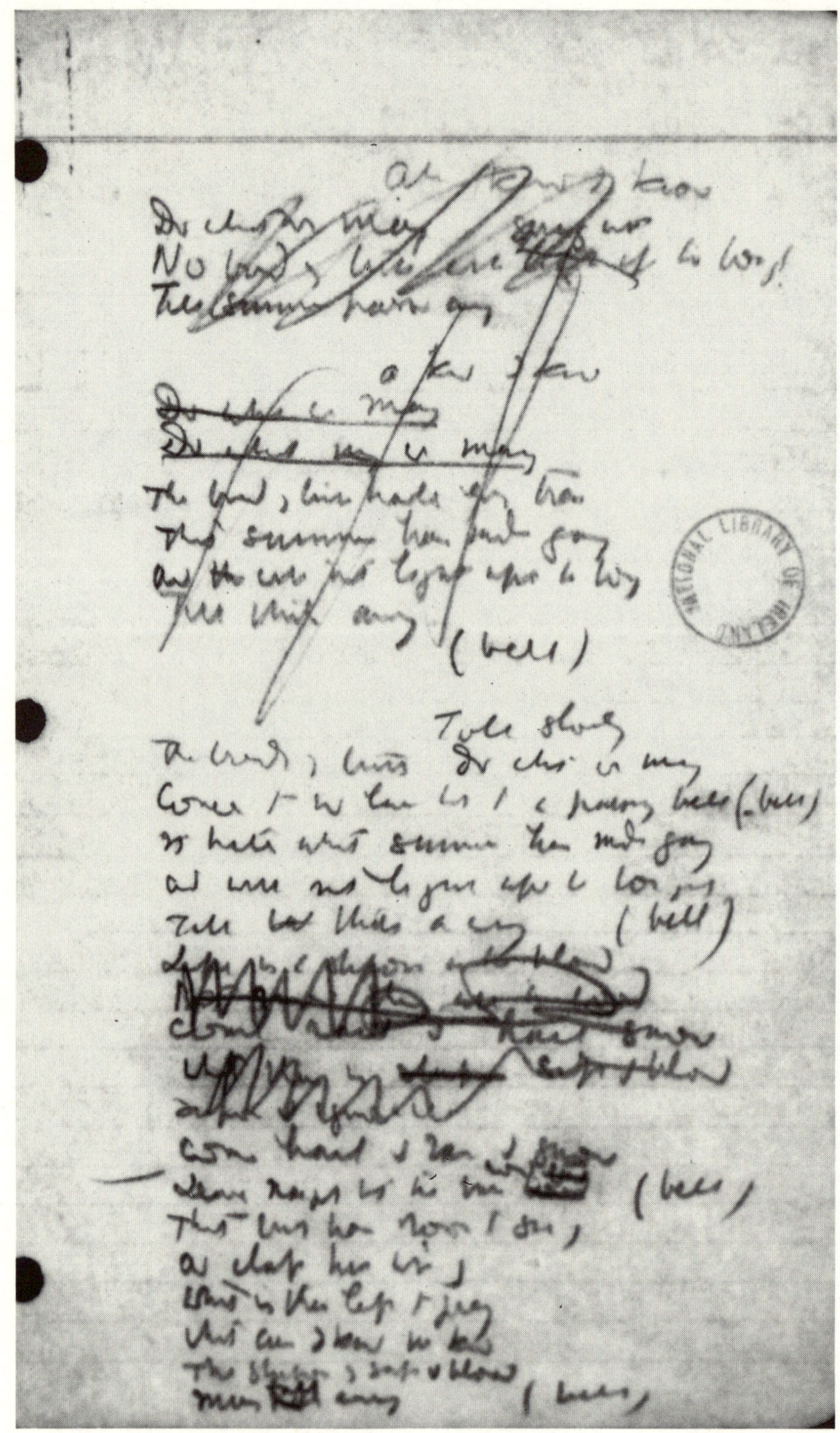

[MS. VH, 2^{r}; 609–624]

Ah know I know
Do what we may
sing upon
No bird of truth will ~~light upon~~ the bough
Till summer passes away

Ah know I know
~~Do what we may~~
~~Do what may we may~~
The bird of truth hates every tree
That summer has made gay
And ~~the~~ will not light upon the bough
Till thats away
(bell)

Toll slowly
The bird of truth do what we may
Comes to no [?*tune*] *but to a passing bell (bell)*
It hates what summer has made gay
And will not light upon the bough
Till ~~but~~ thats away *(bell)*
Life is a stupor in the blood
[?*Not*] *more than* [? ?] *blood*
Come rain & hail snow
What there be ~~stupor~~ sap & blood
Stupor & ignorance
Come hail & rain & snow
——— *wood ~~bough~~*
Leave nought but the bare ~~wood~~ *(bell)*
That bird has [?*room/noon*] *to sing*
And clap his wings
What is there left to [?*say/pray*]
What ever I know we know
The stupor of sap & blood
fall
Must [?~~*pass*~~] *away* *(bell)*

1, 5 WBY evidently meant to write "now I know."

MS. VI

Transcriptions, with facing photographs

15/16 The line was often used by Yeats to mark an interpolation, possibly the passage on 28v which reads:
He s nothing but a bladder for a head
~~And now he s got~~
And now he s got a theory rattling there
Like a dried pea.

[MS. VI, 1r; 1–2, 11–15]

Hour Glass
A big chair with a book open before it, an
hour glass on a bracket upon the wall. Pupils
come in with Teigue the Fool

First Pupil
He has left his big book there

Second Pupil
He told me there is all the wisdom & all the folly
of the world in that book

Third Pupil
I think more of what comes out of his own head
out of
than ~~is in~~ any book

Fourth pupil.
our Master
Yet I would not say that ~~he~~ ^ is wise in everything
Now maybe there was some truth in what the Monk
said.

First Pupil
Do you mean that monk who was the last believer
he was crazy every one said that.

Fourth Pupil.
Well maybe there is some middle course
between those who say there is a god & those who say
there is no god

First Pupil.
Are you going to deny that we have the wisest teacher
in the world.

———— Second Pupil.
Stop quarrelling there our Master said we might choose
~~th~~ the subject for todays lesson ourselves — come
let us choose something out of the book.

Fourth Pupil

[MS. VI, 2^{r}; 3–6, 27–29]

What is the use of our choosing   we havent the wits.
Teigue.
Give me a penny.
First Pupil
That s true, & if we chose wrong he'd make a mock
know what one wants
at us. He said that to ~~question rightly~~ is the half of wisdom.
^

Teigue
Give me a penny — will nobody give a penny to
Teigue the fool
Fourth Pupil
Teigue knows what he wants & yet he is a fool.
Third Pupil
Well we must choose a ~~subject~~ ~~som~~ ~~e~~ [~~?~~]
somehow. What a weight it is — no wonder its
the world s wisdom
Second Pupil.
We can all see if you spread it out on the Fools
back ~~— make him spread out his arms~~.
~~F~~ Third Pupil
Well make him spread out his arms
Second Pupil
Down on your knees — Hunch up your back
& look like a golden eagle in a church.
Teigue (going on his knees)
Give me a penny.
First ~~Third~~ Pupil.
Is that a right cry for an eagle cock — straighten
his arms out. Now keep still — keep still.
Third Pupil.
Let us leave it to chance ~~& then he cant blame~~
~~us~~ for then ~~theres~~ therell be no quarrelling over it

18–19 On the facing verso, 1^{v}, is an interpolation:
Fourth Pupil
[~~?He el? ?~~]
He got that trick of ~~shifting~~ change ~~from~~ his
~~Master~~
[?whoring/whorling] with his master the Babylonian moon.
The last line is also scrawled on VI, 31^{v}: He has gone [?whoring/whorling] with the Babylonian moon

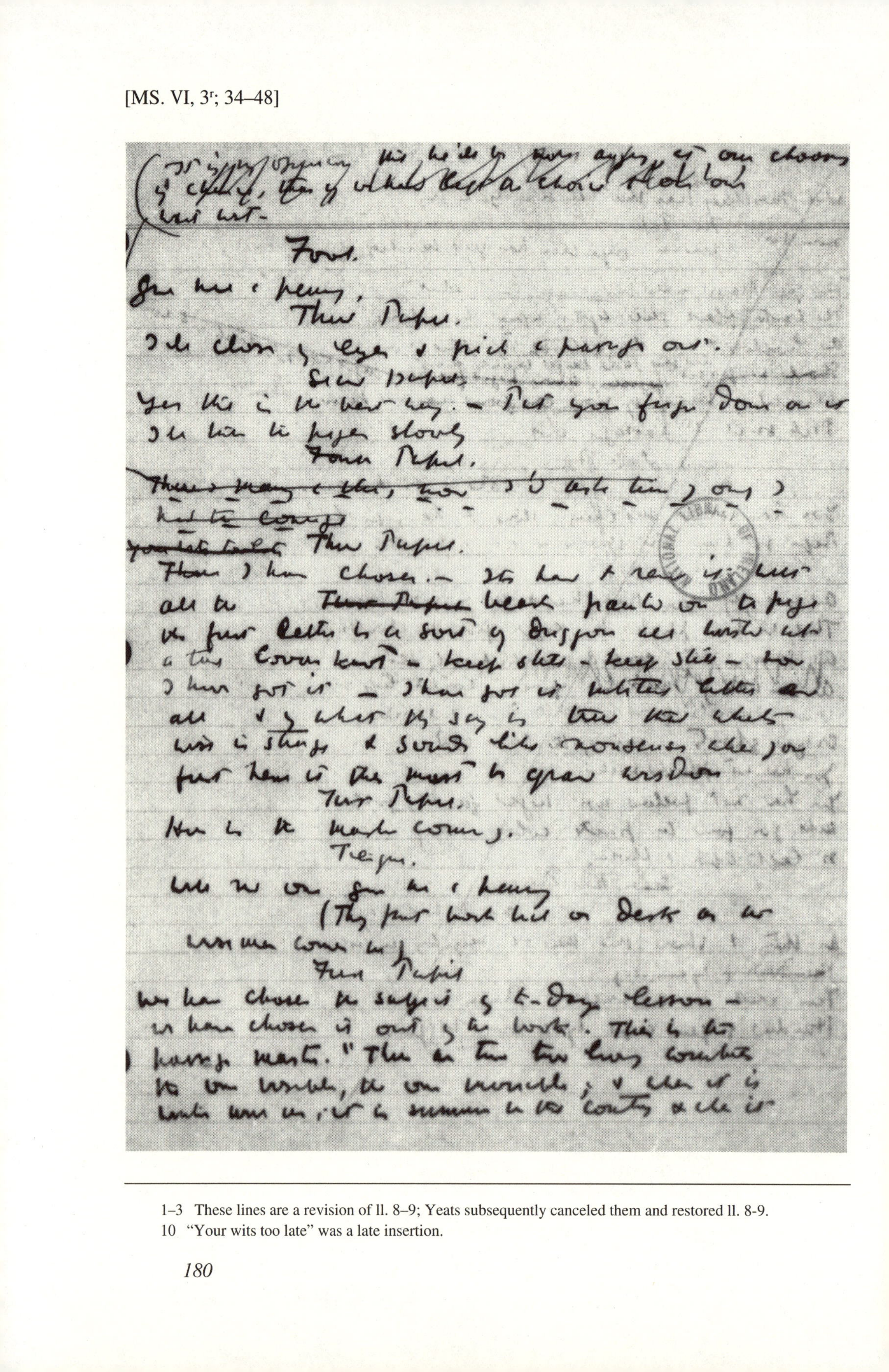

1–3 These lines are a revision of ll. 8–9; Yeats subsequently canceled them and restored ll. 8-9.

10 "Your wits too late" was a late insertion.

[MS. VI, 3^{r}; 34–48]

It is my opinion that he'll be more angry at our choosing
by chance, than if we had left the choice to our own
wwit wit.

Fool.

Give me a penny.

Third Pupil.

I ll close my eyes & pick a passage out.

Second Pupil.

Yes that is the best way. — Put your finger down on it
I ll turn the pages slowly

Fourth Pupil.

~~There s many a thing now I'd ask him~~ if only I
~~had the courage~~

Third Pupil.

~~Your wits too late~~
~~There~~ I have chosen. — Its hard to read it with
all the ~~Third Pupil~~ beasts painted on the page
the first letter is a sort of draggon all twisted into
a true lovers knot — keep still — keep still — now
I have got it — I have got it Initial letter and
all & if what they say is true that whats
wise is strange & sounds like nonsense when you
first hear it this must be grand wisdom

First Pupil.

Here is the Master coming.

Teigue.

Will no one give me a penny
(They put book back on desk as the
Wise Man comes in)

First Pupil

We have chosen the subject of to-days lesson —
we have chosen it out of the book. This is the
passage Master. "There are two true living countries
the one visible, the one invisible; & when it is
winter with us; it is summer in that country & when it

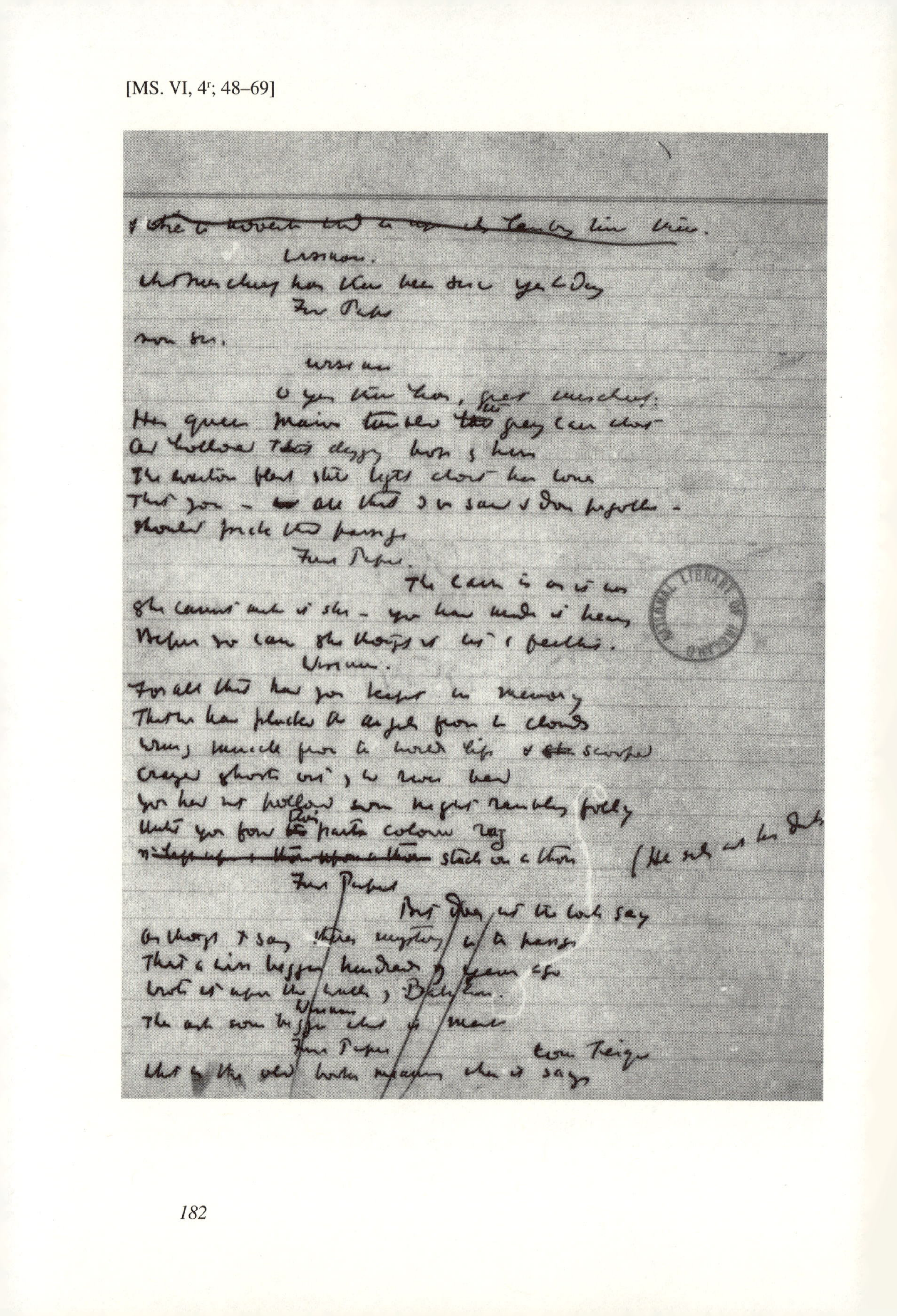

[MS. VI, 4r; 48–69]

[MS. VI, 4^r; 48–69]

~~& when the November wind is up its lambing~~ time there.

Wise man.
What mischief has there been since yesterday

First Pupil
None sir.

Wise man
O yes there has, great mischief
the
Has queen Maive tumbled ~~that~~ grey cairn about
And holloed to that dizzy troop of hers
The wanton flesh still light about her bones
That you — [~~?~~] all that I ve said & done forgotten —
Should pick that passage

First Pupil.
The cairn is as it was
She cannot make it stir — you have made it heavy
Before you came she thought it but a feather.

Wise man.
For all that had you kept in memory
That we have plucked the angels from the clouds
Wrung miracle from the worlds lips & ~~sk~~ scooped
Crazed ghosts out of the river bed
You had not followed some night rambling folly
this
Until you found ~~its~~ parti coloured rag
It ~~left upon a thorn~~ ~~upon a thorn~~ stuck on a thorn
(He sits at his desk)

First Pupil
But does not the book say
As though to say theres mystery in the passage
That a wise beggar hundreds of years ago
Wrote it upon the walls of Babylon.

Wise man
Then ask some beggar what it means

First Pupil
Come Teigue
What is the old books meaning when it says

[MS. VI, 3^{v}; 50–65]

[MS. VI, 3^v; 50–65]

Wise man
What mischief has there been since yesterday

First Pupil
None sir.

Wise man.
O yes there has great mischief
Has Queen Maive tumbled that grey cairn about
The wanton flesh still light upon her bones
And holloed to her dizzy troop? that you
all that I have taught vanished away
~~Should so forget~~, ~~forgetting~~ ~~grow forgetful~~ ~~being forgetful of my work in the~~ world
Should, ~~forgetful of your own good name &~~ mine
Pick such a passage out.

Fourth Pupil
~~She's in her grave~~
You have made that cairn of stone too heavy for her
Before you came she thought it but a feather.

Wise man.
And yet, if you had kept it in your mind
That we have plucked the angels from the clouds
And scooped the crazed spirits from the sea
the
And wrung^miracles from the worlds lips
Wrung miracle from the worlds lips, & scooped
Crazed ghosts out of the river bed
~~You had not plucked~~ ~~picked~~
You had not followed up night fumbling folly
Until you found the parti coloured rag
It left upon a thorn.

~~Second~~ First Pupil
Does not the book say
As though to show that theres a mystery in it
~~Hundreds of years ago~~
Twas written on the walls of Babylon
Hundreds of years ago by a wise beggar.

An experimental revision of VI, 4^r, ll. 2–20, subsequently canceled.

[MS. VI, 5r; 71–84]

[MS. VI, 5^{r}; 71–84]

that drop their lambs when our november howls

That there are sheep in some invisible country
~~Tho That drop their lambs~~ when
~~That when November s howling drop their~~ lambs.

Teig.

To be sure — every body knows, every body in the
Whole world knows — ~~what is the good of an intellect not~~
~~to know that~~. ~~Wh~~ When it is spring with us,
their year lies all a wither, when its summer with us
there snow is a falling, ~~when its autumn wi & when~~ its
~~Autumn with us~~ & havent I heard, on a cold November
day their lambs a bleating — to be sure does not
every body that has an intellect know that, & may be
when its night with us it is broad day there for
~~I have seen~~ many a night I have seen the roads
lighted before me.

Wise man.

~~He who wrote that on Babylon~~
~~The beggar who [?] chose out of the common thought~~
Who wrote that on the walls of Babylon
~~That thought, & wrote it upon Babylon~~ walls
~~the eye~~
~~Meant more than th meets — so deep~~ his folly —
^
is
~~He~~ Meant that there a spiritual state
That can be touched, tasted & understood
Only when all the faculties that ~~keep~~ ~~master~~ whereby
are
Our intellects ~~the~~ masters of the state
must are
Where we ^ live our lives ~~begin to perish~~ perishing
~~As though the autumns~~
~~As though an autumn~~
As though they shivered in the autumn winds
And that we mount into reality
cold
Not by laborious ^ ~~&~~ deliberate thought
is why I called it
But in a frenzy. That ~~why I called the passage~~
~~A foolish passion passage but its more than that~~

---

1 Later revision of ll. 3–4.

16 An arrow drawn in the margin suggests that at one point Yeats intended this line to precede l. 19.

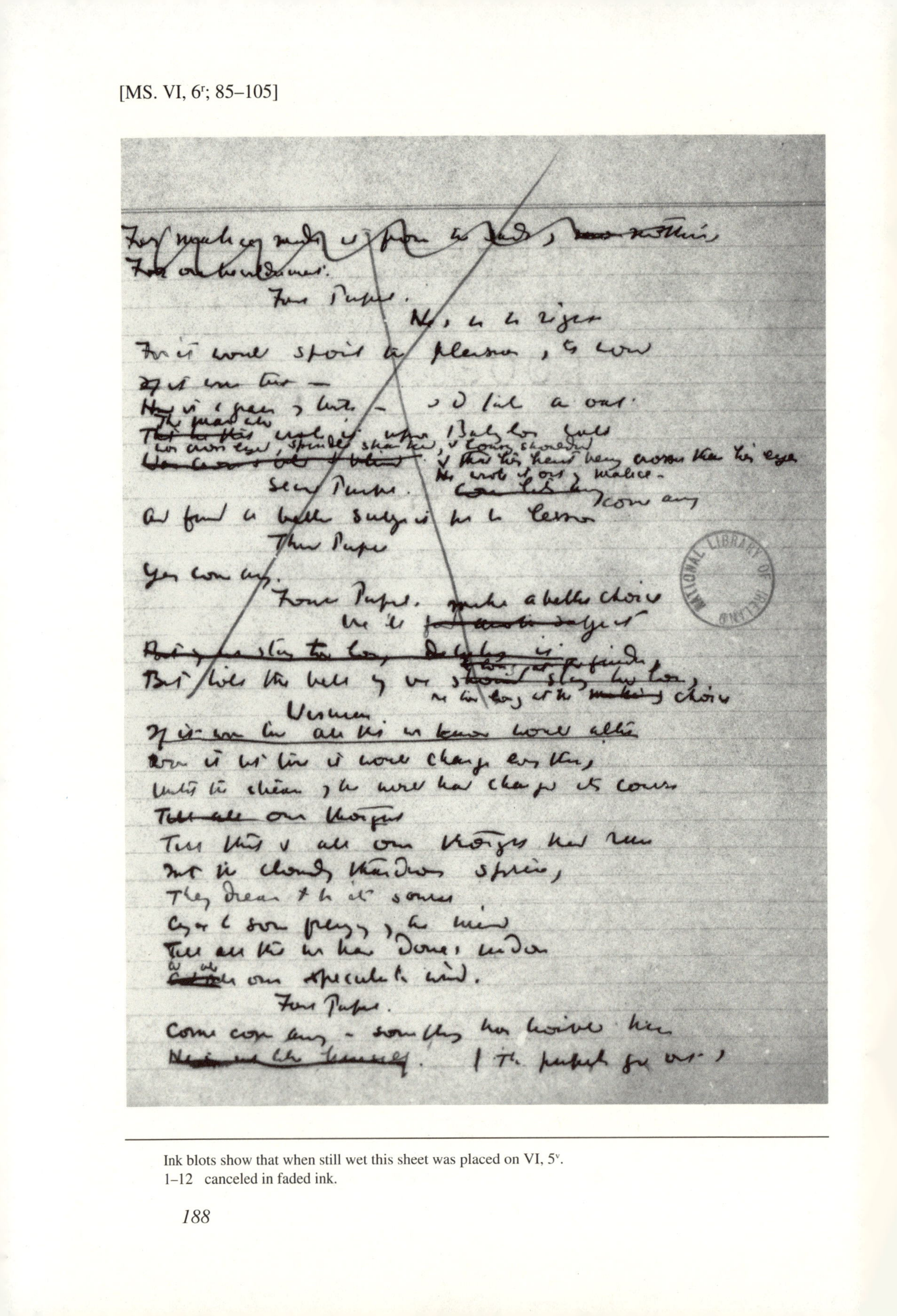

[MS. VI, 6^{r}; 85–105]

Ink blots show that when still wet this sheet was placed on VI, 5^{v}.

1–12 canceled in faded ink.

[MS. VI, 6^{r}; 85–105]

1 ~~For malice made it from the sands of nor nothing~~
2 ~~For our bewilderment~~.

First Pupil.

He s in the right
3 For it would spoil the pleasure of the world
4 ~~If it were true—~~
5 Had it a grain of truth — I d take an oath
The man who
6 ~~That he that~~ wrote it upon Babylons walls
Was cross eyed, spindle shanked, & lousy shouldered
7 ~~Was cross & old & blind~~ & that his heart being crosser than his eyes
8 He wrote it out of malice —

Second Pupil.

~~Come lets away~~
Come away
9 And find a better subject for the lesson

Third Pupil
10 Yes come away.

Fourth Pupil.

make a better choice
We'll ~~find another subject~~
11 ~~But if we stay too long debating it~~
~~too long at the finding~~
12 But toll the bell if we ~~should stay too long~~
are too long at the ~~making~~ choice

Wise man
13 ~~If it were true all that we know would alter~~
14 Were it but true it would change everything
15 Until the stream of the world had changed its course
16 ~~Till all our thoughts~~
17 Till that & all our thoughts had run
18 Into the cloudy thundrous spring
19 They dream to be its sourse
20 Aye to some frenzy of the mind
21 Till all that we have done s undone
And all
22 ~~And all~~ our speculation wind.

Fourth Pupil.
23 Come come away — something has troubled him
24 ~~He is not like himself~~ (The pupils go out)

[MS. VI, 8r; 140–163]

Will this is not the wisdom that has been taught you by your teachers. Wiseman

Run out to the kitchen — my wife gives you something to eat.

Fool.

That is foolish advice for a wiseman to give.

Wiseman

Why Fool.

Fool

What is eaten is gone. I want pennies for my bag. I must buy bacon in the shops & nuts in the market & strong drink for the time when the sun is weak & I want snares to catch the rabbits & the hares & a big pot to cook them in.

Wiseman.

Go away. I have other things to think of now than giving you pennies.

Fool.

Give me a penny & I will bring you luck. The fisher men let me sleep among their nets in the loft in winter time because I bring them luck, & in the summer time the wild creatures let me sleep near their nests & their holes. It is lucky even to look at me or to touch me but it is much more lucky to give me a penny. If I wasn't lucky I'd starve.

Wiseman.

What are the shears for?

Fool

I won't tell you. If I tell you you would drive them away.

but that it was the wisdom they had learned from
Your teaching.

Wise man
~~Wise man~~ Run into the kitchen — my wife
Give you something to eat —

Fool.
That is foolish advice for a wiseman to give.

Wise man
Why Fool.

Fool
What is eaten is gone. I want pennies for my bag
I must buy bacon in the shops & nuts in the
market & strong for the time when the sun is weak
& I want snares to [~~?cathch~~] catch the rabbits &
the hares & a pot to cook them in.

Wise man.
Go away. I have other things to think of now
than giving you pennies.

Fool.
Give me a penny & I will bring you luck.
The fisher men let me sleep among their
nets in the loft in winter time because I
bring them luck, & in the summer time the
wild creatures let me leap near there nests & their
wholes. It is lucky even to look at me or to
touch me but it is much more lucky to give me a
penny. If I wasnt lucky I d starve.

Wise man.
are the
What ~~have you the~~ shears for?

Fool
I wont tell you. If I told you you would drive them
away.

One page is evidently missing ahead of this page.
1–12 Canceled in ink.
2 "will" omitted after "wife".
8 "drink" omitted after "strong".

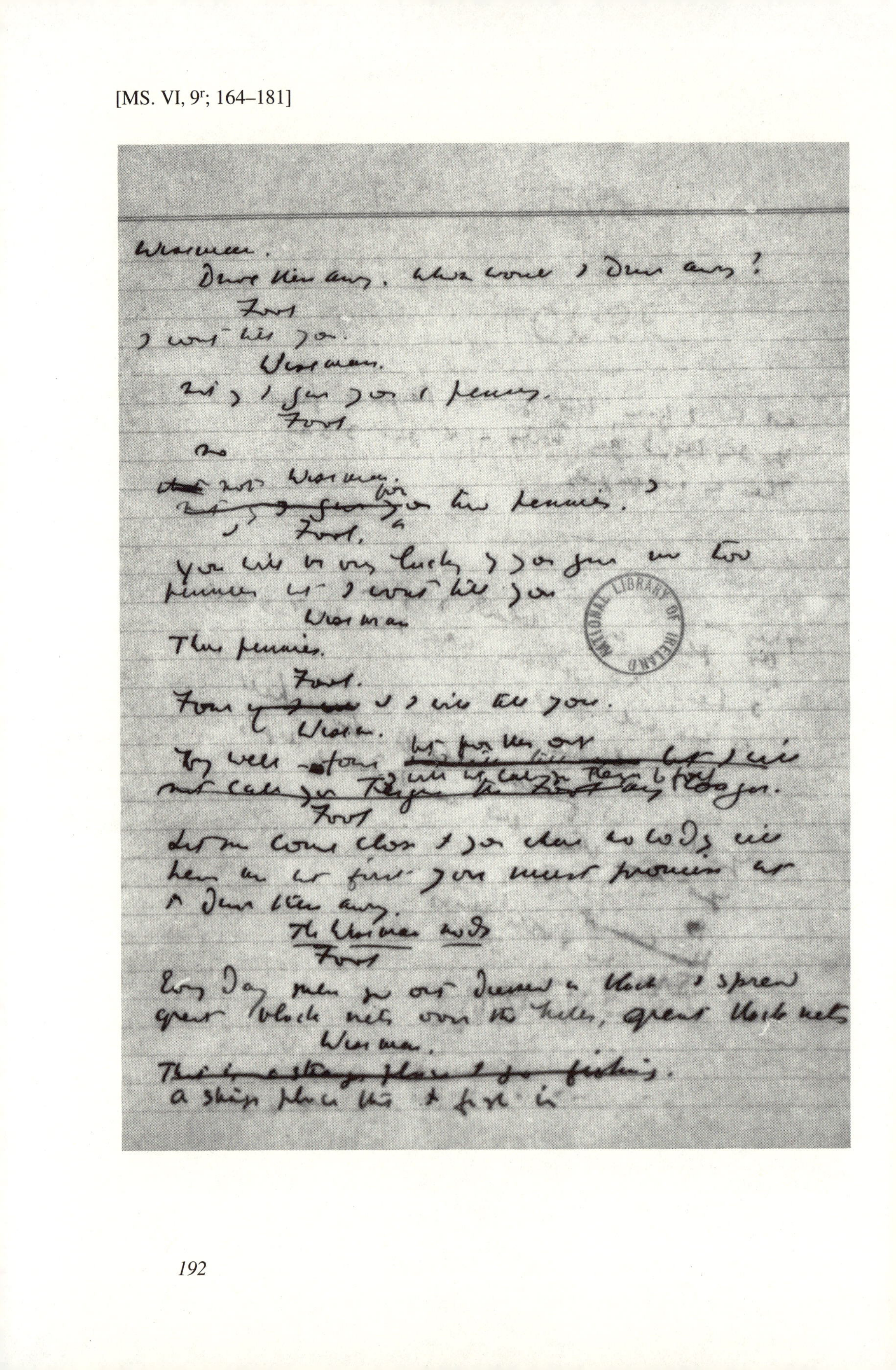

[MS. VI, 9r; 164–181]

[MS. VI, 9r; 164–181]

Wise man.
Drive them away. Whom would I drive away?

Fool
I wont tell you.

Wise man.
Not if I give you a penny.

Fool
No

Wise man.
~~What~~ not for
~~Not if I give you~~ ^ two pennies?

Fool.
You will be very lucky if you give me two
pennies but I wont tell you

Wise man
Three pennies.

Fool.
Four ~~if I will~~ & I will tell you.

Wise man.
{Very but from this out
{F well — four ~~and I will tell you but I~~ will
I will not call you Teigue the fool
~~not call you Teigue the Fool~~ any longer.

Fool
Let me come close to you where nobody will
hear me but first you must promise not
to drive them away.

<u>The Wise man nods</u>
Fool
Every day men go out dressed in black & spread
Great black nets over the hills, great black nets.
Wise man.
~~That is a strange place to go fishing.~~
A strange place that to fish in

[MS. VI, 10r; 182–205]

Fool.

They spread them out on the hill that they may
catch the feet of the angels, But every morning, just
~~[illegible]~~ before the Dawn I go out & cut the nets
with my shears & the angels fly away

Wiseman

ah now I know that you are Teige the Fool. You
have told me that I am wise & I write a whole book
denying that there are angels.

Fool.

I have seen ~~[illegible]~~ plenty of angels.

Wiseman.

no no you have not.

Fool

There are plenty if you but look about you. They
are as thick as the blades of the grass.

Wiseman.

as plenty as the blades of the grass. I heard that phrase
when I was a child & was told folly.

Fool.

When one gets quiet, when one is so quiet that
there is not a thought in ones head maybe there
is something that wakes up inside one — something
happy & quiet, & then all in a minute one
can smell summer flowers, & tall people
go by happy & laughing, ~~& sometimes I[illegible]~~
but they will not let us look at their faces, O no
it is not right that we should look at their faces.

Wiseman.

Oh Fool you ~~should~~ ~~[illegible]~~ have fallen asleep on the hill
side. There are no angels & even though that you saw

[MS. VI, 10r; 182–205]

Fool.

1 They spread them out on the hill that they may
2 catch the feet of the angels, But every morning just
the
3 ~~I come~~ before dawn I go out & cut the nets
4 with my shears & the angels fly away

Wise man

5 Ah now I know that you are Teigue the Fool. You
6 have told me that I am wise & I with my whole soul
7 deny that there are angels.

Fool.

8 I have seen ~~pleny of~~ plenty of angels.

Wise man.

9 No no you have not.

Fool.

10 There are plenty if you but look about you. They
11 are are like the blades of the grass.

Wise man.

12 As plenty as the blades of the grass. I heard that phrase
13 when I was a child & was told folly.

Fool.

14 When one gets quiet, when one is so quiet that
15 there is not a thought in one s head maybe there
16 is something that wakes up inside one — something
17 happy & quiet, & then all in a minute, one
18 can smell summer flowers, & tall people
19 go by happy & laughing, ~~& sometimes there~~
20 but they will not let us look at their faces, O no
21 it is not right that we should look at their faces.

Wise man.

22 Why Fool you ~~should fall~~ have fallen asleep on the hill
23 side. There are no angels & even those that ~~you~~ used

5–7 Revised by ll. 1–3 of the facing verso, VI, 9v. See p. 197, below.
12–13 Revised by ll. 4–6 of the facing verso, VI, 9v. See p. 197, below.
22–23 Revised by ll. 7–11 of the facing verso, VI, 9v. See p. 197, below.

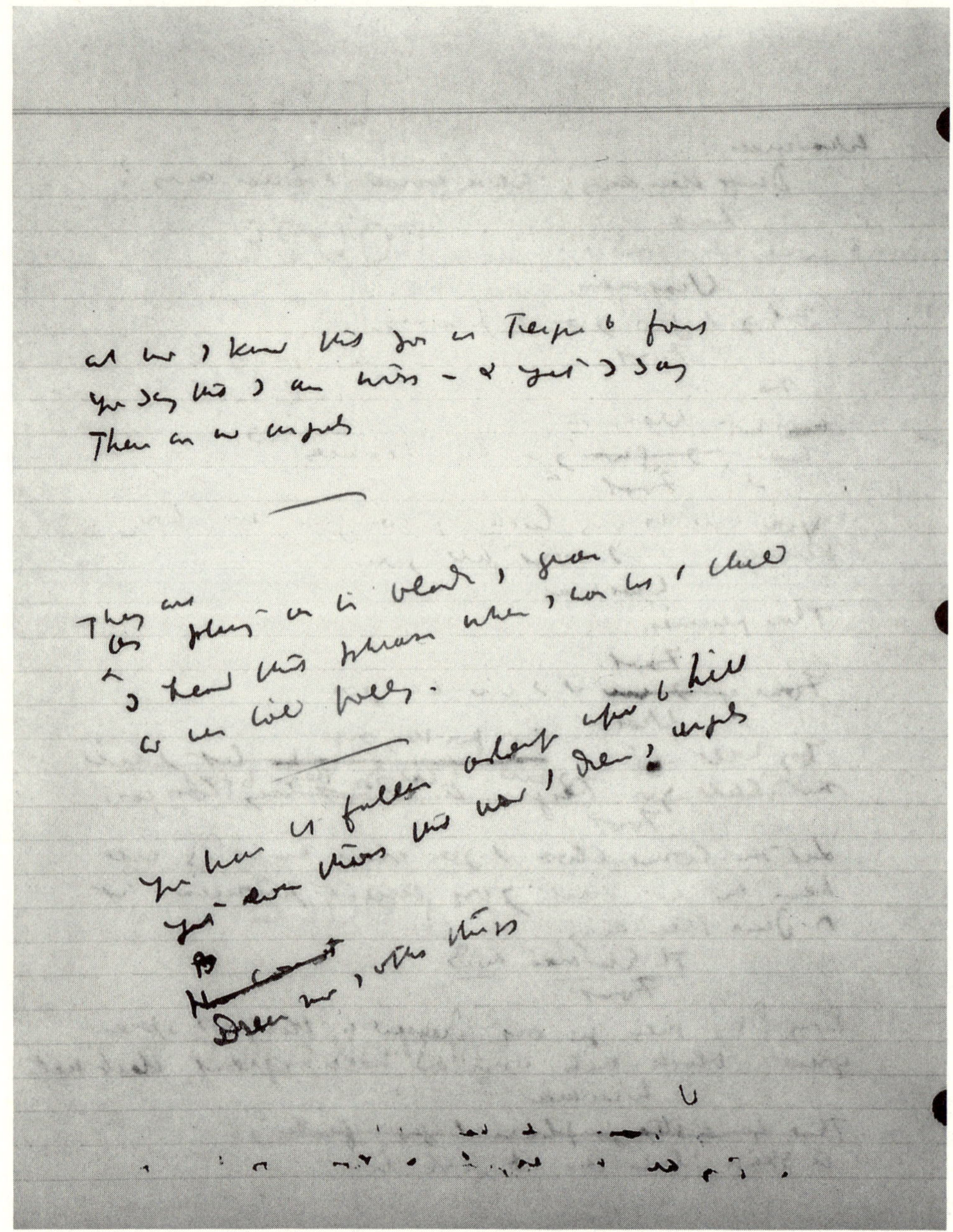

[MS. VI, 9^{v}; 186–188, 193–195, 204–206]

Ah now I know that you are Teigue the fool
You say that I am wise — & yet I say
There are no angels

They are
^As plenty as the blades of grass
I heard that phrase when I was but a child
And was told folly.

You have but fallen asleep upon the hill
Yet even those that used to dream of angels
~~B~~
~~Now cannot~~
Dream now of other things

These are insertions for the facing recto, VI, 10^{r} (transcribed on p. 195, above). Ink blots show that VI, 10^{r}, was wet when placed on VI, 9^{v}, and that ll. 7–11 on VI, 9^{v}, were wet when VI, 10^{r}, was placed on it.

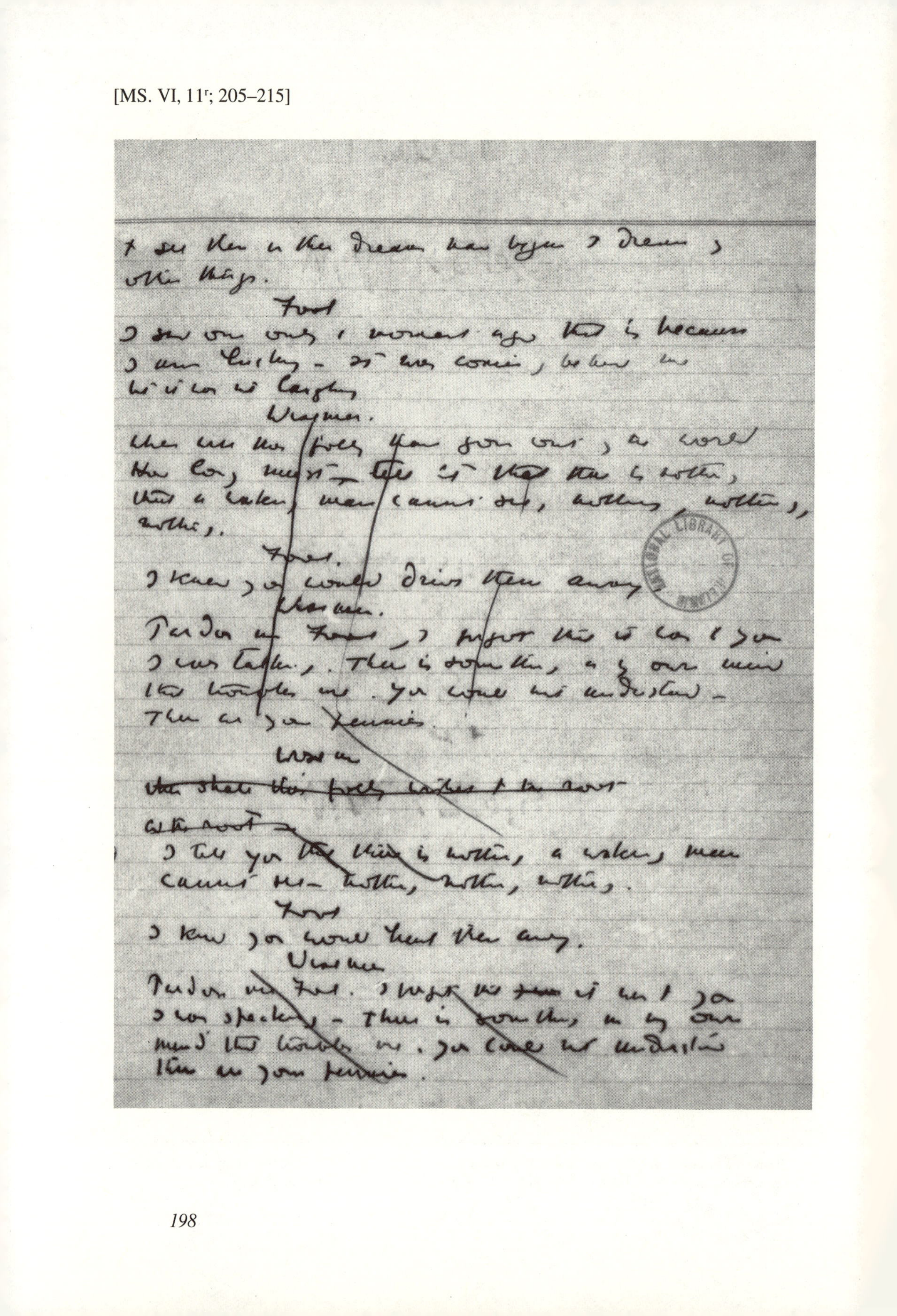

[MS. VI, 11r; 205–215]

[MS. VI, 11^{r}; 205–215]

to see them in their dreams have begun to dream of
other things.

Fool

I saw one only a moment ago that is because
I am lucky — It was coming behind me
but it was not laughing

Wise man.

When will this folly have gone out of the world
How long must — tell it that there is nothing
that a waking man cannot see, nothing, nothing,
nothing.

Fool.

I knew you would drive them away.

Wise man.

Pardon me Fool — I forgot that it was to you
I was talking. There is something in my own mind
that troubles me. You would not understand —
There are your pennies.

Wise man

~~When shall this folly wither to the root~~
~~And the root~~ —

I tell you that there is nothing a waking man
cannot see — nothing nothing nothing.

Fool

I knew you would [?hurl/hunt] them away.

Wise man

Pardon me Fool. I forgot that ~~I was~~ it was to you
I was speaking — There is something in my own
mind that troubles me. You could not understand
there are your pennies.

17–18 On the facing verso, 10^{v}, is a revision:
Theres nothing but what men can see awake
nothing, nothing

[MS. VI, 12A^{r}; 213–223]

[MS. VI, 12A^{r}; 213–223]

Wise man.

1 Pardon me fool.
2 I had forgotten who I spoke to.
3 Well there are your four pennies. Fool you are called
4 And all day long they cry 'Come hither fool'
(fool goes closer)
they
5 or else^ cry 'Fool be gone', ~~or Fool~~
(fool goes to door)
~~or Fool st sit~~ down
(he sits)
6 ~~or~~ or 'Fool stand there'
7 ~~or else,~~
8 or 'fool go sit in the corner' (Fool sits)
and all the while
9 What were they all but fools before I came.
10 What are they now but mirrors that seem men
11 ~~Because my thoughts~~ are
12 ~~Because they have my thoughts~~
13 ~~Because of~~ the
14 Because of my image — 'Fool hold up your head'
(Fool does so)
15 ~~For folly has a new face every day~~
16 For had not they a new face every morning
17 When they were fools like you. What things they told
18 ~~Or be told them~~
19 And trembled with their elbows close together
20 Their shoulders bending to the perishing embers.

VA, 12A^{r}, 13A^{r}, and 14A^{r} are on narrow paper and may well have replaced text no longer extant written on wide sheets.

[MS. VI, 13A^r; 223–248]

[MS. VI, 13A^r; 223–248]

1 What things they told & trembled as they told
2 Bending their shoulders to the perishing embers
3 Stories of ghosts that creep about the room
4 Or fumbled with the bed clothes after dark
5 Or may be were they pious bred of angels
6 That hurried with their messages from heaven
7 And through a mans own door & after that
8 Sollidly to out stare him with unnatural eyes
9 Even on his own floor (angel enters)
Yet it is strange
10 That I should still be haunted by the thought
11 That theres a crisis of the soul where in
12 ~~We get new sight & having~~
13 We get new sight, & how if when it comes
14 That they have some craft to turn it into frenzy
15 Why do you put your finger to your lips
16 And creep away (Fool goes out — he sees angel)
What are you? Who are you

insert here
marked passage on
previous page

crafty

Angel

crafty one that you have called.

17 I am the ~~angel of the most high~~ God

Wise man

How that I called?

18 ~~Why have you come to me~~.

Angel

I am a messenger

~~I bring a message~~

Wise man

19 What message could you bring to one like me

Angel

20 That you will die when the last grain of sand
21 Has fallen through the glass

Wise man

I have a wife

16–17 The passage referred to is on 14A^r. Ink blot shows 14A was placed on 13A^r when cancellation of 13A^r was wet. Further speeches belonging to the dialogue between the Wise Man and the Angel can be found on VI, 26^v.

[MS. VI, 14A^r; 223–243]

[MS. VI, 14A^{r}; 223–243]

~~Bending their shoulders to the perishing embers~~
Stories of ghosts that creaked about the room
Or fumbled with the bed clothes after dark
Or may be were they pious bred of ~~ang~~ angels
That hurried with their messages from heaven
And through a mans own door & after that
Sollidly to outstare him with unnatural eyes
Even on his own floor. (angel enters)
Yet it is strange
That I should still be haunted by the thought
That theres ~~may~~ a crisis of the soul wherein
We get new sigh & how if when it comes
They have some craft to turn it into frenzy
Why do you put your finger to your lips
And creep away. (Fool goes out)
What are you — Who are you
I think I saw some like you in my dreams
When but a child — that thing above your head
That brightness in your hair — that flowering branch
But I have done with dreams. I have done with dreams

The terminating wavy line below the text marks this passage as a discrete section in the revision.

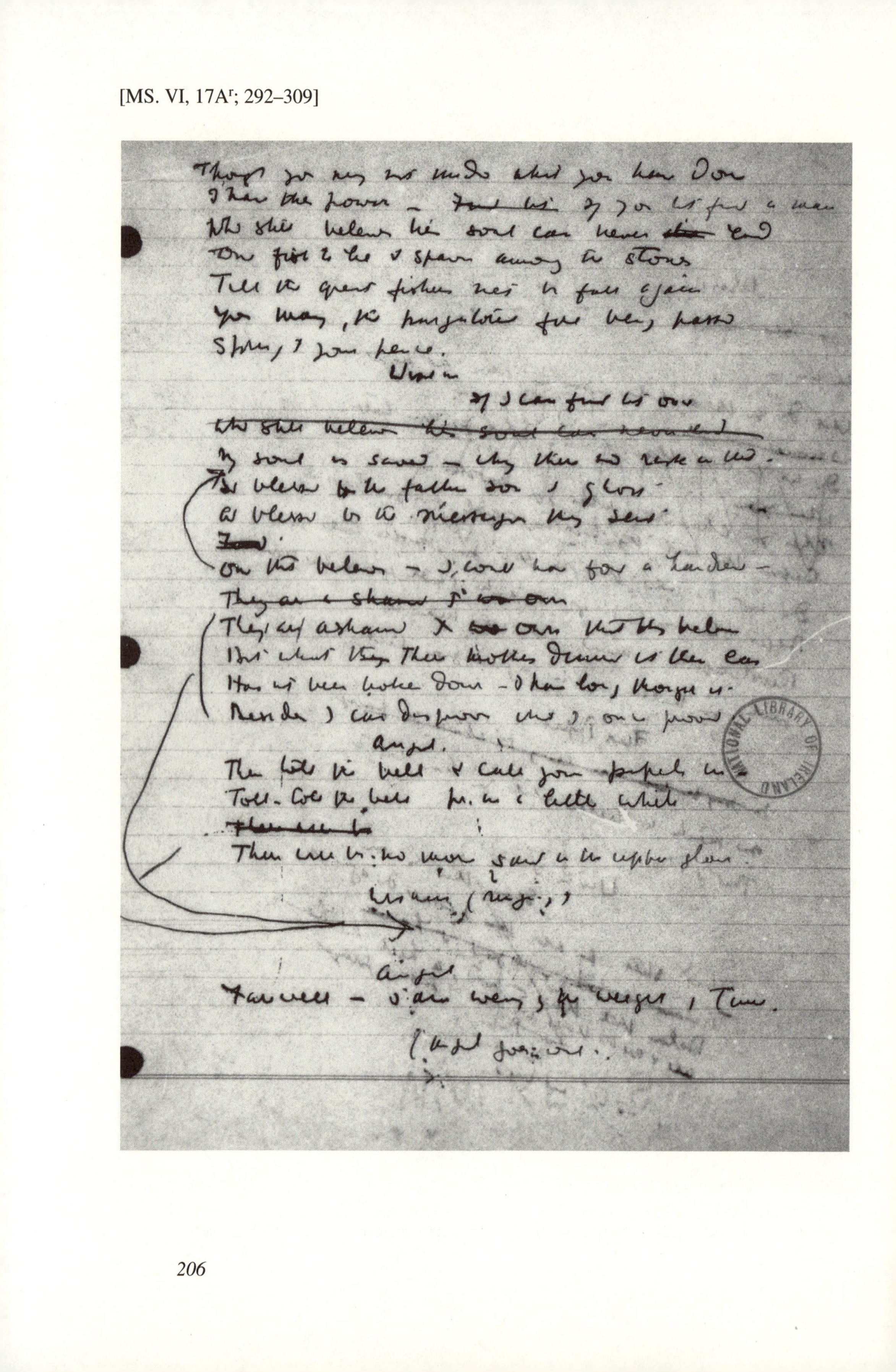

[MS. VI, 17A^{r}; 292–309]

[MS. VI, 17^{r}; 292–309]

Though you may not undo what you have done
I have the power — ~~Find but~~ If you but find a man
Who still believes his soul can never ~~die~~ end
One fish to lie & spawn among the stones
Till the great fishers net be full again
You may, the purgatorial fire being passed
Spring to your peace.

Wise man

If I can find but one
~~Who still believes his soul can never end~~
My soul is saved — why theres no risk in that.
(?So) blessed ~~b~~ be father son & ghost
And blessed be the messenger they sent
~~Find~~
One that believes — I could have found a hundred —
~~They are a shamed to w own~~
They are ashamed to ~~w~~ own that they believe
But what ~~things~~ their mothers dinned into their ears
Has not been broken down — I have long thought it
Besides I can disprove what I once proved.

Angel.

Then toll the bell & call your pupils in —
Toll — toll the bell   for in a little while
~~There will b~~
There will be no more sand in the upper glass.

Wise man (ringing)

Angel

Farewell — I am weary of the weight of Time.

(Angel goes out.

Several pages appear to be missing ahead of this page.

2–7 Variant version can be found on VI, $17A^{r}$.

13 WBY's transposition signal places this after l. 9.

15–18 WBY's transposition signal drops these below l. 22, "Wise man (ringing)".

VI, $17A^{v}$, contains a passage probably meant to be inserted below l. 18 once that had been transposed. The insertion splits l. 23. VCii, 10^{v}, provides another version of ll. 13–18 plus the insertion from VI, $17A^{v}$.

[MS. VI, 17A[r], inverted; 293–298]

[MS. VI, 17A^{r}, inverted; 293–298]

~~that his soul never dies, if you but~~ find
If you but find one soul
That
~~That~~ ~~Who~~ still believes, that it shall never cease
One fish to lie & spawn among the stones
Till the great fishers net is full again
You may the purgatorial fire being passed
Spring to your peace.

[MS. VI, 17A^{v}, inverted; 307–309]

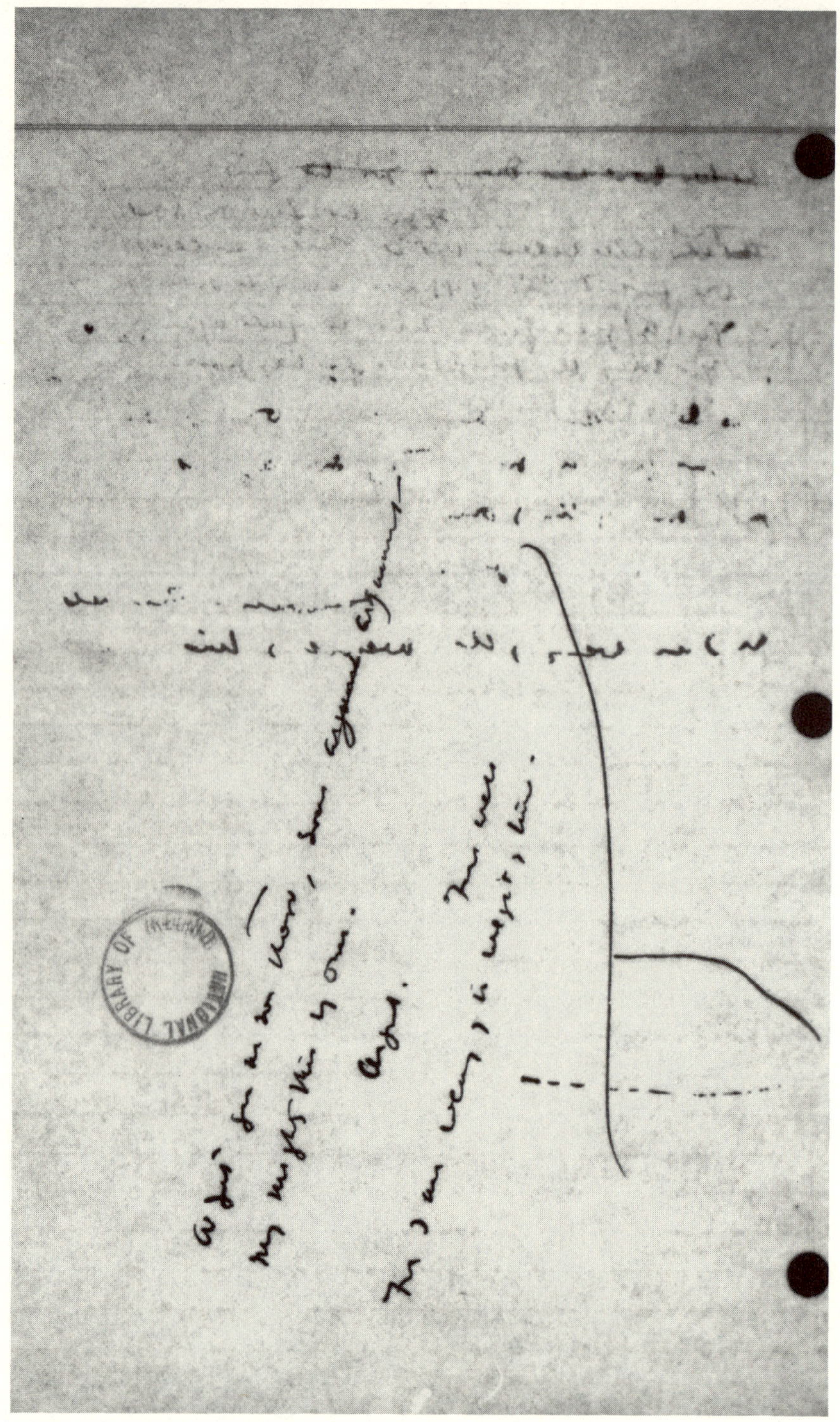

[MS. VI, 17A^{v}, inverted; 307–309]

And yet give me some thought, some ~~argument~~ argument
More mighty than my own.

Angel.

Fare well
For I am weary of the weight of time.

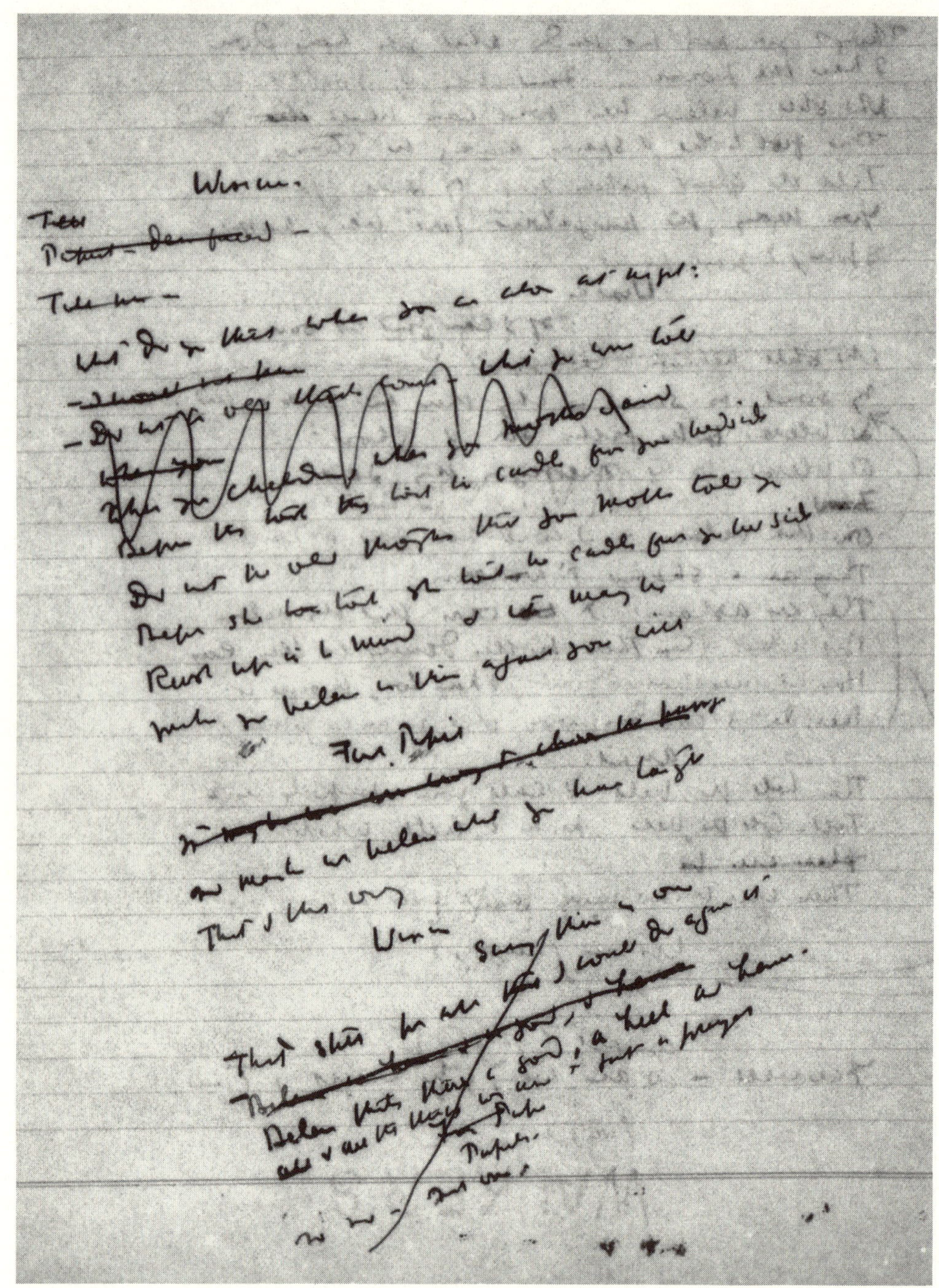

[MS. VI, 17^{v}; 334–345]

Wise man.

~~Tell~~
~~Pupils — dear friends —~~
~~Tell me~~ —
What do you think when you are alone at night.
— ~~I would not have~~
— Do not the old thoughts come — what you were told
~~When you~~
When you children, when your mothers said
Before they took they took the candle from your bedside
Do not the old thoughts that your mother told you
Before she ~~too~~ took she took the candle from your bed side
Rush up in the mind & it may be
Make you believe in them against your will

First Pupil

~~It maybe we were wrong to choose the passage~~
No Master we believe what you have taught
That & that only

Wise man

Surely there is one
That still for all ~~that~~ I could do against it
~~Believes in heaven & in God, & heaven~~
Believes that theres a god, a hell and heaven.
~~All~~ & all the things we used to put in prayers

~~Fourth Pupil~~
Pupils.

No no — Not one.

This passage belongs after VI, 18^{r}. Ink blots show that 18^{r} was placed on 17^{v} when the ink on both pages was still wet. VI, 20^{r} seems to be a revision of this page.

17–21 These lines appear to be revised on VI, 20^{v}.

[MS. VI, 18^{r}; 311–334]

[MS. VI, 18r; 311–334]

Enter pupils with Fool ~~whom they are~~ [?~~there~~]
~~dragging~~ — Pupils dancing round fool
1 ~~What stole your~~ wi
Pupil.
2 Who stole your wits away
3 And where have they gone
4 Run Teigue & find them
5 Up or down.
~~Another Pupil~~.
6 ~~Have they gone up or down Teigue~~
7 ~~Where have they gone Teigue is it up or down~~
~~Another~~.
8 ~~Down~~

Fool
Give me a penny ~~sir~~

Pupil.
9 Come well find your wits

10 Another And when they are found you need not beg for pennies.
11 Theyre hidden somewhere in the badgers ~~who~~ whole
12 ~~And mind~~
13 But you must carry an old candle end
14 If you would find them.

Another pupil.
They are up above the clouds
Fool.
~~Another~~
15 Give me a penny — Give me a penny sir.
16 ~~Lets help him pick up his wits again~~

~~sings~~ sings
17 ~~Who stole your wits away~~ I ll find your wits again Teigue
18 ~~And where have they gone~~ Come for I saw them roll
19 To where old badger mumbles
20 In the black whole.

21 No but an angel stole 'em
22 The night that he was born
23 And now they are but a rag
24 On the moon s horn.
Wise man
25 Be silent.
Pupil
Hush hush — he is about to speak.

[MS. VI, 19r; 334–355]

Wise man

What
~~You~~ do you think when you re alone at night
Do not those things your mother spoke about
Before she took the candle from your bedside
Rush up into the mind, and it may be
Make you believe their truth against your will.

Pupil

We ve no belief but in those things you have taught

Wise man

Why do you say what is ~~inre~~ incredible
To one who knows the world so well as I
For it is certain there is one amongst you
Believes in God, & in some heaven & hell
we
And ~~all those customary things~~
~~We used to put into our prayers at night~~
And all those things we put into our prayers

Pupil.

We ve ~~b~~ rid our minds of all that long ago

Wise man.

You are afraid to tell me what you think
Because I am hot & angry when I am crossed
for it
I do not blame ~~you~~ — But have no fear
For if theres one that sat on smiling there
As though my arguments were sweet as milk
Yet found them bitter I will thank him for it
If he but speak his mind

Pupil.

No one but
There is not one but found them sweet as milk

Wise man.

~~No no no you do not speak the truth~~
All that is taught & reasoned ~~is~~'s but a boat
Drifting above the undebated things
Childhood discovered & our true thought bounds
Out of that glittering sea in a flash of the eye.

VI, 20r contains what may be an alternative version of these lines.

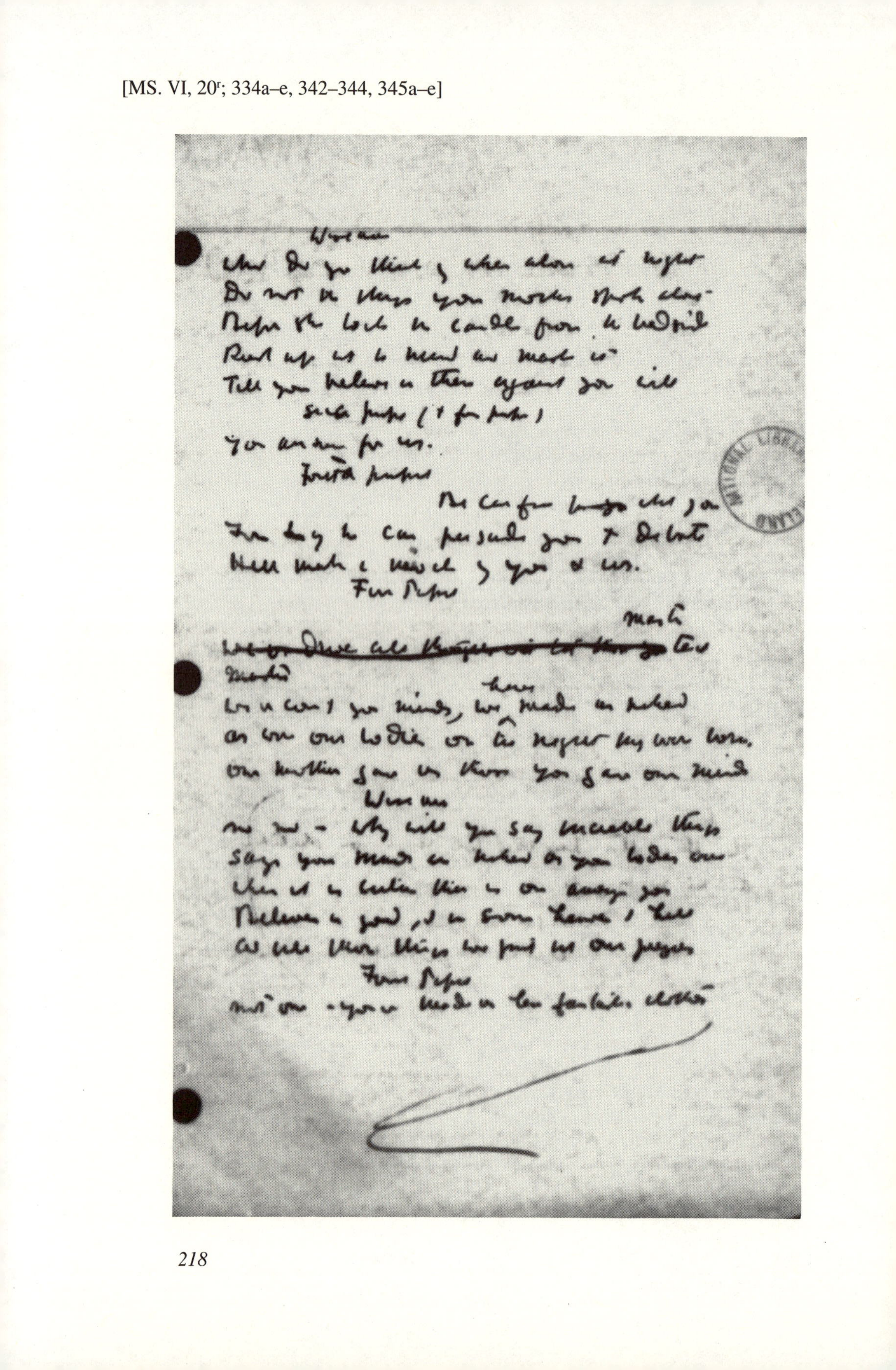

[MS. VI, 20r; 334a–e, 342–344, 345a–e]

Wise man
What do you think of when alone at night
Do not the things your mother spoke about
Before she took the candle from the bedside
Rush up into the mind and master it
Till you believe in them against your will

Second pupil (to first pupil)
You answer for us.

Fourth pupil
Be careful ~~for you~~ what you
For ~~he~~ if he can persuade you to debate
Hell make a mock of you & us.

First Pupil
Master
~~We ve driven all thoughts out but those you~~ teach
~~Master~~
have
We ve come to you minds, we^made as naked
As were our bodies on the night we were born.
Our mothers gave us those you gave our minds

Wise man
No no — Why will you say incredible things
Saying your minds are naked as your bodies were
When it is certain there is one among you
Believes in god, & in some heaven & hell
And all those things we put into our prayers

First Pupil
Not one — you ve made us less fantastic clothes

Arrow below l. 19 shows that this page was intended to be inserted.
11 "with" omitted after "you"?

[MS. VI, 20^{v}; 357–358]

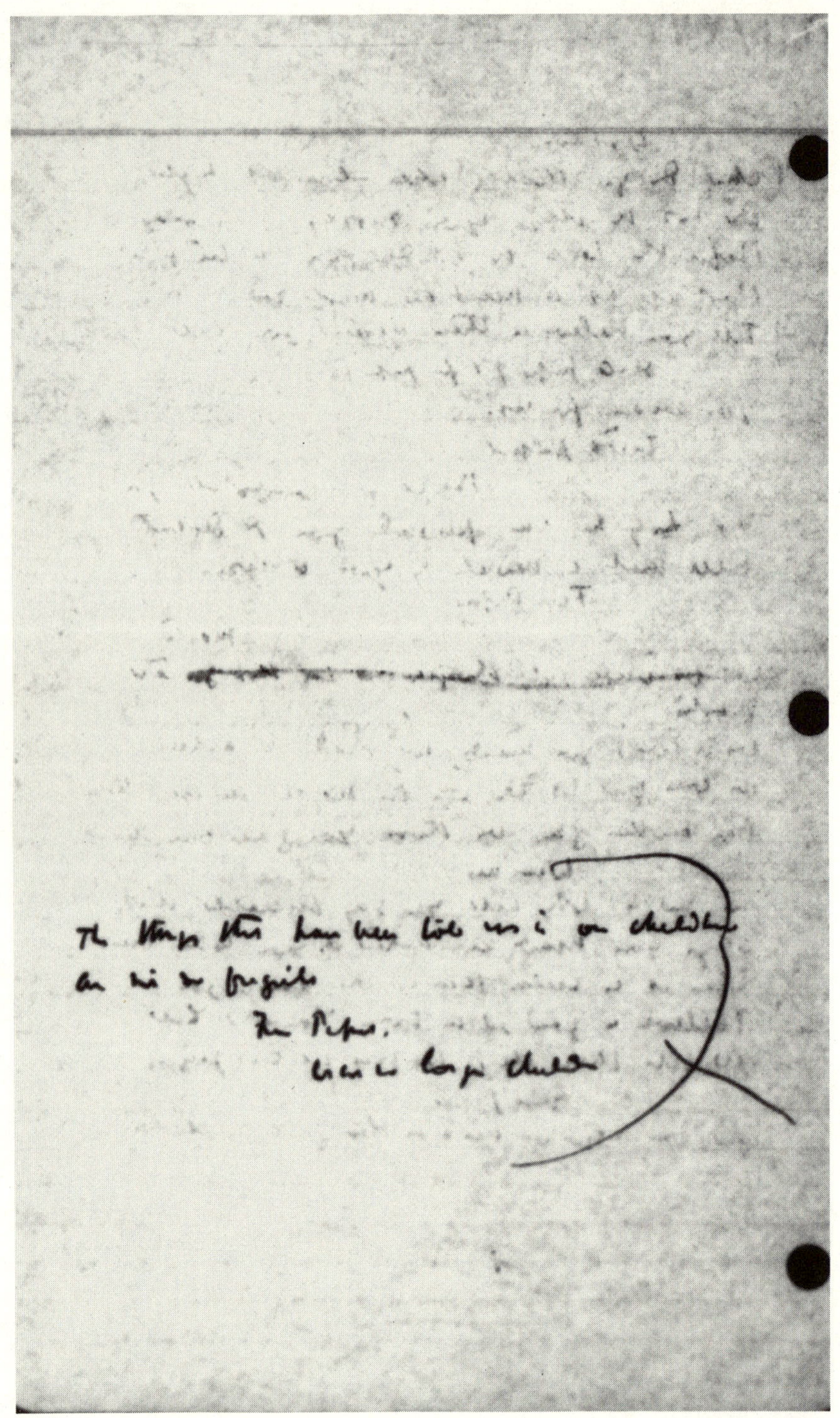

[MS. VI, 20^{v}; 357–358]

The things that have been told us in our childhood
Are not so fragile

First Pupil.

We are no longer children

[MS. VI, 21r; 365, 389–391, 418–434]

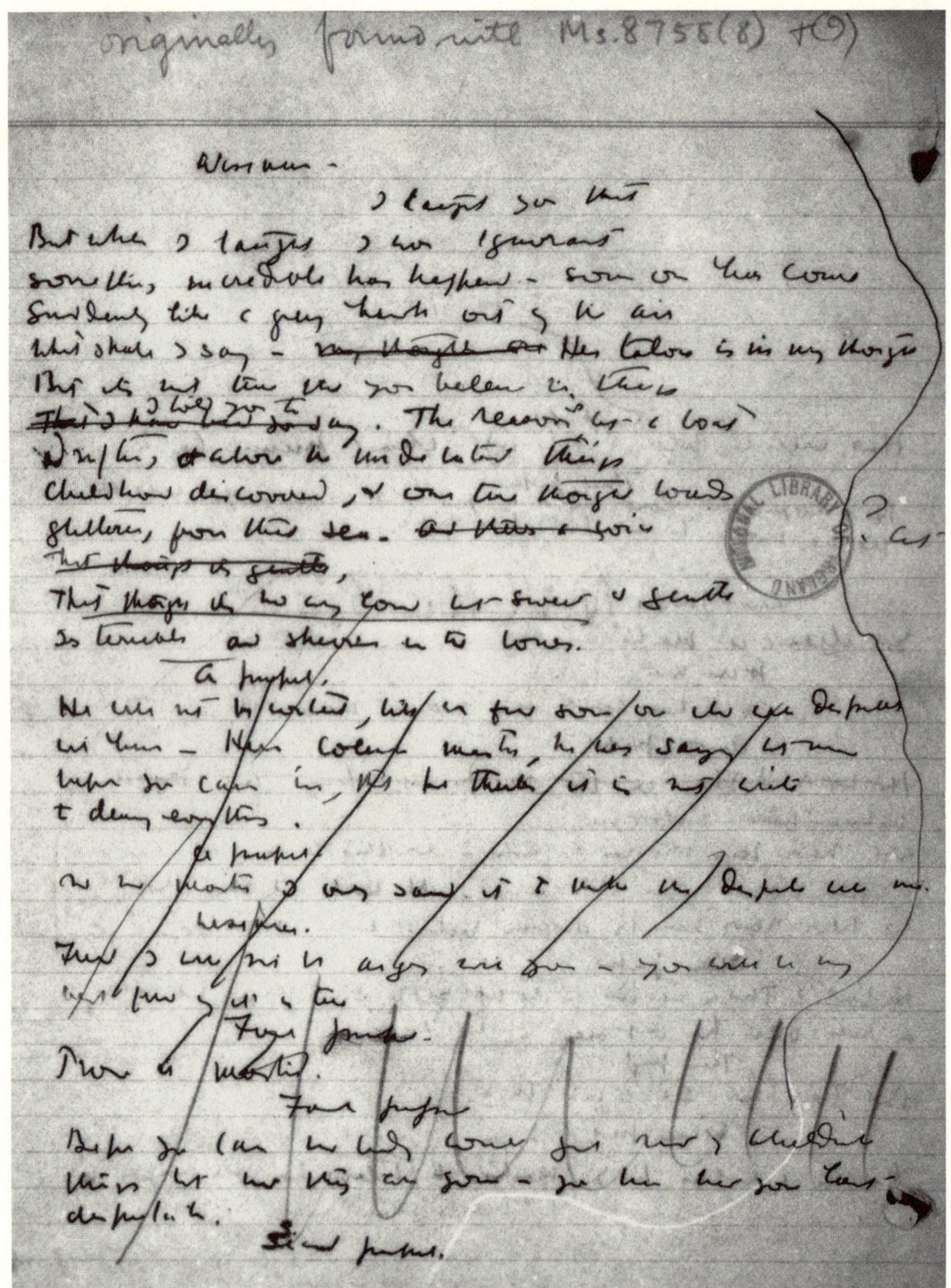
originally found with Ms.8755(8) + (9)

[MS. VI, 21r; 365, 389–391, 418–434]

Wise man.

I taught you that
But when I taught I was ignorant
Something incredible has happened — some one has come
Suddenly like a grey hawk out of the air
What shall I say — ~~my thoughts are~~ His talon is in my thought
But its not true that you believe the things
I told you to is
~~That I have bid you~~ say. The reason ^ but a boat
Drifting ~~eh~~ above the undebated things
Childhood discovered, & our true thought bounds
Glittering from that sea. ~~And theres a voice~~ ?cut
~~That though its gentle~~,
That though its no way loud but sweet & gentle
Is terrible and [?shivers] in the bones.

A pupil.

He will not be content, till we find some one who will dispute
with him — Heres Colum Master, he was saying but now
before you came in, that he thinks it is not write
to deny everything.

A pupil.

No no Master I only said it to make them dispute with me.

Wise man.

Friend I will not be angry with you — you will be my
best friend if it is true

First pupil.

Prove it Master.

Fourth pupil

Before you came no body could get rid of childish
things but now they are gone — you have had your last
disputation.

{S
{Second pupil.

---

12 "in" intended, not "its"?

1–21 A wavy ink line indicates that "?cut" applies to these lines.

19–24 Cancellation in pencil.

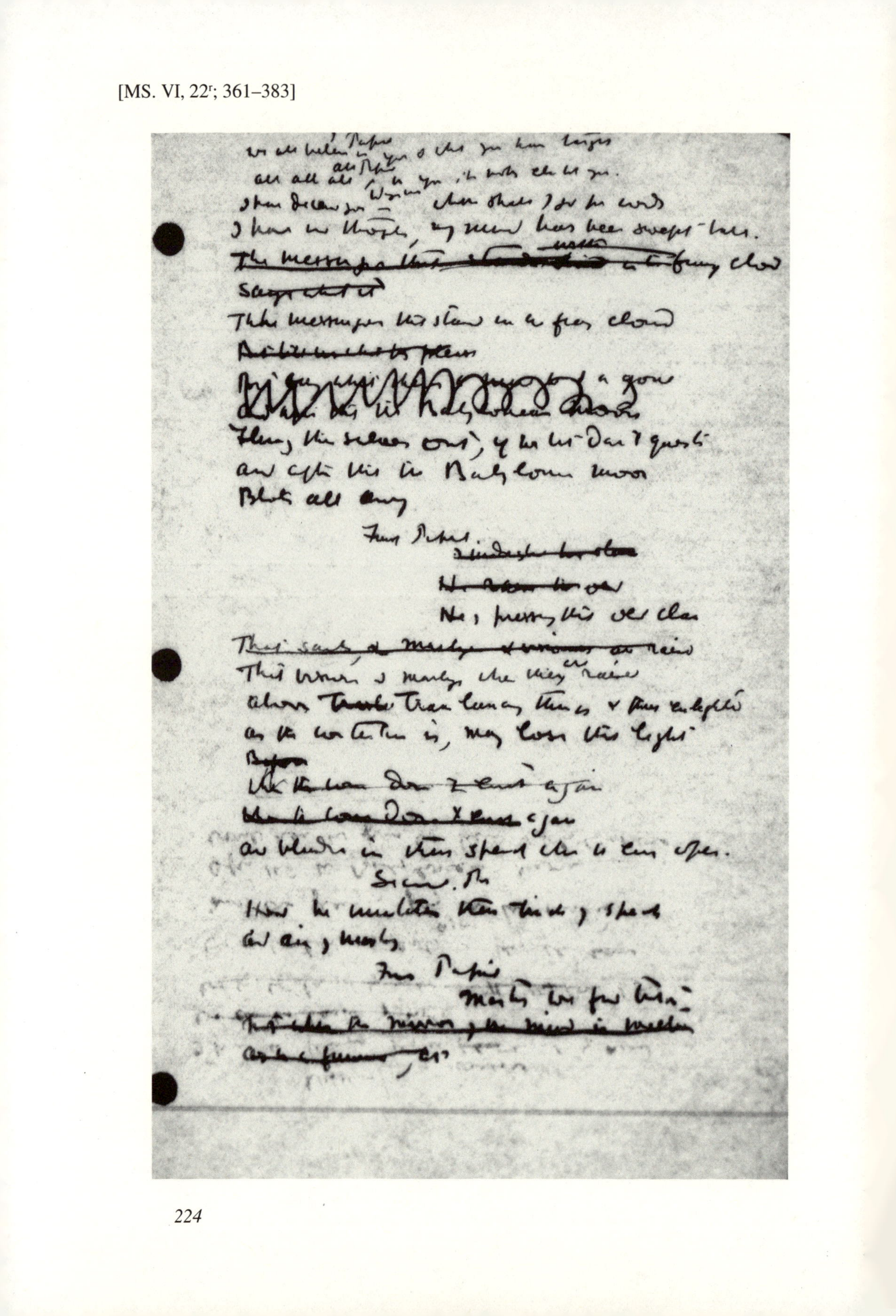

[MS. VI, 22r; 361–383]

[MS. VI, 22r; 361–383]

1 Pupil
We all believe in you & what you have taught

All Pupils
All all all, in you & in nothing else but you.

Wise man
I have deceived you — where shall I go for words
I have no thoughts, my mind has been swept bare.
~~within~~
~~The messenger that stands stood in the~~ fiery cloud
~~says what it~~
[?The] messengers that stand in the fiery cloud
~~But tell us what they please~~
But say what they ve a mind to & are gone
And after that the Babylonian moon
Fling them selves out, if we but dare to question
And after that the Babylonian moon
Blots all away

First Pupil.
~~I understand his claim~~
~~He raises the old~~
He s pressing that old claim
~~That saints, & martyrs & visionaries are raised~~
are
That visionaries & martyrs when they raised
Above ~~Translu~~ Translunary things & there enlightened
As the contention is, may lose that light
~~Before~~
When ~~they come down to earth again~~
~~When they come down to earth~~ again
And blunder in their speech when the eyes open.

Second Pupil
How he imitates their trick of speech
And air of mystery

First Pupil
Master we find truth
~~Not when the mirror of the mind is melting~~
~~As in a furnace, but~~

1–3 Probably inserted later.

4 Lines 1–7 on the facing verso, VI, 22Av, appear to be an experimental version that would have been inserted at l. 4. It was subsequently canceled. See p. 227, below.

[MS. VI, 22A^{v}; 366–370]

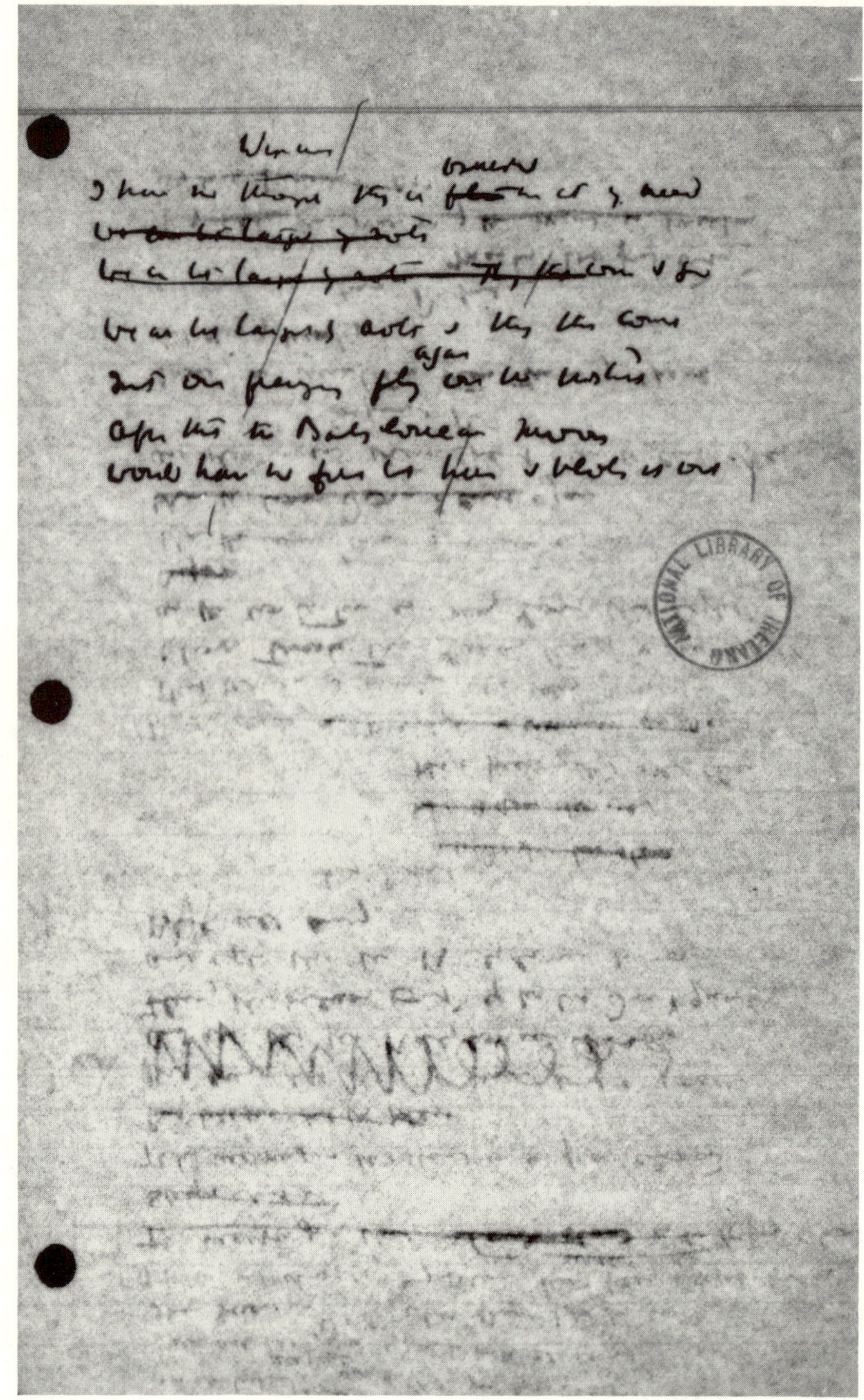

[MS. VI, 22A^{v}; 366–370]

Wise man
vanished
I have no thoughts they've ~~flown~~ at my need
~~We are but [?taught by rote]~~
~~We are but [?taught by rote] They that~~ come & go
We are but [?taught by rote] & they that come
again
Into our frenzy fly on the instant
After that the Babylonian moon
Would have no fire but [?turns] & blots it out

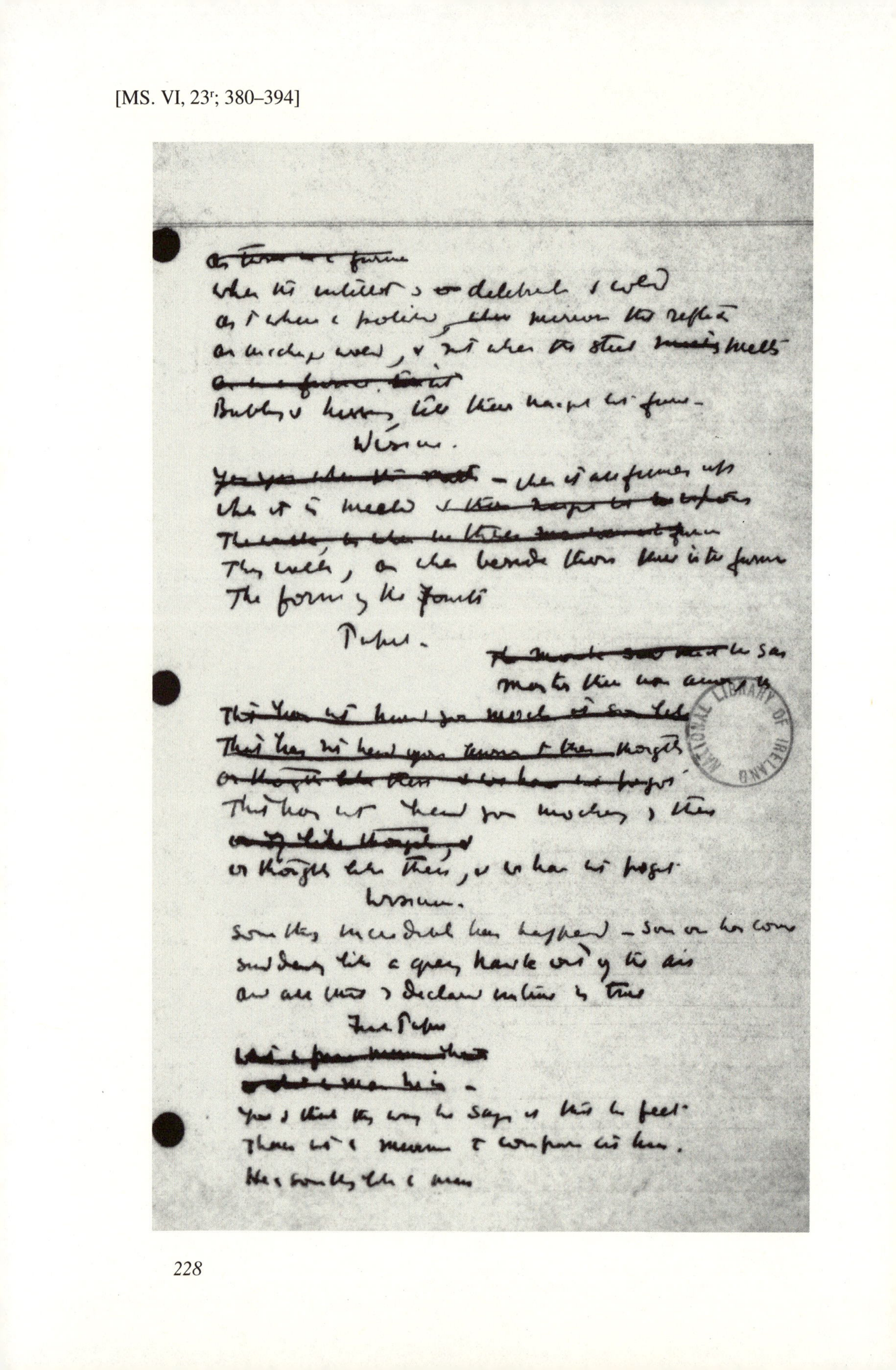

[MS. VI, 23r; 380–394]

[MS. VI, 23^r; 380–394]

~~As twere in a furnace~~
When the intellect s ~~co~~ deliberate & cold
As twhere a polished, ~~wher~~ mirror that reflects
An unchanged world, & not when the steel ~~melts~~ melts
~~As in a furnace till into~~
Bubling & hissing, till theres naught but fumes.

Wise man.

~~Yes yes when that melts~~ — when it all fumes up
When it is melted & ~~theres naught but va vapour~~
~~They walk, as when the three men were in the furnace~~
They walk, as when beside those three in the furnace
The form of the {f / Fourth

Pupil.

~~The monk said much~~ the same
Master theres none among us
~~That has not heard you mock at some like~~
~~That has not heard your answer to these~~ thoughts
~~Or thoughts like these & we have not forgot~~
That has not heard your mockery of these
~~Or of like thoughts, &~~
Or thoughts like these, & we have not forgot

Wise man.

Something incredible has happened — some one has come
Suddenly like a grey hawk out of the air
And all that I declared untrue is true

First Pupil

~~What a fine mummer he is~~
~~And what a man he is~~ —
You d think the way he says it that he felt
Theres not a mummer to compare with him.
He s something like a man

[MS. VI, 21^{v}; 393–408]

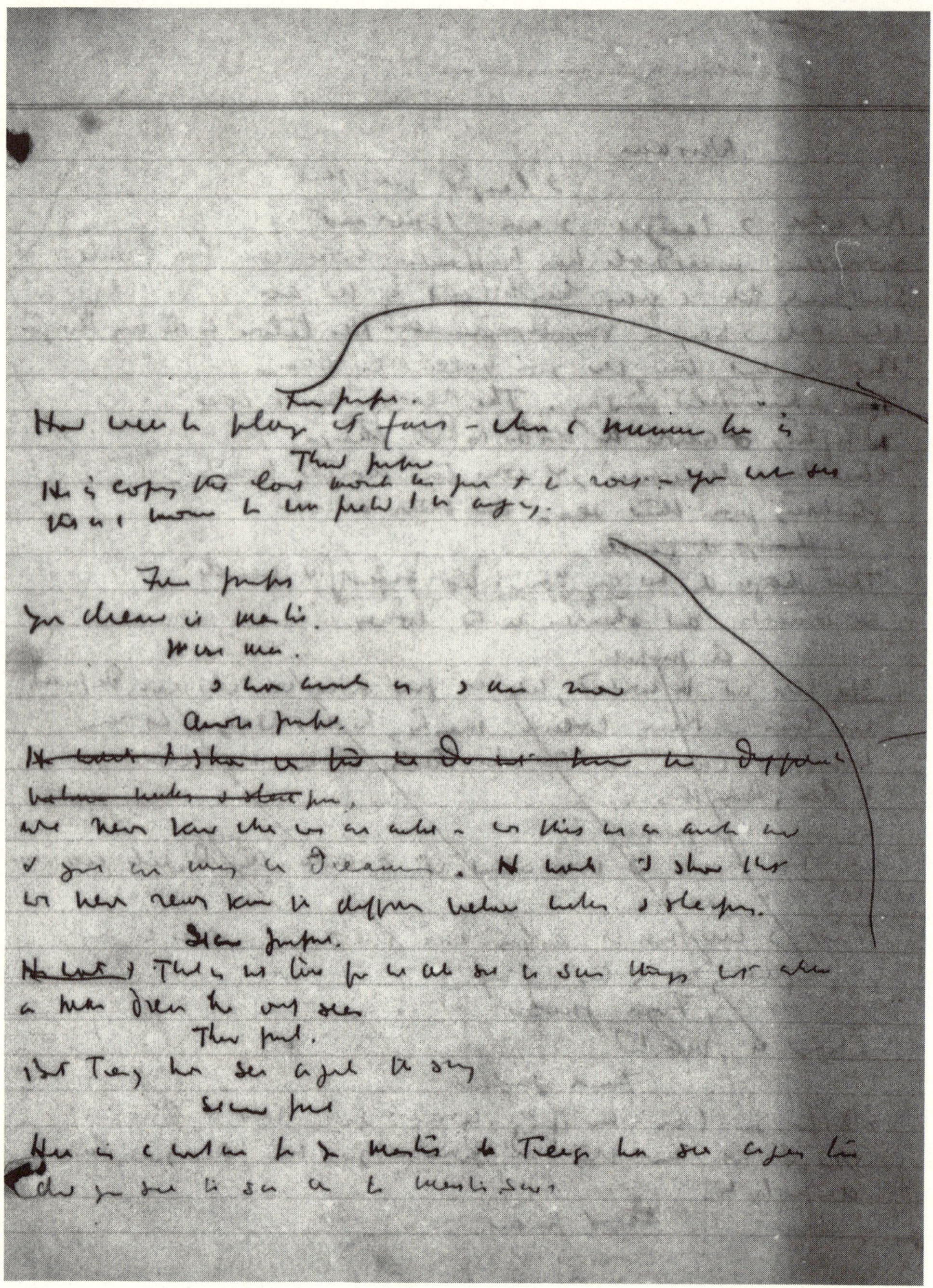

[MS. VI, 21^{v}; 393–408]

First pupil.
How well he plays at faith — what a mummer he is

Third pupil
He is copying that last monk he put to the rout — you will see
that in a moment he will pretend to be angry.

First pupil
You dreamed it Master.

Wise man.
I was awake as I am now

Another pupil.
~~He wants to show us that we do not know the difference~~
~~between waking & sleeping~~
We never know when we are awake — we think we are awake now
& yet we may be dreaming. He wants to show that
We never really know the difference between waking & sleeping.

Second pupil.
~~He wants~~ to That is not true for we all see the same things but when
a man dreams he only sees

Third pupil.
But Teig has seen angels he says

Second pupil
Here is a witness for you Master ~~t~~ Teigue has seen angels too
did you see the same one the Master saw?

This passage belongs after VI, 23^{r}.
4–10 Lines suggest that this passage was intended to replace a canceled section perhaps no longer extant.

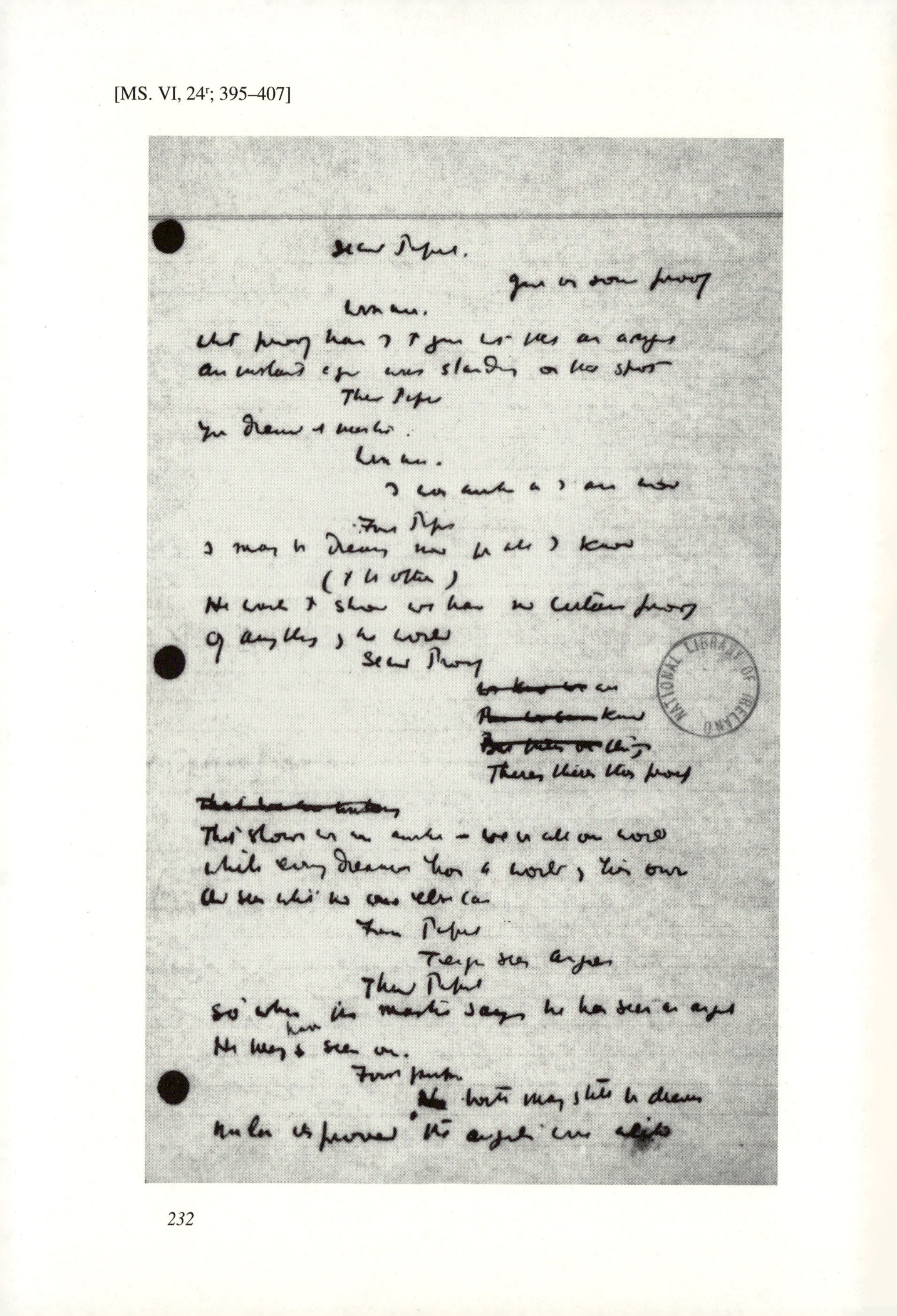

[MS. VI, 24r; 395–407]

[MS. VI, 24[r]; 395–407]

Second Pupil.

1 Give us some proof

Wise man.

2 What proof have I to give but that an angel
3 An instant ago was standing on that spot

Third Pupil

4 You dreamed it Master.

Wise man.

I was awake as I am now

First Pupil

5 I may be dreaming now for all I know
(to the others)
6 He wants to show we have no certain proof
7 Of anything in the world

Second Proof

~~We know we~~ are
8 ~~But we can~~ know
9 ~~But theres one~~ thing
10 Theres theres this proof
11 ~~That we are waking~~
12 That shows we are awake — we ve all one world
13 While every dreamer has a world of his own
14 And sees what no one else can

Fourth Pupil

Teigue sees angels

Third Pupil

15 So when the Master says he has seen an angel
have
16 He may ~~s~~ seen one.

First pupil

~~No~~ both may still be dreaming
17 Unless its proved the angels were alike

7 "Proof" written in error for "Pupil."

[MS. VI, 25[r]; 408–419]

[MS. VI, 25^{r}; 408–419]

Second Pupil

What sort are the angels Teigue

First Pupil

O thats no use

For all we know prolonged obedience
Has made them all as like to one another
As they were eggs.

Fourth Pupil.

The Masters silent now

~~He knows that if he should dispute~~ with us
T'was
~~It was no more sport than reason with himself~~
For he has found that to dispute with us
Seeing that he has taught us what we know
Is but to reason with himself — come lets away
And find if there is one believer left
Who ll put some heart into the argument

Wise man.

~~Yes Yes — go out~~
~~Go out~~
Yes Yes — find me but one that still believes
The things that we believed when we were children

Third pupil

Our Master ll mock and maul him.

Fourth Pupil

From the First

~~I knew that he was set on some debate~~
I knew he'd have us find some disputant

Ink blots show that this page was still wet when placed on VI, 24^{v}.

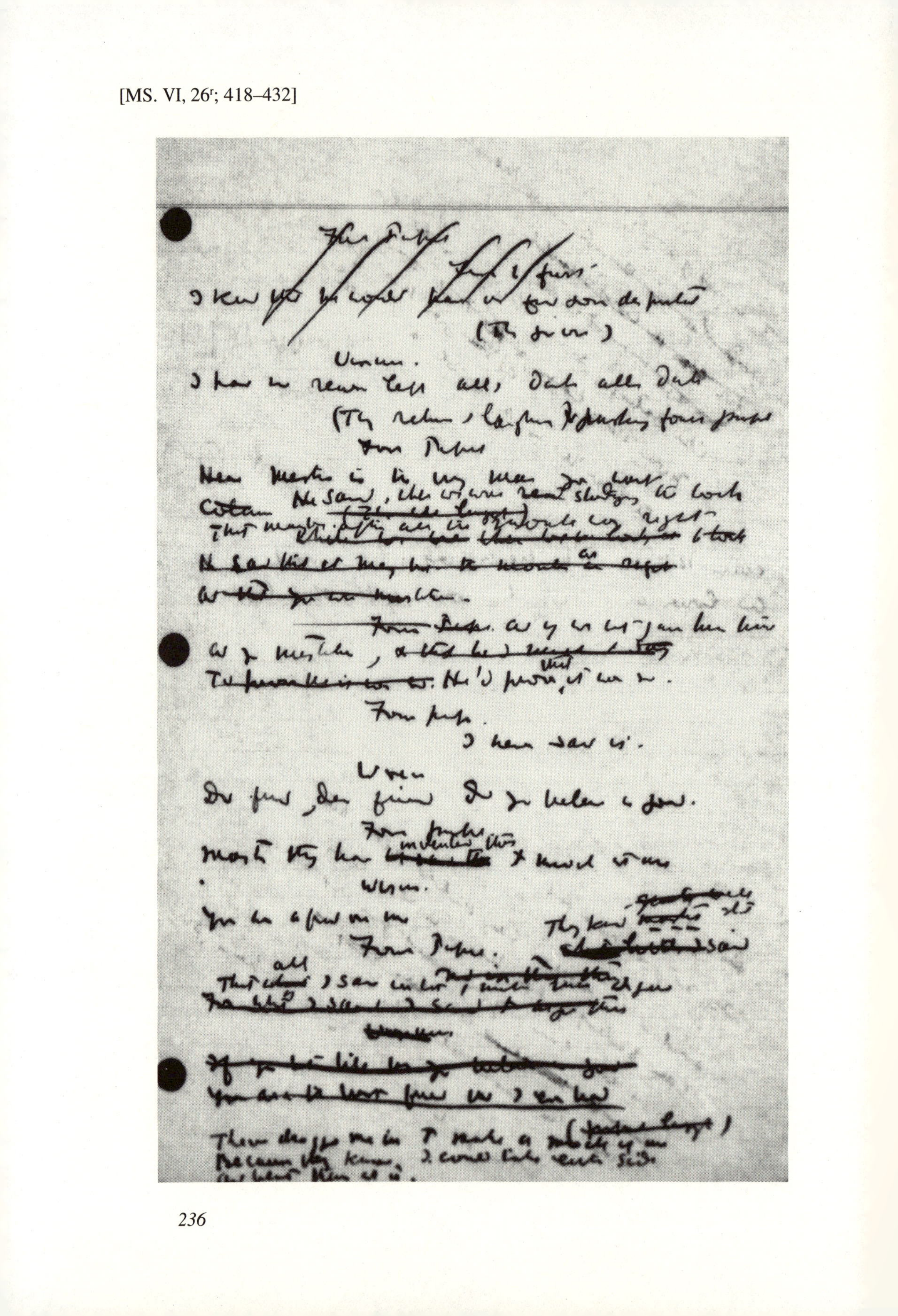

[MS. VI, 26r; 418–432]

[MS. VI, 26^r; 418–432]

First Pupil
From the first
I knew that he would have us find some disputant
(They go out)
Wise man.
I have no reason left all s dark alls dark
(They return, laughing {& /)} pushing fourth pupil
First Pupil
Here Master is the very man you want
He said, when we were ~~read~~ studying the book
~~Colum~~ ~~(They all laugh)~~
That maybe after all the monk was right
~~While we were When we were looking at~~ the ~~book~~
are
~~He said that it may be the monks is right~~
~~And that you were mis~~taken.

~~Fourth Pupil~~ And if we but gave him time
And you mistaken, ~~& that he d much to say~~
that
~~To prove that it was so~~. He'd prove ^ it was so.
Fourth pupil.
I never said it.
Wise man
Dear friend, dear friend do you believe in God.
Fourth pupil.
invented this
Master they have ~~but said this~~ to mock at me
Wise man.
You are afraid of me ~~quite well~~
They know ~~Master~~ stet
Fourth Pupil. ~~what little I~~ said
all ~~Not in this thing~~
That ~~what~~ I said was but to make them argue
~~For what I said I said to anger them~~
~~Wise man.~~
~~If you but tell me you believe in God~~
~~You are the best friend~~ that I ever had
~~(pupils laugh)~~
They ve dragged me in to make a mock of me
Because they know I could take either side
And beat them at it.

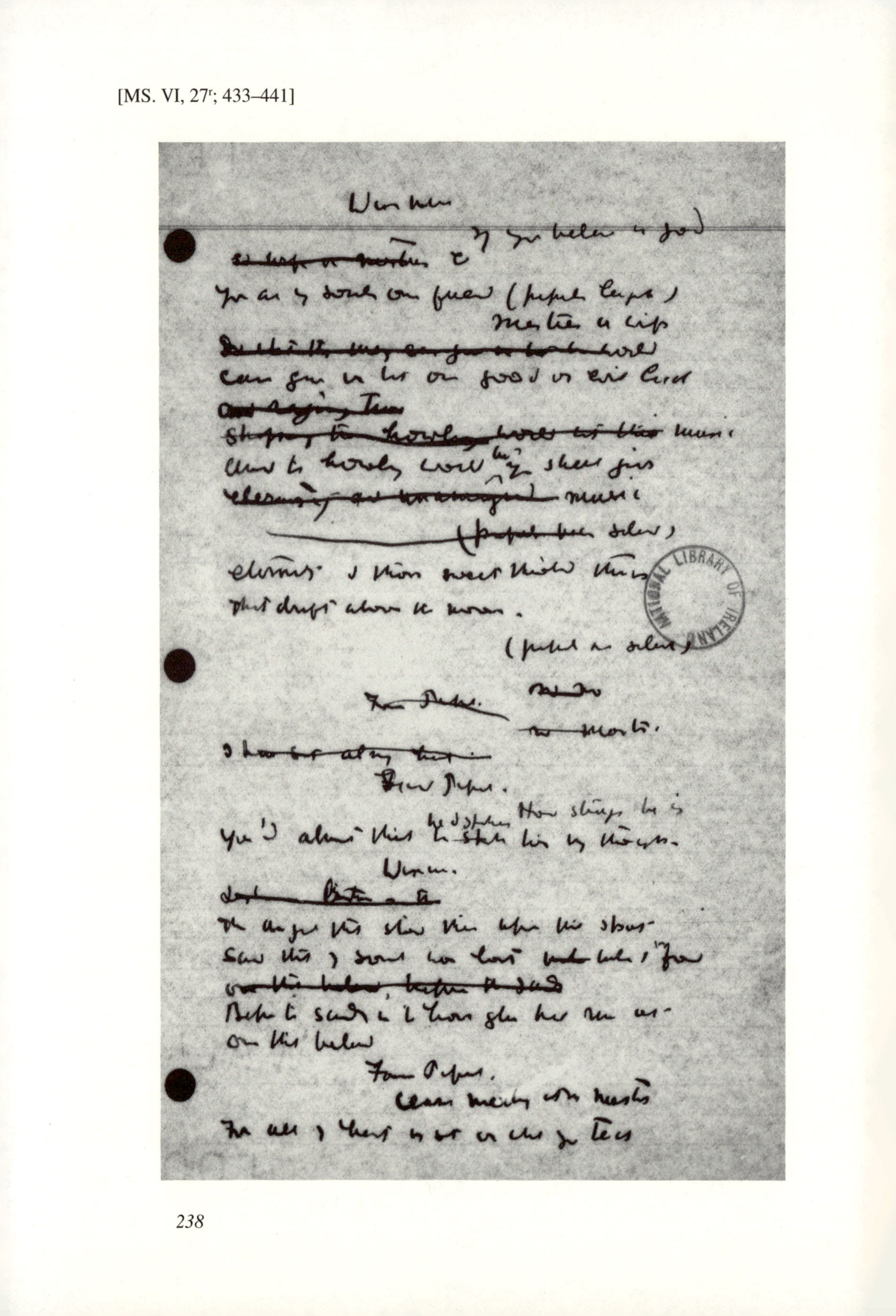

[MS. VI, 27r; 433–441]

[MS. VI, 27^{r}; 433–441]

Wise man

If you believe in God
~~A wife or mistress~~ e
You are my souls one friend (pupils laugh)
Mistress or wife
~~Do what they may can give us but the world~~
Can give us but our good or evil luck
~~And raging turn~~
~~Shaping the howling world into their~~ music
but
Amid the howling world ^ you shall give
~~Eternity and unimagined~~ music
~~———————(pupils become~~ silent)
Eternity & those sweet throated things
That drift above the moon.
(pupils are silent)
~~No No~~

~~Fourth Pupil.~~
~~No Master~~.

I ~~have set all my heart~~

{Second
{F Pupil.
How strange he is
he d spoken
You'd almost think he ~~spoke~~ his very thoughts

Wise man.

~~Listen — listen — th~~
The angel that stood there upon this spot
Said that my soul was lost ~~unles~~ unless I found
~~One that believed before the sands~~
Before the sands in the hour glass had run out
One that believed

Fourth Pupil.
Cease mocking at me Master
For all my heart is set on what you teach

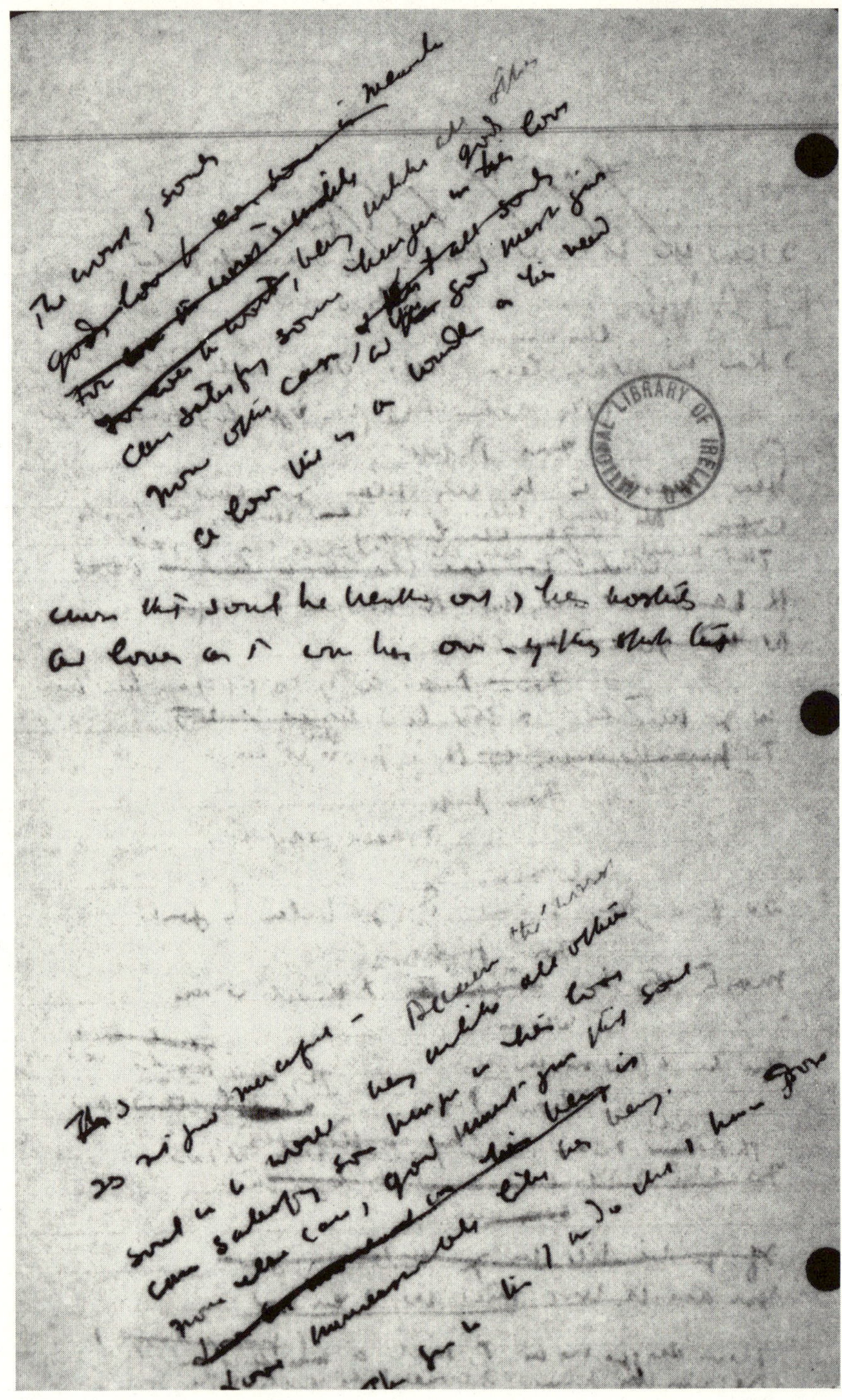

[MS. VI, 26v]

The worst of souls
~~Gods love for every soul is~~ measureless
~~For even the worst s unlike~~
~~For even the worst,~~ being unlike all others
                                        Gods
Can satisfy some hunger in ~~his~~ love
None other can, ~~& thus to all souls~~
                              thus
                    And ~~that~~ God must give
A love that is as boundless as his need

Curse that soul he breathes out of his nostrils
And loves as it were his own — if they spoke true.

~~The~~ s
Is not God merciful —
                                        Because the worst
Soul in the world being unlike all others
Can satisfy some hunger in his love
None else can, God must give that soul
~~Love as unmeasured as his being~~ is
Love immeasureable like his being.

Then give me time to undo what I have done

Ink blots show that the ink on this page was still wet when VI, 28r was placed on it.

8–9 Revisions of ll. 9–10 on VI, 28r.

1–7 and 11–17 were evidently intended for the dialogue between the Wise Man and the Angel.

[MS. VI, 28^{r}; 442–454]

~~And all my thoughts are~~ yours
I ~~believed~~
~~I am so certain theres no God nor~~ heaven
~~That if you will I ll curse~~ them.

Wise man.

Out I say
I am so certain that there is no God
I ll curse him if you will & after
that
Knowing ^ there is nothing here to suffer
~~Curse the beloved~~
Curse the beloved soul that has been breathed
From his own nostrils — if they but spoke the truth.
Wise man.
~~Out of my sight, out of sight I~~ say
I ve but a moment to find that I seek
And you stand there debating laughing wrangling
Out of my sight ~~I say~~ out of my sight I say
(He drives them out).
~~I ll call my wife~~ —
~~I ll call my wife — for women that~~ [?give suck]
~~And carry us in the darkness of their bodies~~
~~Mock at our reason~~
~~Mock~~
Ill call my wife for what can women do
That carry us in the darkness of their bodies
But mock the reason that lets nothing grow
Unless it grow in light — Bridget, Bridget
A woman never ceases to believe
Say what we will — Bridget — come quickly Bridget

An ink line above l. 5 was probably intended to cancel "Wise Man./Out I say".

9–10 See VI, 26^{v} for draft revision of these lines.

[MS. VI, 29r; 455–472]

[MS. VI, 29r; 455–472]

~~Come~~
Bridget tell me the truth & do not say
What ever you imagine would best please me.
~~Do you not say your prayers at night~~
Do you not sometimes when I am not by
Say ~~pr~~ prayers.

Wife

Prayers. No you taught me to leave them off
long ago. At first I was angry but I
am glad now for I am sleepy in the evenings

Wise man

~~But do you~~ not
Do you believe in God.

Bridget

Oh a good wife only believes what her
husband ~~told her~~ tells her.

Wise man.

But sometimes when the children are asleep
And I am in the the school do you not think
About the martyrs & the saints & angels
'd
And all the things that you ~~d~~ belief in once.
What do you think of when you are alone.

Bridget

I think about nothing — sometimes I wonder
If the linen is bleaching white, or I go
Out to see if the crows are picking up
the chickens food

Wise man.

What can I do, ~~What can I do — I'll~~ go
I will go out my self

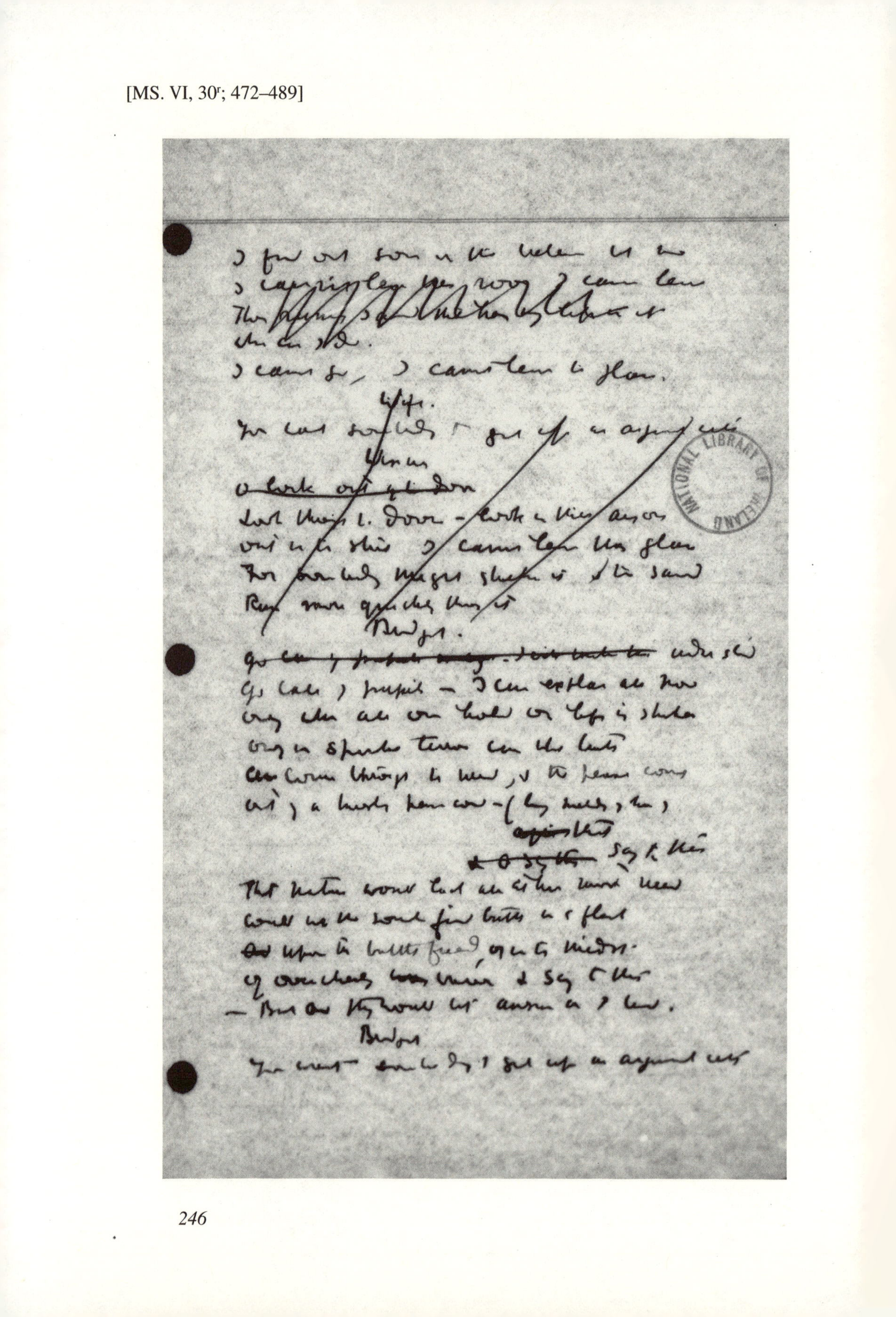

[MS. VI, 30r; 472–489]

[MS. VI, 30r; 472–489]

& find out some one that believes but no
I cannot leave the room I cannot leave
This running sand that has my life in it
What can I do.
I cannot go, I cannot leave the glass.

Wife.

You want somebody to get up an argument with

Wise man

~~O look out of the door~~
Look through the door — look is there anyone
Out in the street   I cannot leave this glass
For somebody might shake it & the sand
Run more quickly through it

Bridget.

~~Go call my pupils in again — I will make them~~ understand
Go call my pupils — I can explain all now
Only when all our hold on life is shaken
Only in spiritual terror can the truth
~~Com~~ Come through the mind, as the pease come
Out of a bursting pease cod — ([?taking hold] of her)
~~after~~ that
~~& O say that~~ say to them
That Nature would lack all at her most need
Could not the soul find truth in a flash
~~And~~ Upon the battlefield, or in the midst
Of overwhelming ~~way~~ waves & say to them
— But no they would but answer as I bid.

Bridget

You want somebody to get up an argument with

[MS. VI, 31r; 490–500]

[MS. VI, 31^{r}; 490–500]

Wise man
O look out of the door, look is there any one
There in the street — I cannot leave the glass
For somebody might shake it & the sand
~~Run quickly throg through~~ it.
~~The sand~~
If it were shaken might run down on the instant.

Bridget
I dont understand a word you are saying —
Theres a crowd of people talking to your pupils

Wise man
Run out & find of if they have found a man
Who did not understand me when I taught
Or did not listen.

Bridget.
It is a hard thing to be married to a man of
learning that must always be having arguments
Do not be meddling with the bread children while
I am out.

[MS. VI, 32r; 501–510]

[MS. VI, 32^r; 501–510]

Dont be meddling with the bread children while I am out.

Wise man.

~~Strange that the~~
Strange that I should [?I] be blind to the great secret
And that so simple ~~that~~ a man might write it out
If ~~he wrote neatly on a blade of grass~~
~~of any~~
~~With juice out a berry & laugh to himself~~
~~Writing it out because it was so simple~~
With but a berries juice & laugh to himself
Writing it out because it was so simple

Upon a blade of grass or bit of rush
With naught but berry juice, & laugh to himself
Writing it out because it was so simple
Enter Fool & Bridget.

~~F~~ Fool
Give me something; give me a penny
to ~~by~~ buy bacon in the shops, & nuts in the market
And strong drink for the time the sun is weak
And I want snares to catch the rabbits &
the squirrels & the hares & a pot to cook
them in.

Bridget
I have no pennies (To the Wise man) Your
pupils cannot find anybody to argue with
you. Theres nobody in the whole country

10–12 Revise ll. 5–9.

[MS. VI, 33r; 510–525]

[MS. VI, 33r; 510–525]

~~has enough belief to stuff a pipe with to~~ curse
~~by~~ belief enough for a curse, or a
lovers oath — cant you be quiet now
and not always wanting to have arguments.
It must be terrible to have a mind like
that.

Wise man.

~~I am lost — I am lost.~~
~~Then I am lost, lost~~
Then I am lost indeed.

Bridget

Leave me alone now I have to make the
bread for you & the children.

Wise man.

Children children.

Bridget.

Your father wants you run to them.

Wise man.

~~They say that when you come into the world~~
~~You~~
Children, theres a story among men
That when but newly come into the world
We have some memory, some light with us
More than we find there, ~~& if we tell it~~
Children come to me — do not be afraid
~~Tell me the tr~~
I want to know if you believe in heaven
God or a soul — ~~And do not be~~ afraid
~~Say what you will & I shall~~ not be angry
~~But do not tell me yet~~ no — do not tell me yet
You need not be afraid I shall be angry

12 "them" written in error for "him."

19 WBY's transposition signal places "children" after "me."

[MS. VI, 34r; 523–537]

[MS. VI, 34r; 523–537]

~~No what matter what you say I will but~~ thank you
Say what you please, so that it is your thought.
I wanted you to know before you spoke
That I shall not be angry.

First Child
We have not forgotten father.

Second Child
O no father

~~(speak~~
both Together
There is nothing we cannot see nothing we cannot
touch.

First Child
Foolish people used to say there was but
You have taught us better.

Wise man.
Go to your mother go — yet do not go
~~She cannot teach~~ you
~~For she can tell you nothing and if I do~~ not
~~You shall be torn from all & cast~~ away
~~Beyond the edge of the world of the world~~ & the skies
— ~~The s~~
can tell
For she ~~can~~ you nothing — if I am ~~silent~~ dumb
You shall be lost amid the woods of nothing
And I because the sands are running out
Have but a moment to show it all in — children
~~If but The grass blades would~~
~~The blades of grass would wither if they doubted~~
The sap would drie out of the blades of grass
Had they a doubt — ~~They understand it all~~
~~Being the go fingers of Gods certainty~~

[MS. VI, 35r; 536–552]

[MS. VI, 35^r; 536–552]

~~They u~~
1 They understand it all
2 Being the fingers of Gods certainty
3 Yet can but make their sign in the air
4 ~~But had they tongues~~
5 ~~But could they find their tongues — could they but find~~ their
6 But could they find their tongues they show it all —
7 But what have I to say that am but one
8 When they are millions & they will not speak —
9 ~~Why do you run~~ aw
10 But they are gone — what made them run away
wi
(The fool comes ~~in blowing~~
dandelion)
11 Look at me — tell me if my face is changed
the
12 Is there a notch of ^ fiends nail upon it
13 ~~Already — has it grown terrible~~
14 Already — is it terrible to the sight —
15 ~~Because of the moment that is coming~~ up
16 Because the moments near (goes to glass
I dare not look.
17 I dare not know the moment when they come
18 To carry me away (covers glass)
~~Therell be a step at the door~~
Therell be a footstep
19 ~~But the~~
20 No — they are shadows & will make no sound

~~Fool (blowing dandelion)~~
21 What are you doing ~~there~~

Fool.
22 Wait a moment — four five six

21–22 On the facing verso, 34^v, WBY drafted an insertion:
Will there be a foot fall
~~Like a mans foot or there be a tearing sound~~
Or will there be a sort of tearing sound
~~Or~~
Or else a cracking as though an iron claw
~~had gripped the threshold, till~~
had gripped the wooden threshold but no not that
~~There~~ For they will come without a sound being shadows
Blots show that the ink was still wet on both pages when VI, 35^r was placed on VI, 34^v.

[MS. VI, 36^r; 553–571]

Wise man.
What are you doing that for.

Fool.
I am blowing the dandelion to find out what
hour it is.

Wise man.
You have heard everything & that is why
You d find what hour it is — you find that out
That you may see them coming through the door
To carry me away — Out out with you
I will have no one here when they come in
I will have no one sitting there — out out
~~But wait — for there is something strange in you~~
~~But no no~~ —
No no no — there is something strange about you
Are you the one I seek do you believe
~~undying~~
In God & the soul — ~~in that undying stuff~~
in that undying stuff
of
That all things have been made from the first.

Teig
So you ask me now — I thought when
You were asking your pupils, will he
Ask Teigue the fool, ~~no~~ yes he will he
Will, no he will not — yes he will
But Teigue will say nothing, Teigue will
Say nothing

Wise man.
~~Spe~~ Tell me quickly

Teigue.
the green eyed cats
I said Teigue knows everything, not even ∧
& The ~~cats &~~ hares that milk the cows

6–7 Short cancellation mark. On the facing verso, 35^v, WBY drafted a revision:

~~That you may see~~
That you may look upon a fleet of shadows
Dragging my soul away

[MS. VI, 37r; 572–587]

But Teigue will not speak, he says nothing.

Wise man

Speak — speak — for underneath the cover there
{~~when~~
~~The grains are falling,~~ {~~&~~
~~The sand falls, when~~
~~Sand falls, & when the last s fallen~~
~~The sands are falling — when the last grain~~ falls
I ~~shall be lost unless I have have one~~
The sand is running from the upper glass
And when the last grains through, I shall be lost
~~Unless I have found someone that believes~~
Unless I have lit upon unshaken faith
Somewhere in somebody —

Teigue.

~~Teigue will not~~ sp
I will not speak — I will not tell you
what is in my mind & I wont tell you
what is in my bag — you might [?slip]
away my thoughts I met a bodach on the
road yesterday & he said 'Teigue
tell me how many pennies are in your
bag — I will wager three pennies that there are
not twenty pennies in your bag — let me
put in [?~~it~~] my hand & count them' But
I ~~pulled th~~ I gripped the bag the tighter
at
& when I go to sleep ~~by~~ night I hide
it but where nobody knows.

Wise man (going to cover)

No I have not the courage — [?~~Yes~~]
~~For~~ If you are not he I seek I am
lost for the time is at an end.

[MS. VI, 38r; 588, 597–600, 641–643, 612–617]

[MS. VI, 38r; 588, 597–600, 641–643, 612–617]

See duplicate next page.

Teigue

Teigue knows Teigue knows what what a lot the
~~fool knows but he says nothing~~
(he goes out & then
looks back at the cover)

Wise man.

The last hopes gone & now that I am lost
I ~~see it all — we live~~
I see it all — to live is to forget
We perish into god, & sink away
Into reality — the rests a dream
Man cannot know the truth for its God
~~Who knows the truth~~
His body in our body his eyes in ours
Who knows the truth in man

Fool

I hear the wind a blow
~~&~~ I hear the grass grow
And all they know I know

~~Wise man.~~ (he goes over on his toes
~~Now~~ & looks under cover on glass)

Wise man.

~~And now that the last grain of sand is falling~~
Now that the last grain of sand is fallen
And live flows out — I understand it all
I know what fixed the stations
For star & cloud
And knowing all I cry
That what so God has willed
~~May~~ upon the instant be fullfilled
Though it be my damnation

The following page is missing. Ink blots show that "See duplicate next page" was still wet when VI, 38r was placed on VI, 37v, but VI, 37v has additional blots that were not made by VI, 38r.

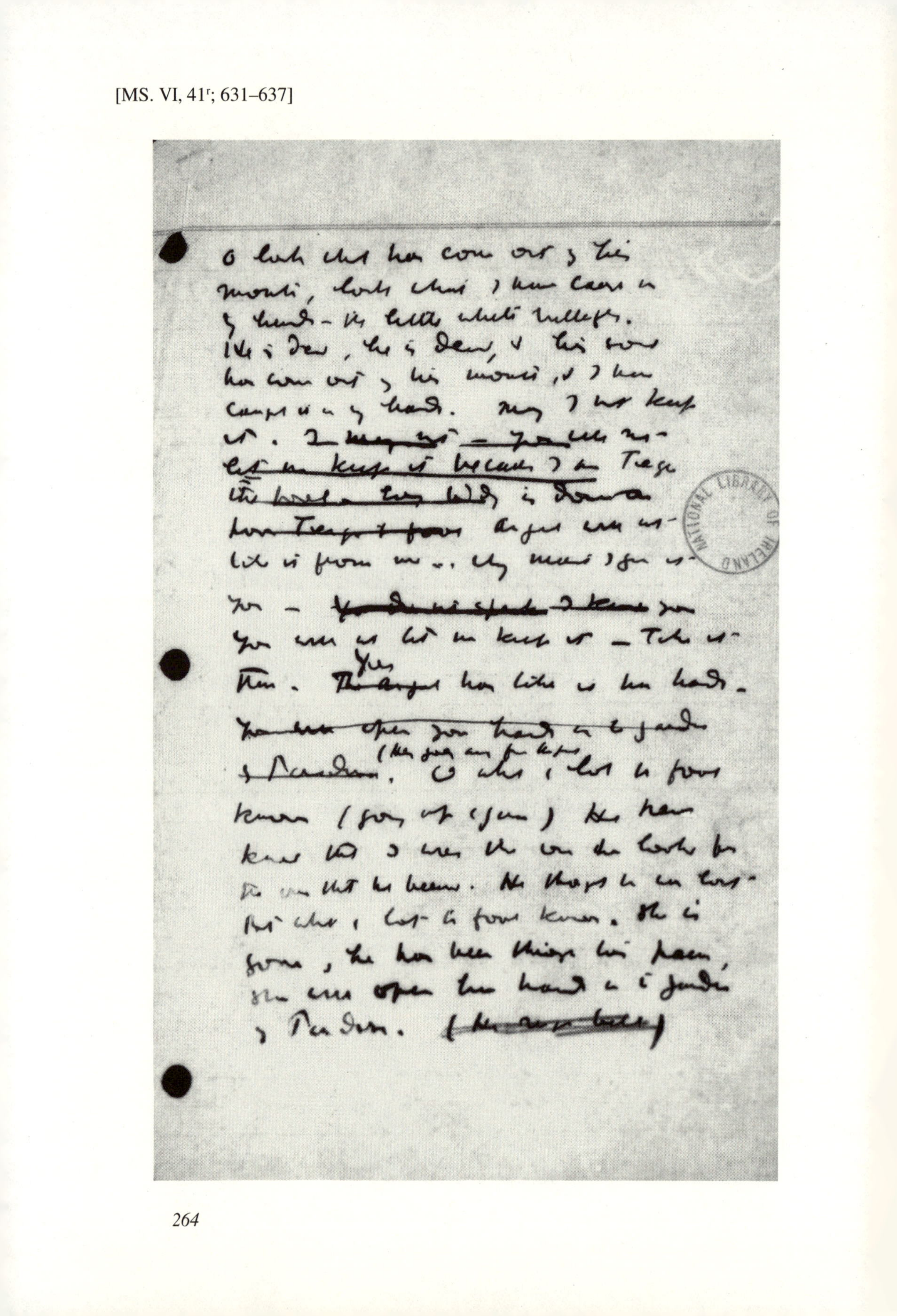

[MS. VI, 41r; 631–637]

O look what has come out of his
mouth, look what I have caught in
my hands — the little white butterfly.
He is dead, he is dead, & his soul
has come out of his mouth, & I have
caught it in my hands. May I not keep
it. ~~I may not — you~~ will not
~~let me keep it~~ because I am Teigue
~~the fool — every body~~ is down on
~~poor Teigue the fool~~ Angel will not
take it from me... Why must I give it
You — ~~You do not speak I know~~ you
You will not let me keep it — Take it
You
then. ~~The Angel~~ has taken in her hands.
~~You will open your hands in the Garden~~
(He goes away from Angel
~~of Paradise~~. O what a lot the fool
knows (going [?up/off] again) He never
knew that I was the one he looked for
the one that he needed. He thought he was lost
But what a lot the fool knows. She is
Gone, he has been through his pain,
She will open her hands in the Garden
of Paradise. ~~(He rings bell)~~

Several pages apparently missing ahead of this page.

MS. VJ

Transcriptions

[MS. VJ, 1; 1–15]

(1

Hour Glass.

The wise mans house — an Hour glass on a stand & a big chair with a great book on a desk before it. Enter pupils.

First
~~Fourth~~ Pupil

He said we might choose the subject for the lesson.

~~Fourth Pupil~~
Second Pupil

There is none of us wise enough to do that

Third Pupil

It would need a great deal of wisdom to know what we want to know.

Fourth Pupil.

I will question him.

First Pupil

You.

Fourth Pupil

Last night I dreamt that someone came & told me to question — I want to say to him [?~~me~~] you were wrong to ~~close the churches & drive the monks~~ say theres no god & no soul — may be ~~if~~, if there is not much of either there is yet some ~~rag, some~~ tatter, some tag in the wind, some [~~?~~] rag so to speak of divinity. I will ~~ge~~ argue with him — not that I believe it but I

[MS. VJ, 2; 16–26]

(2

dreamt that I was to say it & you will see
how well I shall argue

First Pupil

I'd as soon listen to dried peas in a
bladder as listen to your thoughts

Second Pupil

Here is his big book let us
choose out a passage & ask to give
the lesson upon it. How heavy it is.

~~[?First] Pupil~~.

~~I should be afraid to choose~~

Fool (who has come in)

Give me a penny.

First Pupil

No I have a better plan — I will
spread it on Teigues back

~~See~~ ~~F~~

(Fool comes in

Fool

Give me a penny.

Second Pupil

Let us choose a subject by chance
Here is his big book — Let us turn over
the pages slowly, & let one of put
down his finger without looking — the
passage his finger lights on will be
the subject for the lesson

Fool

Give me a penny

---

6 "him" probably omitted after "ask".

15 "us" omitted.

[MS. VJ, 3; 27–41]

(3

Third Pupil

How heavy it is

Fourth Pupil

Spread it on Teigues back & then we
can all stand round & see the choice

Second Pupil

Make him spread out his arms.

Fourth Pupil

Down on your knees Hunch up your
back — spread your arms out now &
look like a golden eagle in a church.
keep still, keep still

Fool

Give me a penny sir.

Third Pupil

Is that the right cry for an eagle cock

Second Pupil

you
I ll turn the pages —‸close your eyes
& put your finger down

Third Pupil

Thats it & then he cannot blame us
for the choice

First Pupil

There I have chosen ~~but it is hard~~ to
read ~~with the letters all twisted~~
~~up like lovers knots~~ There s a big
~~first letter all gold & clour~~ colour
& ~~twisted like a lovers knot~~ — It should
be ~~wise~~ ——
— Fool keep still — & if what s wise

[MS. VJ, 4; 41–62]

(4

is strange & sounds like nonsense
we ve made a good choice.

First Pupil

Here is the master coming [~~?~~]

Fool

Will nobody give a penny to a fool

First Pupil.

We have chosen the passage for the lesson
Master — There are two living countries
one visible & one invisible
and when it is summer there it is
winter here & when it is november with
us it is lambing time there.

Wise Man That passage, that passage

What mischief has there been since yesterday

First Pupil

None master

Wise man

O yes there has, some crazy ness
has fallen from the air, or
risen from the graves of old men
that you should that subject. (He ~~takes book~~
& goes to desk)

Fourth Pupil

I knew that it was folly but they would
have it.

~~F~~ Third Pupil

Had we not better say we picked it by
chance

Second Pupil

No he [~~?~~] would say we were children still

---

11 "That passage, that passage" is a later addition.

17 "choose" omitted.

[MS. VJ, 5; 63–82]

(5

~~I have~~ First Pupil
I have found a sentence under that one
that says as though to show it had a ~~hi~~
hidden meaning, a beggar wrote it
upon the walls of Babylon.

Wise man.
Then find some beggar and ask him what
it means for I will have nothing to do
with it.

First Pupil
Come Teigue what is the old books
meaning when it says that there are
sheep that drop there lambs in
november.

Fool.
To be sure — everybody knows, everybody
in the world knows, when it is spring
with us, the trees are withering there, when
it is summer with us the snow is falling
there & have I not myself heard
there lambs a bleating on a cold
november day — to be sure does not
everybody with an intellect know that
and be when its night with us it is
day with them for many a time I
have seen the ~~rads~~ roads lighted
before me.

Wise man
wrote that on Babylons walls
meant that there is a spiritual ~~state~~
kingdom that cannot be seen

---

21 "may" omitted.
25 Line missing? Other copies read "The beggar who wrote . . .".

[MS. VJ, 6; 82–95, 105]

(6

or known till the faculties where by we
master the kingdom of this world
wither away, like green things in winter
a monkish thought, the most
mischievous thought that ever passed out
of a mans mouth. They have always
had the same dream that we come
at truth not by ~~cold~~ laborious, cold
deliberate thought, but by a sort of
frenzy, inspiration they call it

First Pupil.

If he meant all that I will take an oath
that he was spindle shanked & cross eyed
and had a louzy itching shoulder & that his
heart was crosser than his eyes and that
he wrote it out of malice.

Second Pupil

Lets come away & find a better subject

Fourth Pupil

And maybe now you ll let me choose.

First Pupil

Come — (~~They go out~~

6 Cancellation begins at "They have always".

18 Wavy leading stroke below line to lead to following page; this page evidently replaced an earlier version, no longer extant.

[MS. VJ, 7; 96–118]

(7

Wise man

t'would alter

Were it but true ~~it would change~~ everything
Until the stream of the world had changed its course
And that and all our thought had run
Into some cloudy thunderous ~~source~~ spring
They dream to be its ~~sourse~~ source
Aye to some frenzy of the mind
Till all that we have dones undone
Our speculation wind.
I have dreamed it ~~tw~~ twice

First Pupil

~~Come come away~~. Something has troubled him.
(pupils go out)

Wise man

Twice have I dreamed it in a morning dream
Now nothing serves my pupils but to come
With a like thought. Reason is growing dim
A moment more & Frenzy ~~will~~ will beat his drum
And laugh aloud & scream
And I must dance in the dream
No no but it is like a hawk, a hawk, a hawk
It has swooped down & this swoop makes the third
And what can I but tremble like a bird

Fool

Give me a penny

Wise man

That I should dream it ~~twie~~ twice & after that
That they should pick it out

Fool

Wont you
^ Give me a penny

---

9 Clearly added later.

[MS. VJ, 8; 119–128]

(8

Wise man

What do you want. What can it be to you
Whether the words I am reading
Be wisdom or sheer folly

Fool

Such a great wise teacher as you are will
not refuse a penny to a fool

Wise man

Seeing that everybody is a fool
When he is asleep and dreaming
Why do you call [?] ~~w~~ me wise

Fool

O I know — I know. I know what I have
seen.

Wise man

Well to see rightly is the whole of wisdom
What ever [?~~world~~] dreams be with us

---

12 Wavy leading stroke below line to lead to following page. The page evidently replaces an earlier version.

[MS. VJ, 9; 129–153]

Fool. (9

the
When I went by Kilcluan where ~~the~~ bells used
to be ringing at the break of every day I
could hear nothing but the people snoring
vanack
in their houses. When I went by Tubber ~~vanach~~
where climbing
~~where~~ the young men used to be ~~climbing~~ the
hill to the blessed well — they were sitting at
the cross roads playing cards. When I went
Carric orus
by ~~Carrig orus~~, where the friars used to be
serving
fasting & ~~serving~~ the poor I saw them
wine
drinking ~~wine~~ & obeying their wives & when
^ brought
I asked what misfortune had ~~brought~~ all these
changes said it was no misfortune
the wisdom
but that it was ~~the wisdom~~ they had learned from your
teaching.

Wise man.

Run
~~Run~~ to the kitchen food
My wife will give you ~~food~~ & drink.
^

Fool.

wise man
That s foolish advice for a ~~wise man~~ to give.

Wise man

Why Fool.

Fool

What is eaten is gone — I want pennies for my
bacon
bag. I must buy ~~bacon~~ in the shops, & nuts
in the market & strong drink for the time the
sun is weak
~~sun is weak~~ & snares to catch the rabbits
And the hares & a big pot to cook them in.

Wise man.

I ve more to think about than giving
pennies
~~Than giving pennie~~s to ~~your like~~ your like
So run away

This page is evidently a replacement, incorporated at the same time as pp. 16 and 17.

[MS. VJ, 10; 154–172]

(10

Fool

Give me a penny and I will bring you luck. The fisher men let me sleep among their nets in the loft because I bring them luck & in the summer time the wild creatures let me sleep near their nests and their holes. It is lucky even to look at me but it is much more lucky to give me a penny. If I was not lucky I would starve.

Wise man

What are the shears for.

Fool

I wont tell you. If I told you you would ~~driv~~ drive them away.

Wise man

Drive them away. Who would I drive away.

Fool

I wont tell you.

Wise man

Not if I give you a penny

Fool

No.

Wise man

Not if I give you two pennies

Fool

You will be very lucky if you give me two pennies ~~bu~~ but I wont tell you

Wise man

Three pennies

[MS. VJ, 11; 173–190]

11

Fool.

Four and I will tell you.

Wise man

Very well — four but from this out
I will not call you Teigue the fool.

Fool

Let me come close to you, where nobody
will hear me but first you must
promise not to drive them away.

nods
(The Wise man { ~~nods~~ / m)

Fool.

Every day men go out dressed in black and
spread great black nets over the hills
great black nets.

Wise man

A strange place that to fish in

Fool

They spread them out on the hills
~~to catch the~~ that they may catch
the feet of the angels; but every
morning just before the dawn I go out
and ~~catch the nets~~ cut the
nets with the shears & the angels fly away.

Wise man

Ah now I know that you are Teigue the Fool
You say that I am wise & yet I say
There are no angels.

Fool

I have seen plenty of angels

Wise man

No no you have not

[MS. VJ, 12; 191–209]

(12

Fool

They are plenty if you but look about you.
They are like the blades of grass.

Wise man

They are plenty as the blades of grass.
I heard that phrase when I was but a child
And was told folly

Fool

When one gets quiet. When one is so
quiet that there is not a thought in
one s head maybe there is something
that wakes up inside one — something
happy and quiet & then all in a
minuit one can smell summer
flowers & tall people go by happy
and laughing but they will not let us
look at ~~them~~ their faces. O no it
is not right that we should look at
their faces.

Wise man

{F
Why {fool you have fallen asleep on
the hill side. There are no angels
and even those that used
~~You hav~~
You have fallen asleep upon a hill
And even those that used to dream of angels
Dream now of other things

Fool

I saw one only a moment ago that
is because I am lucky. It was
~~be~~ coming behind me but it was not laughing

13

Wise man

see when they are
awake
1 Theres nothing but what men can ~~see when awake~~
2 Nothing, nothing. ^

Fool

3 I knew you would drive them away

Wise man

4 Pardon me Fool
5 I had forgotten who I spoke to called
6 Well there are your four pennies. Fool you are ^
hither
7 And all day long they cry 'come ~~hith~~ fool'
(Fool goes close to him)
8 Or else its 'Fool begone'
(He goes further away)
Or 'fool stand there'
(He straightens himself)
9 Or 'fool go sit in the corner'
(Fool sits in corner)
And all the while
10 What were they all but fools before I came
mirrors
11 What are they now but ~~mirrors~~ that seem men
12 Because of my image. *Fool hold up your head)
(He does so)
13 ~~For had not they a new face every morning~~
14 Have they not told trembling beside each other
15 ~~And trembled with their elders~~
16 Their shoulders bending in the perishing ashes
17 Stories of ghosts that creaked about the room
18 Or fumbled with the bed-clothes after dark
19 Or may be where they pious bred of angels
20 That hurried with their messages from heaven
21 And through a mans own door & after that

---

4 On the verso of p. 12 WBY wrote: "from here on it is verse" and drew a marker pointing to l. 4.
19 "where" written for "were".

1 What foolish stories they have told of the ghosts
2 That fumbled with the clothes upon the bed
Or
3 ~~Or~~ creaked & shuffled in the corridor
4 Or else if they were pious bred
5 Of angels from the skies
6 That came through a man s door
7 ~~And~~ & it maybe standing there
8 Would solidly outstare
steadiest eyes
9 The ~~strongest man~~ with their unnatural eyes
10 Aye even on his own floor.
(Angel has come in)
11 Yet it is strange — the strangest thing I have known
12 That I should still be haunted by the fancy

---

1 Revised on verso of p. 14:
~~How many foolish stories did they tell~~
H

12 Vertical wavy leading stroke below line to lead to following page. This page was incorporated when passages on pages 13 and 15 were canceled.

[MS. VJ, 15; 230–248]

(15

Solidly to outstare him with unnatural eyes
even on his own floor
(angel enters)
Yet it is strange
That I should still be haunted by a thought
That there s a crisis of the soul wherein
We get new sight & how if when it comes
They have some craft to turn it into frenzy
Why do you put your finger to your lips
And creep away (Fool goes out.
Wise man sees angel)
What are you? Who are you?
I think I saw some like you in my dreams
When but a child — that thing about your head
That brightness in your hair — that flowering branch
But I have done with dreams — I have done with dreams

Angel

crafty have called
I am the ~~[?crazy] one [?crazy]~~ one that you ^

Wise man

How that I called?

Angel

I am a messenger

Wise man

What message could you bring to one like me

Angel

That you will die when the last grain of sand
Has fallen through this glass.

Wise man.

I have a wife

[MS. VJ, 16; 249–267]

(16

Children & pupils that I cannot leave
Why must I die my time is far away

Angel

You are to die because no soul has passed
The heavenly threshold since you have opened school
But grass grows there, & rust s upon the hinge
And they are lonely that must keep the watch.

Wise man.

And whither shall I go when I am dead

Angel

You have denied the ~~pur~~ purgatorial fire
Therefore that gate is closed: You have denied
~~You have denied the heavenly~~
~~The heavenly [?] threshold & you may~~ not pass
That theres a heaven & that gate is closed

Wise man.

Where then — I have denied there is a hell.

Angel.

Hell is the place of those who have denied
They find there what they planted & what dug
A lake of spaces & a wood of nothing
And wander there & drift & never cease
Wailing for sustance

Wise man.

Pardon me blessed angel
I have denied & taught the like to others
Believing nothing but what sense has taught
And the minds abstract.

Angel

It is too late for pardon

Pages now numbered 9, 16, and 17 were evidently written later, replacing earlier versions no longer extant.

[MS. VJ, 17; 268–294]

(17

Wise man

Had I but seen your face as now I see it
But how can you that live but where we go
In the uncertainty of dizzy dreams
Know why we doubt. Disease & death
The rotting of the grass, tempest & drouth
These were the messengers that came to me
Why are you silent? you carry in your hands
Gods pardon & you will not give it me.
Why are you silent? Were I not afraid
I d kiss your hands — no — no the hem of your dress

Angel

Only when all the world has testified
May soul confound it crying out in joy
Whats dearth & death & sickness to the soul
That knows no virtue but it self nor could it
So trembling with delight & mother naked
Live unabashed if the arguing world stood by.

Wise man.

It is as hard for you to understand
Why we have doubted as it is for us
To put our doubt away — What have I said
There can be nothing that you do not know
Give me a year — a month — a week — a day
I would undo what I have done — an hour —
Give me until the sand has run in the glass

Angel

Though you may not undo what you have done
I have this power — ~~if you find a man~~
~~who still believes what he believed in childhood~~
~~[?And that] he has a soul~~

[MS. VJ, 18; 293–311]

(18

If you but find one soul
That still believes that it shall never cease
One fish to lie & spawn among the stones
is
Till the great fishers net ~~be~~ full again
You may, the purgatorial fire being passed
Spring to your peace.

pupils (sing without)
Who stole your wits away
~~they go~~ they gone
And where are ~~(Pupils sing without~~)

Wise man

My pupils come
Before you have begun to climb the sky
I shall have found belief — They say they doubt
But what their mothers dinned into their ears
Has not been broken down — I have long thought it
Besides I can disprove what I once proved
And yet give me some thought some argument
More mighty than my own.

Angel.

Fare well — farewell
For I am weary of the weight of time

(Angel goes out — Wise man makes a start to follow & pauses — pupils come in at other side)

First pupil

Master — Master you must choose the subject

Second pupil

No here it is — Where have the Fools

[MS. VJ, 19; 312–329]

(19

enter the pupils with Fool about whom
they dance.

Pupils

Did your wits run off
1 ~~Who stole your wits away~~
on their own pair of shoes
2 ~~And where have they gone~~
or who was it dragged them
3 ~~Run Teigue to find them~~
4 ~~Up and down~~. Where no one knows.

Fool.

5 Give me a penny.

1 Pupil

The Master will find
6 ~~The Master will tell us where~~ y
your wits
7 ~~Come we will find your wits~~

2 Pupil

8 And when they are found you need not beg
9 ~~for pennies~~ for pennies

3 Pupil hole

10 They are hidden somewhere in the badgers
11 ~~hole but~~
12 ~~And~~ But you must carry an old candle end
13 If you would find them.

4 Pupil

They are up above the clouds

Fool

14 Give me a penny, give me a penny Teigue.

~~5 Pupil~~

Pupils

1

15 I ll find your wits again
16 Come for I saw them roll
17 To where old badger mumbles
18 In the black hole

2

19 No but an angel stole em

This and the following two pages appear to belong to a later stage of composition.

[MS. VJ, 20; 330–341]

(20

1 The night that you were born
2 And now they are but a rag
3 On the moons horn.

Wise man.

4 Be silent

1 Pupil

Can you not see that he is troubled
~~Hush hush he is about to speak~~

Wise man

5 What do you think of when alone at night
6 Do not the things your mother spoke about
7 Before she took the candle from the bedside
8 Rush up into the mind & master it
9 Till you believe in them against your will.

[~~?~~] 2 Pupil (to 1 Pupil)

10 You answer for us.

3 Pupil (in a whisper)

Be careful what you say

11 ~~For if he can~~
12 If he persuade you to an argument
13 He ll make a mock of you & us.

1 Pupil.

~~Master~~

We have made

14 Our minds as naked as our bodies were

us

15 ~~When they were born — [?Your] mothers gave [?] those~~
16 When we were born that you may give us thought.
17 Our bodies were our mothers work

Wise man.

No ~~w~~ no

18 ~~Why will you say what is untrue~~
19 You answer with incredible things. It is certain
20 ~~That there is one — though may one man only~~
21 That there is one though it may be but one
22 Believes in god & in some heaven & hell
23 And all those things we put into our preyers

---

15 "Our" clearly intended rather than "Your."

20 "be" omitted.

[MS. VJ, 21; 347–371]

(21

~~Mast~~ Pupils

No one — you ve made us less fantastic clothes

Wise man

You are afraid to tell me what you think
Because I am hot and angry when I am crossed
I do not blame you for it but have no fear
For if there is one that sat on smiling there
As though my arguments were sweet as milk
Yet found them bitter I will thank him for it
If he but speak his mind

1 Pupil.

In very truth
There is not one but found them sweet as milk

Wise man

The things that have been told us in our childhood
Are not so fragile.

2 Pupil

We are no longer children

3 Pupil

We all believe in you & in what you have taught

Other Pupils.

All, all, all, all. In you, nothing but you

Wise man.

I have deceived you. Where shall I go for words
I have no thoughts — my mind has been swept bare.
The messengers that stand in the fiery cloud
Fling themselves out if we but dare to question
And after that the Babylonian moon
Blots all away.

First Pupil. (to other pupils)

That visionaries & martyrs when they are raised

[MS. VJ, 22; 372–388]

(22

1 above translunary things & there enlightened
2 As the contention is may lose the light
3 And blunder in their speech when the eyes open.

Second Pupil

trick
4 How well he imitates their ~~trick~~ of speech
5 ~~And air of mystery~~

Third Pupil.

6 Their air of mystery [?~~that~~]

Fourth Pupil.

~~The look in the eyes~~
7 ~~Their em The empty gaze~~
8 Their empty gaze
9 As though ~~the d~~ they d looked upon some winged thing
10 ~~And found all else~~
11 [?~~Tu~~]
mankind
12 And would not condescend to ~~mankind~~ after.

First Pupil.

learned
13 Master we have learned that truth is ~~found~~
14 When the intellect is deliberate and cold
15 As it were a polished mirror that reflects
16 An unchanged world & not when the steel melts
17 Bubbling & hissing till there s naught but fume

Wise man

fumes
18 When it is melted, when it all ~~fumes~~ up
19 They walk, as when beside those three in the furnace
20 The form of the fourth

First Pupil

Master there s none among us
21 That has not heard your mockery of these
22 Or thoughts like these & we have not forgot.

[MS. VJ, 23; 389–404]

(23

Wise man.
1 Something incredible has happened — some one
has come
2 Suddenly like a grey hawk out of the air
3 And all that I declared untrue is true

First Pupil (to other pupils)
4 You d think the way he says it that he felt it
5 There s not a mummer to compare with him
6 He s something like a man.

Second Pupil.
Give us some proof

Wise man
7 What proof have I to give but that an angel
8 An instant ago was standing on that spot

Third Pupil
9 You dreamed it Master

Wise man.
I was awake as I am now

First Pupil
10 I may be dreaming now for all I know
(to the others)
11 He wants to show we have no certain proof
12 Of anything in the world

Second Pupil.
There is this proof
13 That shows we are awake — we have all one
world
14 While every dreamer has a world of his own
15 And sees what no one else can.

Third Pupil
Teigue sees angels

[MS. VJ, 24; 405–420]

(24

Third Pupil

1 So when the Master says he has seen an
angel

2 He may have seen one.

First Pupil

~~Both~~ Both may still be dreamers

3 Unless its proved the angels were alike

Second Pupil

4 What sort are the angels Teigue.

Third Pupil.

That would prove nothing

5 For all we know prolonged obedience

6 Has made one angel like another angel

7 As they were eggs.

First Pupil.

The Masters silent now

8 For he has found that to dispute with us

9 Seeing that he has taught us what we know

10 Is but to reason with himself. Let us go

11 And find if there is one believer left

Wise man

12 Yes yes. Find me but one that still believes

13 The things that we believed when we were children

Third Pupil

14 Our master'll mock and mawl him.

Fourth Pupil.

From the first

15 I knew he'd have us find some disputant

(They go)

Wise man

16 I have no reason left all dark, all dark

[MS. VJ, 25; 421–438]

(25

(pupils return laughing. They push fourth
~~third~~ pupil forward)

First Pupil.

Here master is the very man you want.
He said, when we were studying the book
That maybe after all the monk was right
And you mistaken & if we but gave him time
He d prove that it was so.

Fourth Pupil

I never said it

Wise man

Dear Friend, dear friend do you believe in God

Fourth Pupil

Master they have invented this to mock me

Wise man

You are afraid of me.

Fourth Pupil

They know well Master
That all I said was but to make them argue
~~They~~ p
They've pushed me in to make a mock of me
Because they know I could take either side
And beat them at it

Wise man

If you believe in god
You are my souls one friend (pupils laugh)
Mistress or wife
Can give us but our good or evil luck
Amid the howling world but shall give
Eternity & those sweet throated things
That drift above the moon.

(The pupils are silent)

---

16 "you" omitted after "but"?

[MS. VJ, 26; 438–458]

(26

Second Pupil

How strange he is
You'd almost think he'd spoken his own thought

Wise man

The angel that stood there upon that spot
Said that my soul was lost unless I found
Before the sands in the hour glass had run out
One that believed.

4th Pupil

Cease mocking at me Master
I am so certain that there is no god
I ll curse him if you will & after curse
The soul that has been breathed out of his nostrils
If but these lies are true. Will that convince you
That I have set my heart on what you teach

Wise man

The giddy glass is emptier every moment
And you stand there debating laughing & wrangling
Out of my sight, out of my sight I say.
(He drives them out)
I ll call my wife for what can women do
That carry us in the darkness of their bodies
But mock the reason that lets nothing grow
Unless it grow in light. Bridget, Bridget
A woman never ceases to believe
Say what we will. Bridget come quickly Bridget.
(Bridget comes in~~)~~— wearing
her apron. Her sleeves turned up from her
floury arms.)
Wife what do you believe in — tell the truth
~~nothing~~
And not, as is the habit with you all,
Something you think will please me. Do you prey
Some times when youre alone in the house do you prey.

[MS. VJ, 27; 459–482]

(27

Bridget

Preyers — no — you taught me to leave them off
long ago. At first I was sorry but I
am glad now for I am sleepy in the
evenings.

Wise man.

Do you believe in God.

Bridget

Oh a good wife only believes in what
her husband tells her

Wise man

But sometimes when the children are asleep
And I am in the school do you not think
About the Martyrs & the Saints & Angels
And all the things that you believed in once
What do you think of when you are alone

Bridget

I think about nothing — sometimes I wonder
linen
if the ~~lin linnen~~ 's bleaching white
or I go out to see if the crows are picking
up the chickens food.

Wise man.

My god — my god — I will go out my self
My pupils said that they would find a man
That had the old belief — they may have found him
There-fore I will go out — but If I go
The glass will let the sands run out unseen
I cannot go — I cannot leave the glass.
Go call my pupils — I can explain all now
Only when all our hold on life is shaken
Only in ~~the~~ spiritual terror can the truth
Come through the broken mind as the pease burst
Out of a broken pease cod.

~~Th~~ (He clutches her as she is going)

[MS. VJ, 28; 482–500]

(28

Say to them
That nature would lack all at her most need
Could not the soul find truth in a flash
Upon the battle field or in the midst
Of overwhelming waves & say to them —
But no they would but answer as I bid.

Bridget
You want somebody to get up an argument
with

Wise man
~~Look through the door~~ &
Look out & see if there is any one
There in the street — I cannot leave the glass
For somebody might shake it and the sand
If it were shaken might run down on the instant.

Bridget.
I dont understand a word you are saying
There's a crowd of people talking to your
pupils.

Wise man
~~Run out &~~
Go out & find if they have found a man
Who did not understand me when I taught
Or did not listen.

Bridget
It is a hard thing to be married to a
man of learning ~~but that~~ that must
always be having arguments. ~~Child~~
children dont be meddling with the
bread while I am out (she goes out)

[MS. VJ, 29; 501–517]

(29

Wise man

Strange that I should be ~~bl~~ blind to the great secret
write
And that so simple a man might ~~right~~ it out
Upon a blade of grass or bit of rush
With naught but berry juice & laugh to himself
Writing it out because it was so simple.

(Enter Fool & Bridget)

Fool.

Give me something; give me a penny to buy
bacon in the shops & nuts in the market
And strong drinks for the time when the
sun is weak.

Bridget.

I have no pennies (to wise man) Your
pupils cannot find anybody to
argue with you. There s nobody in the
whole country with ~~enough~~ belief enough
for a curse or a lovers oath. Cant
you be quiet now & not always
wanting to have arguments. It must be
~~terrible~~ terrible to have a mind like
that.

Wise man

Then I am lost indeed.

Bridget

Leave me alone now I have to make
the bread for you and the children

~~Wise man~~ ~~she goes~~ out
(She goes into kitchen)

Wise man

Children children.

[MS. VJ, 30; 518–538]

(30

Bridget

Your father wants you run to him.

(The children run in)

Wise man

Come to me children. Do not be afraid
I want to know if you believe in heaven
God or the soul — no do not tell me yet
You need not be afraid I shall be angry
Say what you please so that it is your thought
I wanted you to know before you spoke
That I shall not be angry.

First child.

We have not forgotten father

Second child.

O no father ~~O no father~~

Both children (as if repeating a lesson)

There is nothing we cannot see, nothing
we cannot touch.

First child

Foolish people used to say that there was but
You have taught us better.

Wise man

Go to your mother go yet do not go
For she can tell you nothing — If I am dumb
You shall be lost among the woods of nothing
And I because the sands are running out
Have but a moment to show it all in. Children
The sap would die out of the blades of grass
Had they a doubt. They understand it all
Being the fingers of gods certainty
Yet can but make their sign into the air

[MS. VJ, 31; 539–554]

31

[?~~Their own answer~~]
But could they find their tongues — they show it all
But what am I to say that am but one
When they are millions & they will not speak
(The children have run out)
But they are gone what made them run away
(The Fool comes in with a ~~dan~~
dandelion)
Look at me — tell me if my face is changed
Is there a notch of the fiends nail upon it
Already? — is it terrible to sight
Because the moments near
(going to glass)
I dare not look
I dare not know the moment when they come
To carry me away. (covers glass)
Will there be a footfall
Or will there be a sort of tearing sound
Or else a cracking as though an iron claw
~~Had gripped the~~
~~Had gripped the threshold stone Oh no not that~~
Had gripped the threshold stone.
(The Fool has begun to blow the
dandelion)
What are you doing?

Fool.

Wait a ~~min~~ minuit — four — five — six

Wise man

What are you doing that for?

Fool

I am blowing the dandelion to find out what

[MS. VJ, 32; 554–576]

(32

what hour it is.

Wise man

You have heard every thing & that is why
You d find what hour it is — you d find that out
~~That you may see them comin~~
That you may look upon a fleet of devils
Dragging my soul away. Out out with you
I will have no one here when they come in
I will have no one sitting there — out — out
No no — there is some thing strange about you
Are you the one I seek? Do you believe
In god & the soul in the undying stuff
That all things have been made of from the first

Fool

So you ask me now. I thought when
You were asking your pupils, will
he ask Teigue the fool. Yes he will, he
will, no he will not — yes he will
But Teigue will say nothing, Teigue
will say nothing.

Wise man

Tell me quickly

Fool

I said Teigue knows everything not
even the green eyed cats & the hares that
milk the cows have Teigues wisdom but
Teigue will not speak, he says nothing.

Wise man

Speak speak for underneath the cover there
The sand is running from the upper glass
And when the last grains through I shall be lost
Unless I have lit upon unshaken faith
somewhere in somebody

[MS. VJ, 33; 577–587]

(33

Fool

I will not speak. I will not tell you what
is in my mind. I wont tell you what
is in my bag. You might steal away
my thoughts. I met a bodach on
the road yesterday & he said ‘Teigue
tell me how many pennies are in your
bag. I will ~~wat~~ wager three pennies
that there are not twenty pennies in
your bag. Let me put in my hand
and count them’ But I gripped
~~my~~ the bag the ~~tighter~~ tighter & when
I go to sleep at night I hide
the bag where nobody knows.

Wise man (going near Hour Glass)

~~No I have not the courage~~. If you
are not ~~him~~ him I seek ~~I~~ I am
lost for ~~the time is at an end — I~~
there is scarcely a grain left.

Fool.

O what a lot the Fool knows ~~but~~ but
he says nothing.

Wise man.

I kneel to you — You are the man
that I have saught. You alone can
save me.

Wise man ([~~? ? ? Hour Glass~~]

~~There is scarce one grain that has not fallen~~
’s
There‸ ~~is~~ but one pinch of sand — ~~I am lost~~
And I am lost
If you are ~~not~~ not him I seek

[MS.VJ, 34; 588–617]

(34

Fool

O what a lot the fool knows but he says
nothing.

Wise man (seizing him)

I kneel to you — you are the man I have saught
You alone can save me.

Fool.

No no what should poor Teigue know
Teigue that is out in all weathers, Teigue
that sleeps in the fishers loft, poor
Teigue the Fool ~~(he breaks away & goes
out)~~ (He breaks away)

Wise man.

The last hope is gone
And now that it is too late I see it all
We perish into god & sink away
Into reality — The rests' a dream
Man does not know the truth for it is god
That sees the ~~truth~~ truth in Man

Fool peering in

I hear the wind blow
And the grass a grow
And all that they know I know.

Wise man

~~The sands have fallen~~
I understand the world now that I leave it
I know what fixed the station
Of star and cloud
And knowing all I cry
That what so God has willed
On the instant be fullfilled
Though that be my damnation

[MS. VJ, 35; 597–626]

(35

(The Fool goes out

Wise man

The last hope is gone
And now that it s too late I see it all
We perish into god & sink away
Into reality — the rests a dream

Fool (coming back on tip toe
& peering under cover of ~~glass~~
Hour Glass & singing in a low voice)

I hear the wind ~~a~~blow
And the grass a grow
And all that I know I know

Wise man

~~I understand the world now that I leave it~~
I know what fixed the station
Of star & cloud
And knowing all I cry
That what so God has willed
On the instant be fullfilled
Though that be my damnation
The world has changed its course
And every stream has run
Into some cloudy thundrous spring
Aye to its own mountain sourse
Even to some frenzy of the mind
For all we have done s undone
Our speculation wind

(He dies)

Fool

Master, Master. ~~There is some thing~~ I
~~will tell you if you give me a penny~~

1–4 On the verso of p. 34 WBY drafted a revision or addition:
and my life ebbs — pull a passing bell
call in

[MS. VJ, 36; 626–643]

(36

~~I believe~~ — I
It is me, poor Teigue the Fool
that you are looking for — but now
You must give me a penny.
Why dont you speak — why dont you
Say 'There is a penny for you
Teigue'

Angel enters.

O look what has come from your
mouth — O look what I have
caught in my hands — The white
butterfly. He is dead, he is dead
and I have taken his soul in my
hands.

Angel holds out her hands

There then I will give it you
You will open your hands in the
Garden of Paradise. Come in
everybody — everybody in the world &
look at, I was the one the Wise
man was looking for [?it] & he did not
know it (Angel goes) He is gone
but I am here & I know all.

---

14 "to" omitted before "you".

18 "me" omitted.

[MS. VJ, 37; 641–644]

37

You and I. We are the two fools
We know everything but we will not
speak
    I hear the wind a blow
    I hear the grass a grow
    And I know what I know

W B Yeats

The Mask (1913)

Transcription, with apparatus criticus
of variants in MSS. VK, VN, VP, VQ, and VR

[*Mask*]

THE HOUR GLASS by W.B. Yeats.

A PREFACE TO THE NEW VERSION.

I took the plot of "The Hour Glass" from an Irish Folk Tale but tried to put my own philosophy into the words. An action on the stage, however, is so much stronger than a word that when the Wise Man abused himself before the Fool I was always ashamed. My own meanings had vanished and I saw before me a cowardly person who seemed to cry out "the wisdom of this world is foolishness" and to understand the words not as may a scholar and a gentleman but as do ignorant preachers.

I began a revision of the words from the moment when the play converted a music hall singer and sent him to mass and to confession ; but no revision of words could change the effect of the Wise Man down on his knees before the Fool; so last year I changed action and all.

I made a new play of it and when I had finished discovered how I might have taken the offence out of the old by a change of action so slight that a reader would hardly have noticed it. I shall let "our second company" go on playing the old version thus amended in Irish provincial towns but think the new one better for myself and my friends.

W.B.Yeats.

[*Mask*]

THE HOUR GLASS

SCENE: THE WISE MAN'S house. An Hour-glass on a stand and a big chair with a great book on a desk before it.

(ENTER PUPILS)

1st PUPIL. **He said we might choose the subject for the lesson.**

2nd PUPIL. **There is none of us wise enough to do that.**

3nd PUPIL. **It would need a great deal of wisdom to know what we want to know.**

4th PUPIL. **I will question him.**

5th PUPIL. **You ?**

4th PUPIL. **Last night I dreamt that someone came and told me to question him. I was to say to him, " you were wrong to say there is no God and no soul.... maybe, if there is not much of either, there is yet some tatters, some tag on the wind, some rag.... so to speak of divinity, some bob-tail of a god ". I will argue with him,... nonsense**

---

title THE HOUR-GLASS. / By W. B. Yeats. *typed carbon on one separate sheet. Title at start of play and another separate cover sheet read:* THE HOUR-GLASS *VK* THE HOUR-GLASS *below which is added in ink* NEW VERSION *VN* — THE HOUR-GLASS/ NEW VERSION — *with date* 1912 *added below in ink VP* THE HOUR-GLASS *VQ, VR*

no preface VK, VN, VP, VQ, VR

stage directions underlined VK; at line ends, with square initial bracket, no closing bracket, and period VQ, VR

character idents spelled out in caps and centered VN, VP, VQ, VR

single quotes throughout VP, VQ, VR

long dashes instead of three dots throughout VK, VN, VP, VQ, VR

THE PERSONS OF THE PLAY / WISE MAN. / BRIDGET, his wife. / TEIGUE, a fool. / ANGEL. / Children and Pupils. *VN, VP, so VQ but* WISE MAN PERSONS IN THE PLAY *VR* A as in VPl.III *added in ink before* WISE MAN / . . . Wife / . . . Fool / CHILDREN and PUPILS *no periods,* TEIGUE *circled in ink, accepted by WBY VR Pencil tick beside the list VQ*

scene The Wise man's *VK omitted VN, VP, VQ*

/1 PUPILS.) *VK* Pupils come in and stand before the stage curtain which is still closed. One pupil carries a book. *VN, VP* curtain, *VQ,* When played at the Abbey Theatre [*del* the *(rev in ink to* The*) then marked in ink* stet. This can stand in this edition] stage is brought out into the orchestra so as to leave a wide space in front of the stage curtain. Pupils [*note in ink reads:* caps?] come in and stand before the stage curtain, which is still closed. One pupil [pupil *circled, note in ink reads:* caps *both caps accepted by WBY*] carries a book. *VR*

1, 2 *character idents lightly underlined in pencil VR*

3 3rd *rev in ink to* 1st *VK* what it is we *VN, VP, VQ, VR*

6 5th *rev in ink to* 3rd *VK*

7 some one *VQ, VR*

8 You *VQ, VR*

10 some *e inserted in ink VK*

11 wind — so to speak — some rag upon a bush, some *VN, VP, VQ, VR*

12 god.' *VN* him — *VR*

though it be... according to my dream, and you will see how well I can argue, and what thoughts I have.

1st PUPIL. **I'd as soon listen to dried peas in a bladder, as listen to your thoughts.**

(FOOL comes in)

FOOL. **Give me a penny.**

2nd PUPIL. **Let us choose a subject by chance. Here is his big book. Let us turn over the pages slowly, let one of us put down his finger without looking, the passage his finger lights on will be the subject for the lesson.**

FOOL. **Give me a penny.**

3rd PUPIL. **(taking up book) How heavy it is.**

4th PUPIL. **Spread it on Teigue's back, and then we can all stand round and see the choice,**

2nd PUPIL. **Make him spread out his arms.**

4th PUPIL. **Down on your knees. Hunch up your back. Spread your arms out now, and look like a golden eagle in a church. Keep still, keep still.**

FOOL. **Give me a penny.**

3rd PUPIL. **Is that the right cry for an eagle cock ?**

2nd PUPIL. **I'll turn the pages.... you close your eyes and put your finger down.**

3rd PUPIL. **That's it, and then he cannot blame us for the choice.**

1st PUPIL. **There, I have choosen. Fool, keep still.... and if what's wise is strange and sounds like nonsense, we've made a good choice.**

5th PUPIL. **Here is the master coming.**

FOOL. **Will anybody give a penny to a fool ?**

---

15 bladder, *comma del VR*

16 Teigue the *inserted in ink before* FOOL *VR*

19 slowly. Let *VN, VP, VQ, VR*

20 looking. The *VN, VP, VR, so VQ but surface of page torn so that* loo *from* looking, s *from* lights *and* on *are missing, all then added by WBY in ink in the margin*

23 (Taking *VQ*

24 Teigue's *circled in ink, with* stet *(not WBY) marked in margin VR*

25 choice. *VK, VN, VP, VQ, VR*

29 still, Keep *VK, VN, VP, VQ*

31 3rd *rev in ink to* 1st *VK* eagle-cock *hyphen inserted in ink (WBY) VR*

35 chosen *VN, VP, VQ, VR*

38 5th. PUPIL. Here is the master coming. *del in ink to* 2nd *rev then continues in pencil* 5 *(5 then del in ink)* Pupil. Hush. The Masters there. *VK* The master has come. *VN, VP, so VQ, VR but* Master

39 fool? (One of the pupils draws back the stage curtain showing the Master sitting at his desk. One pupil puts the book before him) *VN, VP, so VQ, VR but* desk. There is an hour-glass upon his desk or in a bracket on the wall. One *VR also reads* curtains *and idents are circled with* caps? *written in margin in ink; WBY has canceled* ?s, *accepting change*

39 fool?] F *suggested but del (editor) VR*

(WISE MAN comes in)

1st PUPIL. **We have chosen the passage for the lesson, Master. " There are two living countries, one visible and one invisible, and when it is summer there, it is winter here, and when it is November with us, it is lambing-time there. "**

WISE MAN. **That passage, that passage ; what mischief has there been since yesterday ?**

1st PUPIL. **None, Master.**

WISE MAN. **Oh, yes, there has; some craziness has fallen from the wind, or rises from the graves of old men, and made you choose that subject. (he goes to desk)**

4th PUPIL. **I knew that it was folly, but they would have it.**

3rd PUPIL. **Had we not better say we picked it by chance ?**

2nd PUPIL. **No, he would say we were children still.**

1st PUPIL. **I have found a sentence under that one, that says.... as though to show it had a hidden meaning.... a beggar wrote it upon the walls of Babylon.**

WISE MAN. **Then find some beggar and ask him what it means, for I will have nothing to do with it.**

4th PUPIL. **Come, Teigue, what is the old book's meaning when it says that there are sheep that drop their lambs in November ?**

FOOL. **To be sure.... everybody knows, everybody in the world knows, when it is Spring with us, the trees are withering there, when it is summer with us, the snow is falling there, and have I not myself heard the lambs that are there all bleating on a cold November day.... to be sure, does not everybody with an intellect know that ; and maybe when it's night with us, it is day with them, for many a time I have seen the roads lighted before me.**

---

45 passage! what *VN, VP, VQ, so VR but* W ? *added in pencil in margin*

47 *line typed on directly (ribbon, not carbon) VK*

48 *character ident typed on directly (ribbon, not carbon) VK* Oh yes, *VQ* Oh *del in ink to* O *VR*

49 rises *rev in ink to* risen *VN,* risen *VP, VQ, VR*

50 (He *VK* *stage direction omitted VN, VP, VQ, VR* *in VQ, period after* subject *rev in ink to dash, and ink insert then reads* Diem noctemque contendo, sed quos elegi, quos amavi, in tirocinium vel hi labuntur. *with clarification of* cinium *is written in parens on the line below, rev adopted VR, which has* ital? *written in margin, del ink WBY*

53 No; *VQ, VR*

54 *no comma VN, VP, VQ, VR*

59 Teigue, *circled,* stet *written by WBY in margin VR*

63 Spring *ink note in margin reads* lc *VR, pencil note, mostly erased, reads:* l.c. cf p and previous page, *accepted WBY*

64 Summer *VQ, so VR but ink note in margin reads* lc, *accepted WBY*

67 that; *semicolon rev in ink to* ? And *VR, accepted WBY*

WISE MAN. **The beggar who wrote that on Babylon wall meant that there is a spiritual kingdom that cannot be seen or known till the faculties whereby we master the kingdom of this world wither away, like green things in winter. A monkish thought, the most mischievous thought that ever passed out of a man's mouth.**

1st PUPIL. **If he meant all that, I will take an oath that he was spindle-shanked, and cross-eyed, and had a lousy itching shoulder, and that his heart was crosser than his eyes, and that he wrote it out of malice.**

2nd PUPIL. **Let's come away and find a better subject.**

4th PUPIL. **And maybe now you'll let me choose.**

1st PUPIL. **Come.**

WISE MAN. **Were it but true t'would alter everything.**
Until the stream of the world had changed its course,
And that and all out thoughts had run
Into some cloudy thunderous spring.
They dream to be its source....
Aye, to some frenzy of the mind,
Till all that we have done's, undone
Our speculative wind,
I have dreamed it twice.

1st PUPIL. **Something has troubled him.**

(PUPILS go out)

WISE MAN. **Twice have I dreamed it in a morning dream,**
Now nothing serves my pupils but to come
With a like thought. Reason is growing dim.
A moment more and Frenzy will beat his drum

---

70 beggar, . . . wall, *commas del VR*

72 faculties, *VR*

73 world, wither away like *VR*

75 *ink insertion after* mouth. *reads:* virgas ~~colligunt aves~~ ut partus educant, [colligunt aves *inserted*] mens hominis nugas *VQ* mouth. — Virgas ut partus educant colligunt aves, mens hominis nugas. *VR*

83 true, *comma added ink VR* 'twould *VR* eveything *VN, VP, VQ, VR* everything, *VK*

85 our *VK, VN, VP, VQ, VR*

86 spring. —*period del and dash added in pencil VK* spring *VN, VP, VQ, VR*

88 mind; *VN, VP, VQ,VR*

89 done's, *comma del in pencil VK* And all that we have done would be undone, *VP, VQ, VR, so VN but comma added in pencil*

90 speculative *overwritten in pencil to* speculation *VK* On [*del and rev in ink to* Our] speculation [as the *inserted in ink*] wind. (A pause) *VN* Our speculation as the wind. (A pause) *VP* Our speculation but as the wind. (A pause. *VQ, VR*

91 Pupils *circled pencil, ink note (WBY) in margin reads* caps *VR*

94 dim; *VQ, VR*

And laugh aloud and scream.
And I must dance in the dream,
No, no, but it is like a hawk, a hawk of the air,
It has swooped down... and this swoop makes the third...
And what can I, but tremble like a bird ?

FOOL. **Give me a penny.**

WISE MAN. **That I should dream it twice, and after that,**
That they should pick it out.

FOOL. **Won't you give me a penny ?**

WISE MAN. **What do you want ? What can it matter to you whether the words I am reading, are wisdom or sheer folly ?**

FOOL. **Such a great wise teacher will not refuse a penny to a fool.**

WISE MAN. **Seeing that everybody is a fool when he is asleep and dreaming, why do you call me wise ?**

FOOL. **O, I know,... I know, I know what I have seen.**

WISE MAN. **Well, to see rightly is the whole of wisdom, whatever dream be with us.**

FOOL. **When I went by Kilcluan, where the bells used to be ringing at the break of every day, I could hear nothing but the people snoring in their houses. When I went by Tubbervanach, where the young men used to be climbing the hill to the blessed well, they were sitting at the crossroads playing cards. When I went by Carrigoras, where the friars used to be fasting and serving the poor, I saw them drinking wine and obeying their wives. And when I asked what misfortune had brought all these changes, they said it was no misfortune, but that it was the wisdom they had learned from your teaching.**

WISE MAN. **And you too have called me wise .... you would be paid**

---

96 scream; *VQ, VR*

97 dream. *VQ, VR*

100 I *inserted (ribbon) VK*

102–103 that, that *VN, VP, VQ, VR* out. *del ink to* out! *VR, accepted WBY*

106 *no comma VQ, VR*

107 great, *VQ, VR*

108–109 *l.c.* fool *accepted unchanged by WBY VR*

111 know. — I *VK*

117 Tubber-vanach, *hyphen inserted and marginal note in ink reads:* one word or hyphened as in VPl.III p.5 *VR WBY cancels* one word, *marks hyphen*

117–128 Tubber- *ends page VQ. Pencil note on p. 132 not in WBY's hand reads* 'Page 131 awanting / (Set from other side)'. *An attempt to unstick the page was made, tearing its surface, and some words had to be written in in black ink. But the larger sheet is translucent and p. 131 can be read through it. There are no alterations to its text.*

119 cross-roads *VK, VN, VP, VR but pencil note questioning it erased* Carrigoras, *ink note in margin reads* Carrick-orus — in VPl. III, p.5 *VR WBY cancels* in VPl. III, p.5 *and revises (in ink)* g *to* c — *and* as *to* us

125 And you too *added (ribbon) VK*

for that good opinion doubtless .... Run to the kitchen, my wife will give you food and drink.

FOOL. **That's foolish advice for a wise man to give.**

WISE MAN. **Why, Fool ?**

FOOL. **What is eaten is gone...I want pennies for my bag. I must buy bacon in the shops, and nuts in the market, and strong drink for the time the sun is weak, and snares to catch the rabbits, and the hares, and a big pot to cook them in.**

WISE MAN. **I have more to think about than giving pennies to your like, so run away.**

FOOL. **Give me a penny and I will bring you luck. The fishermen let me sleep among their nets in the loft because I bring them luck, and in the summer time, the wild creatures let me sleep near their nests and their holes. It is lucky even to look at me, but it is much more lucky to give me a penny. If I was not lucky I would starve.**

WISE MAN. **What are the shears for ?**

FOOL. **I won't tell you. If I told you, you would drive them away.**

WISE MAN. **Drive them away, who would I drive away ?**

FOOL. **I won't tell you.**

WISE MAN. **Not if I give you a penny ?**

FOOL. **No.**

WISE MAN. **Not if I give you two pennies ?**

FOOL. **You will be very lucky if you give me two pennies, but I won't tell you.**

WISE MAN. **Three pennies ?**

FOOL. **Four, and I will tell you.**

WISE MAN. **Very well ... four, but from this out I will not call you, Teigue the Fool.**

FOOL. **Let me come close to you, where nobody will hear me, but first you must promise not to drive them away. (WISE MAN nods) Every day men go out dressed in black and spread great black nets over the hills, great**

---

126 doubtless. *period inserted VR* kitchen, *comma rev in ink to semicolon VR*
128 give, *VK, VN*
133 rabbits and *VQ, VR*
139 luck; *VQ, VR* summer-time, *hyphen inserted VR*
146 away! Who *VQ, so VR but ink note* m *inserted in margin, pencil note:* ? Accusative cf p. 13
155 you *VQ, VR*
156 Teigue *circled and* stet *written in margin in ink (WBY) VR*
157 me; *VQ, VR*
159 nods. *VR, so VQ but parens*

black nets.

WISE MAN. **A strange place that to fish in.**

FOOL. **They spread them out on the hills that they may catch the feet of the angels ; but every morning just before the dawn, I go out and cut the nets with the shears and the angels fly away.**

WISE MAN. **(speaking with some excitement) Ah, now I know that you are Teigue the Fool. You say that I am wise, and yet I say, there are no angels.**

FOOL. **I have seen plenty of angels.**

WISE MAN. **No, no, you have not.**

FOOL. **They are plenty if you but look about you, they are like the blades of grass.**

WISE MAN. **They are plenty as the blades of grass .... I heard that phrase when I was but a child and was told folly.**

FOOL. **When one gets quiet. When one is so quiet that there is not a thought in one's head maybe, there is something that wakes up inside one, something happy and quiet, and then all in a minute one can smell summer flowers, and tall people go by, happy and laughing, but they will not let us look at their faces. Oh, no, it is not right that we should look at their faces.**

WISE MAN. **You have fallen asleep upon a hill, yet, even those that used to dream of angels dream now of other things.**

FOOL. **I saw one but a moment ago... that is because I am lucky. It was coming behind me, but it was not laughing.**

WISE MAN. **There's nothing but what men can see when they are awake. Nothing, nothing.**

FOOL. **I knew you would drive them away.**

WISE MAN. **Pardon me, Fool,**
I had forgotten who I spoke to.
Well , there are your four pennies ... Fool, you are called

---

164 morning, *comma inserted in ink by WBY VR*

167 (Speaking *VQ* with excitement) *VN, VP, VQ,VR*

168 Teigue *circled VR* Fool, You *VN, VP*

169 say, *comma del? VR, accepted by WBY*

172 you. They *VN, VP, VQ, VR*

181 Oh no, *VQ* Oh [*del to* O] no, *VR*

183 hill, yet, *commas del? VR, accepted by WBY*

187 is *del and rev in ink to* it *VN*

191 who] whom *VQ, VR, but underlined in pencil,* stet *marked, then changes erased*

192 Fool you . . . called, *VQ, VR*

193 **And all day long they cry, " come hither, Fool.**
(FOOL goes close to him)
194 **Or else it's, " Fool, be gone " (FOOL goes further off)**
195 **Or, " Fool, stand there " (FOOL straightens himself)**
196 **Or, " Fool, go sit in the corner " (FOOL sits in the corner)**
And all the while
197 **What were they all but fools before I came.**
198 **What are they now, but mirrors that seem men.**
199 **Because of my image. Fool, hold up your head. (FOOL**
does so)
200 **What foolish stories they have told of the ghosts**
201 **That fumbled with the clothes upon the bed,**
202 **Or creaked and shuffled in the corridor,**
203 **Or else, if they were pious bred,**
204 **Of angels from the skies,**
205 **That came through a man's door,**
206 **Or, it maybe, standing there,**
207 **Would solidly out stare**
208 **The steadiest eyes with their unnatural eyes,**
209 **Aye, even on his own floor.**
(ANGEL has come in)
210 **Yet it is strange, the strangest thing I have known,**

---

193 Come *VQ, VR* Fool, *but* Fo *missing, circled in pencil VQ* Fool.' *VR*

193, 194 (The fool *VN, VP, VQ, VR*

193–196 (The FOOL The *underlined in pencil, ink mark in margin in preparation for correction of l. 199 VR*

194 gone.' *VQ, VR*

195 there'. *VQ, VR* (The fool . . . himself up) *VN, VP so VQ, VR but* up.

196 Fool go *VN* corner'. *VQ,VR* (The fool . . . in the *VN, VP, VQ, VR*

197 came? *VQ, VR*

198 now, *comma del? VR, accepted by WBY* men, *VK, VN, VP, VQ* men *VR*

199 image? *VQ, VR* The *inserted in ink before* FOOL *VR*

202 corridor, *comma circled in pencil, margin* ?; *VR*

203–204 (angel comes) *inserted in ink in margin VK*

205 That coming through the door, *VN, VP, VQ, VR*

206 may be, *VR*

207 out-stare *VR*

209 Aye, on a man's own *VN, VP, VQ, VR* (ANGEL has come in) *circled in ink VK*

(An angel [has *inserted in ink*] comes [*del to* come] in. It should be played by a man if a man can be found with the right voice, and may wear a little golden mask or [*del and rev in ink to* and] a halo made of metal.) *VN; VP follows revised VN*

(An angel has come in. It should be played by a man if a man can be found with the right voice, and may wear a little golden domino and a halo made of metal. Or the whole face may be a beautiful mask, in which case the last sentence on page 136 [*ie. ll. 181-2*] should not be spoken. *VQ*

(An angel [angel *circled, ink note in margin reads:* caps? *accepted by WBY*] has come in. It may be played by a man if a man can be found with the right voice, and in that case 'she' should be changed to 'he' throughout, and may wear a little golden domino and a halo made of metal. Or the whole face may be a beautiful mask, in which case the sentence in lines ~~14~~ and ~~15~~ on page ~~339~~ [*blue ink note in margin reads:* 20 *del to* 17/18/306; *all del in red ink to* 20 21 12 *written below* 14, 15 *&* 339 *respectively, i.e. ll. 181–182*] should not be spoken. *VR*

211 That I should still be haunted by the notion
212 That there's a crisis of the soul wherein
213 We get new sight, and how if when it comes
214 They have some craft to turn it into frenzy.
215 Why do you put your finger to your lips,
216 And creep away ? (FOOL goes out)
(WISE MAN sees ANGEL) What are you ? Who are you ?
217 I think I saw some like you in my dreams,
218 When but a child. That thing about your head,
219 That brightness in your hair .... that flowery branch ....
220 But I have done with dreams ... I have done with dreams.
221 ANGEL. I am the crafty one that you have called.
222 WISE MAN. How that I called ?
ANGEL. I am the messenger.
223 WISE MAN. What message could you bring to one like me ?
224 ANGEL. That you will die when the last grain of sand
225 Has fallen through this glass.
WISE MAN. I have a wife,
226 Children and pupils that I cannot leave,
227 Why must I die, my time is far away ?
228 ANGEL. You are to die because no soul has passed
229 The heavenly threshold since you have opened school,
230 But grass grows there, and rust upon the hinge ;
231 And they are lonely that must keep the watch.
232 WISE MAN. And whither shall I go when I am dead ?
233 ANGEL. You have denied the purgatorial fire
234 Therefore that gate is closed ; you have denied
235 That there's a heaven, and that gate is closed.

---

212 soul] spirit *VN, VP, VQ, VR*
213 and that they know some trifle *(*trifle *del and rev in ink to* trick*) VN VP, VQ, VR follow VN as revised*
214 To turn our thoughts for their own ends to frenzy, *VN, VP, so VQ, VR but* frenzy.
215 lips, *del to* lip, *VN* lip, *VP, VQ, VR*
216 The *inserted in ink before* FOOL *VR* out. *underlined in ink, note in margin reads:* ital *VR*
218 head,— *VN, VP, VQ, VR*
219 branch *VN,VP* branch; *VQ, VR*
220 dreams, I *VN, VP, VQ, VR*
224 ANGEL (turning the hour-glass) *VQ, VR*
225 (turns glass) *inserted in ink after* glass. *VK*
226 leave: *VQ, VR*
228 are] have *VN, VP, VQ*
233 fire, *VK* denied there is a purgatory, *VN, VP, VQ, so VR with ink note* P *in margin*
235 There is . . . and so that *VN, VP, VQ, so VR with ink note* H *in margin*

WISE MAN. **Where then ? I have denied there is a hell.**
ANGEL. **Hell is the place of those who have denied,**
They find there what they planted and what dug,
A lake of spaces, and a wood of nothing,
And wander there and drift and never cease,
Wailing for substance.
WISE MAN. **Pardon me, blessed Angel,**
I have denied and taught the like to others.
Believing nothing but what sense has taught,
And the mind's abstract.
ANGEL. **It is too late for pardon.**
WISE MAN. **Had I but seen your face as now I see it,**
But how can you...that live but where we go,
In the uncertainty of dizzy dreams...
Know why we doubt. Parting, disease and death,
The rotting of the grass, tempest and drouth,
These are the messengers that came to me.
Why are you silent ? You carry in your hands,
God's pardon, and you will not give it me,
Why are you silent ? Were I not afraid,
I'd kiss your hands, no, no, the hem of your dress.
ANGEL. **Only when all the world has testified,**
May soul confound it, crying out in joy.
What's dearth and death and sickness to the soul,
That knows no virtue but itself, nor could it,
So trembling with delight and mother naked,

---

236 I . . . hell.] For I have said there is no hell. *VN, VP, VQ, so VR with ink note* H *in margin*
237 denied; *VN, VP, VQ, VR*
239 A lake of spaces, and a wood of nothing, *with ink note in margin* L/S/W/N/ *VN* A Lake of Spaces, and a Wood of Nothing, *VP, VQ, VR*
240 drift, and . . . cease *VN, VP, VQ, VR*
243–244 But how could I believe before my sight
Had come to me? *VN, VP, VQ, VR* pardon, *VK*
245 but met your gaze as now I met it — *VQ, so VR but* meet it —
246 you that . . . go *VN, VP, VQ, VR*
247 dreams *VN, VP, VQ, VR*
248 doubt? *VQ, VR* disease] sickness *VN, VP, VQ, so VR but* sickness,
249 tempest, *VR*
251 hands *VN, VP, VQ, VR*
252 me. *VQ, VR*
254 hands — no, *VQ, VR*
256 joy. *period rev in ink to comma VN* joy, *VP, VQ, VR*
256/257 And laughing on its lonely precipice. *VN, VP, VQ, VR*
257 soul *VQ, VR*
258 itself? Nor *VQ, VR*
259 mother-naked, *hyphen inserted VN* mother-naked, *VP, VQ, VR*

Live unabashed if the arguing world stood by.
WISE MAN. **It is so hard for you to understand**
Why we have doubted, as it is for us
To put our doubts away ... what have I said,
There can be nothing that you do not know,
Give me a year ... a month ... a week ... a day,
I would undo what I have done...an hour...
Give me until the sand has run in the glass.
ANGEL. **Though you may not undo what you have done,**
I have this power ... if you but find one soul,
That still believes that it shall never cease,
One fish to lie and spawn among the stones
Till the great fisher's net is full again,
You may, the purgatorial fire being passed,
Spring to your peace.
PUPILS. **(sing in the distance) " Who stole your wits away**
And where are they gone ? "
WISE MAN. **My pupils come,**
Before you have begun to climb the sky
I shall have found belief ... they say they doubt,
But what their mothers dinned into their ears
Has not been broken down ... I have long thought it,
Besides, I can disprove what I once proved,
And yet give me some thought, some argument,
More mighty than my own.
ANGEL. **Farewell ... farewell,**

---

261 so] so *del and rev in ink to* as *VN* as *VP, VQ, VR*

262 doubted, *comma del? VR accepted WBY*

263 To banish doubt — what folly have I said? *VN, VP, VQ, so VR but with ink note* . stet W? *in margin*

264 know: *VQ* know: *colon del and period marked* ? *in margin, VR, accepted WBY*

267 Give me until the sand has run in the glass. *del in ink VK*

269 before *written in ink above* find one soul *then del VK*

270 that it shall never cease *del in ink to* before the hour has ended *VK* Before the sands have fallen, that still believes, *VQ, VR*

272 fisher's. *with pencil note* ? caps *del in ink to* F *in margin VR*

274–275 *vertical pencil line in left margin and a tick beside verse VQ* (pupils sing *VN, VP, VQ no parens VR* Pupils *ink note by WBY in margin reads:* caps *VR* Who . . . gone? . . . come, *comma rev in ink to period, accepted WBY VR*

277 found that soul. They *VN, VP, VQ, VR*

279 Has . . . it.)] Cannot have been so lightly rooted up, *VN, VP; so VQ, VR but* up;

280 proved — *VN, VP, VQ, VR*

For I am weary of the weight of time.
(ANGEL goes out, WISE MAN makes a Step to follow and pauses. PUPILS come in at other side.)

1st PUPIL. **Master, Master, you must choose the subject.**
(ENTER other PUPILS with FOOL, about whom they dance.)

2nd PUPIL. **Here is a subject .... where have the Fool's wits gone ?**
(Singing) "Who dragged your wits away
Where no one knows ?
Or have they run off
On their own pairs of shoes ? "

FOOL. **Give me a penny.**
1st PUPIL. **The Master will find your wits.**
2nd PUPIL. **And when they are found, you must not beg for pennies.**
3rd PUPIL. **They are hidden somewhere in the badger's hole,**
But you must carry an old candle end,
If you would find them.
4th PUPIL. **They are up above the clouds.**
FOOL. **Give me a penny, give me a penny, Teigue.**
1st PUPIL. **(singing) " I'll find your wits again,**
Come, for I saw them roll,
To where old badger mumbles
In the black hole.
2nd PUPIL. **(singing) " No, but an angel stole them**
The night that you were born,
And now they are but a rag,

283/284 step . . . side. *VK* out. Wise . . . step *VN, VP, VQ, VR* Some of his pupils come . . . side of the stage.) *VN, VP, VQ, so VR but* pupils *circled and marginal note in ink reads* caps ? *accepted WBY*

284 subject . . . dance) *VK* Master, master, . . . dance; all the pupils may have little cushions on which presently they seat themselves) *VN, VP, VQ, so VR but* OTHER *del in ink WBY, marked* lc ital *in ink in margin*

285–289 *del in ink VK* where *with ink note* W *in margin VR* (singing) *VN, VP, VQ, VR*

286 Who *VR* away, *comma del in ink VN*

287–289 *vertical pencil line in left margin and a tick VQ*

289 pair *VK, VN, VP, VQ, VR* shoes?' *quote inserted in ink VN*

291 wits, *VK, VN, VP, VQ*

292 pennies, *VK*

293 *no comma VQ* candle-end *hyphen inserted by WBY VR*

295 Teigue. *del in pencil VK* penny. *VN, VP, VQ, VR*

296 I'll . . . again, *comma rev in ink to period? VR, accepted WBY*

296–299, 300–303 *vertical pencil lines and ticks in the left margin VQ*

297 roll, *comma del? VR, accepted WBY*

299 hole.' *quote inserted in ink VN* hole.' *VQ*

300 *no quotes VR*

301 that *typed (ribbon) VK*

302 rag, *comma del VR, accepted WBY*

On the moon's horn.
WISE MAN. **Be silent.**
1st PUPIL. **Can you not see that he is troubled ?**
WISE MAN. **What do you think of when alone at night ?**
Do not the things your mothers spoke about
Before they took the candle from the bedside,
Rush up into the mind and master it,
Till you believe in them against your will ?

---

303 horn.' *quote inserted in ink VN* horn.' *VP, VQ* horn. *VR*
304 troubled? (all the pupils are seated) *VN, VP, so VQ but* [All All . . . PUPILS are seated. *VR*
305–319 *ink insertion in VQ reads as follows:*

Wise man
nullum esse deum dixi, nullam dei matrem:
mentitus vero: nam recte intellegenti sunt et
deus et ~~de~~ dei mater.
First Pupil
argumentis igitur proba; nam argumenta poscit
qui rationis est particeps.
Wise man
Pro certo habeo e vobis unum quidem in
fide perstitisse, unum altius quam me vidisse.
Third Pupil
You answer for us.
Third Pupil (in a whisper to First Pupil)
Be careful what you say;
If he persuades you to an argument,
He will but turn us all to mockery.
~~Wise m~~
First Pupil
We had no minds until you made them for us.
Wise man
a
quae destruxi, necesse est omnia re‸-edificem.
Haec rationibus nondum natis opinabamur: nunc
vero adolevimus: exuimus incunabula.
~~First Pupil~~
~~We thought those things before our minds~~ were born
~~But this was long ago - we are not ch~~ildren

First Pupil *clue line then inserts* First Pupil *above line* Haec rationibus *VQ*
305 *VR reads as follows:*

Nullum esse deum dixi, nullam dei matrem: mentitus
vero: nam recte intellegenti [*note in margin* i *accepted WBY*] sunt et deus et dei
mater.
FIRST PUPIL
Argumentis igitur proba; nam argumenta poscit qui
rationis est particeps.
WISE MAN
Pro certo habeo e vobis unum quidem in fide per–
stitisse, unum altius quam me vidisse.

310 **2nd PUPIL.** **(to 1st PUPIL) You answer for us.**
3rd PUPIL. **(in a whisper)** **Be careful what you say.**
311 **If he persuades you to an argument**
312 **He will make a mock of you and us.**
1st PUPIL. **You have made our minds,**
313 **Our bodies only, were our mothers' work.**
WISE MAN. **No, no,**
314 **You answer with incredible things. It is certain**
315 **That there is one, ... though it may be but one ...**
316 **Believes in God and in some heaven and hell.**
317 **In all those things we put into our prayers.**
318 **1st PUPIL.** **We thought those things before our minds were born**
319 **But that was long ago ... we are not children.**
320 **WISE MAN.** **You are afraid to tell me what you think**
321 **Because I am hot and angry when I am crossed,**
322 **I do not blame you for it, but have no fear,**
323 **For if there is one that sat on smilling there**

---

310 ~~THIRD~~ PUPIL *ink note in margin reads:* SECOND *VR, accepted WBY*

310 whisper to first pupil) . . . say *VN, VP, so VR but* FIRST PUPIL . . . say;

311 argument, *VR*

312 and us. *del inkVK* will but turn us all to mockery. / FIRST PUPIL / We had no minds until you made them for us; *semicolon inserted in ink VN, so VP but* us;

312–313 He will but turn us all to mockery.
FIRST PUPIL
We had no minds until you made them for us. *VR*
We have made
Our minds as naked as our bodies were,
When we were born, that you may give us thought- *all del in ink to* You have made our minds *then continues* Our bodies were *(*were *del ink to* only were*)* our mothers' work.
WISE MAN ~~No, no,~~ *VK*

313 only, were *comma del in ink VN no comma VP* mother's *VN, VP* No, no, *del ink VK omitted VN, VP*

314–317 *replaced by* Quae destruxi necesse est omnia reaedificem. *VR*

316 hell. *period then rev to dash in pencil VN* hell — *VP*

318 You've made our clothes out of a better cloth. *del and rev in ink to* We thought those things before our minds were born *VK* born, *VN, VP*

319 *line inserted in ink, but* children— *VK*

318–319 Haec rationibus nondum natis opinabamur: nunc
Vero adolevimus: exuimus incunabula. *marginal note in ink reads:* run on lc *referring to* Vero *both accepted by WBY VR*

320–322 Wise man
You are afraid to tell me what you think
Because I am ~~to~~ hot & angry when I am crossed
I do not blame you for it; but have no fear *inserted in ink VQ*

321 crossed. *VR*

322 it; *VR* fear *VN, VP, VR, but period inserted in ink VR, accepted WBY*

323 there's one . . . there, *VN, VP, VQ, so VR but comma del*

As though my arguments were sweet as milk
Yet found them bitter, I will thank him for it,
If he but speak his mind.
1st PUPIL. **There is no one Master,**
There is not one but found them sweet as milk.
WISE MAN. **The things that have been told us in our childhood**
Are not so fragile.
2nd PUPIL. **We are no longer children.**
3rd PUPIL. **We all believe in you and in what you have taught.**
OTHER PUPILS. **All, all, all, all, in you, nothing but you.**
WISE MAN. **I have deceived you ... where shall I go for words,**
I have not thoughts...my mind has been swept bare.

---

324 milk, *comma inserted in ink VR*

326 In very truth, *del and rev in ink to* There is no one Master *VK* one, master, *VN, so VP, VQ but* Master, Master, *comma rev to period VR*

329 We are not children now. *VR*

330 3rd. *rev in ink to* 1st *VK*

329–331 VQ *inserts in ink:* ~~First Pupil~~ Second Pupil
~~Non iam pueri sumus~~;
~~corpus tantumando~~ we are not children now
First
~~Second~~ Pupil
modo
non iam pueri sumus; corpus tantum~~ando~~
ex matre fictum est.
Second Pupil
Docuisti; et nobis persuaditur
Wise man.
¢
mendacie vobis imbui, mintisque simulacre
Second Pupil
nulli non persuasisti
Other Pupils speaking together
nulli, nulli, nulli *and l. 331 del in ink*

329–331 FIRST PUPIL
Non iam pueri sumus; corpus tantummodo ex matre
fictum est.
SECOND PUPIL
Docuisti; et nobis persuadetur.
WISE MAN
Mendacia vobis imbui, mentisque simulacra.
SECOND PUPIL
Nulli non persuasisti.
OTHER PUPILS [speaking together]
Nulli, nulli, nulli. *VR*

331 *omitted VR*

332 words— *VN, VP, VQ* words— *marginal note in ink inserts* ? *VR*

333 no thoughts *VK, VN, VP, VQ, VR Mask text presumably a misprint*

The messengers that stand in the fiery cloud,
Fling themselves out, if we but dare to question,
And after that, the Babylonian moon,
Blots all away.
1st PUPIL. (to other PUPILS) I take his words to mean
That visionaries, and martyrs when they are raised
Above translunary things, and there enlightened,
As the contention is, may lose the light.
And blunder in their speech when the eyes open.
2nd PUPIL. How well he imitates their trick of speech.
3rd PUPIL. Their air of mystery,
4th PUPIL. Their empty gaze.
As though they'd looked upon some winged thing,
And would not condescend to mankind after.
1st PUPIL. Master, we have learnt that all truth is learnt
When the intellect's deliberate and cold,
As it were a polished mirror that reflects
An unchanged world ; and not when the steel melts,
Bubbling and hissing, till there's naught but fume.
WISE MAN. When it is melted, when it all fumes up,
They walk, as when beside those three in the furnace
The form of the fourth.
1st PUPIL. Master, there's none among us
That has not heard your mockery of these,
Or thoughts like these, and we have not forgot.
WISE MAN. Something incredible has happened ... someone has come,
Suddenly like a grey hawk out of the air,
And all that I declared untrue is true.
1st PUPIL. (to other PUPILS)
You'd think the way he says it, that he felt it,

---

334 firey *VK* cloud, *comma del VR, accepted WBY*
336 that, *comma del VR, accepted WBY* moon *VN, VP, VQ, VR*
338 visionaries, *comma del VR* martyrs, *comma inserted in ink VR, both accepted WBY*
340 light, *VN, VP, VQ, VR*
341 blunder *del and rev in ink to* flounder *VN* flounder *VP, VQ, VR*
343 3rd. *rev in ink to* 1st *VK* mystery, *VP* mystery. *VN, VQ, VR* gaze, *VK, VN, VQ, so VR but comma del, accepted WBY*
344 winged *ink note in margin* é?, *WBY rev to* è *VR*
346 have . . . truth] all have learnt that truth *VR*
349 and not . . . melts] not . . . dissolves *VR*
352 walk, *comma del VR, accepted WBY* three *typed (ribbon) VK*
356 some one *VQ, VR* *no comma VQ, VR*
359 think *comma inserted in margin in ink VR, accepted WBY* felt it. *VN, VP, VQ, VR*

There's not a mummer to compare with him,
He's something like a man.
2nd PUPIL. **Give us some proof**
WISE MAN. **What proof have I to give, but that an angel**
An instant ago was standing on that spot.
3rd PUPIL. **You dreamed it, Master,**
WISE MAN. **I was awake as I am now.**
1st PUPIL. **I may be dreaming now for all I know.**
(to the OTHERS) He wants to show we have no certain proof
Of anything in the world.
2nd PUPIL. **There is this proof,**
That shows we are awake ... we have all one world
While every dreamer has a world of his own,
And sees what no one else can.
3rd PUPIL. **Teigue sees angels.**
So when the Master says he has seen an angel,
He may have seen one.
1st PUPIL. **Both may still be dreamers.**
Unless it's proved the angels were alike.
2nd PUPIL. **What sort are the angels, Teigue ?**
3rd PUPIL. **That will prove nothing.**
For all we know, prolonged obedience
Has made one angel like another angel,
As they were eggs.
1st PUPIL. **The Master's silent now :**
For he has found that to dispute with us ...
Seeing that he has taught us what we know ...

---

360 him. *VN, VP, VQ, VR*

361 proof. *VK, VN, VP, Mask text presumably a misprint* Give us some proof. *del to note* Latin D X *which also then del when clue line inserts* Argumentum, domine, profer *written in ink, from foot of page, to replace second half of l. 361 VQ* Argumentum, domine, profer. *VR*

363 spot. (The pupils rise) *VN, VP, VQ, so VR but* ? *inserted in ink in margin*

364 it. *VQ, VR* Master. *VK, VN, VP*

365 (to the others) I may *VN, VP, VQ*

366 others) *VN, VP, VQ*

367 proof *VQ, VR*

370 Teigue, *VK* Teigue *circled, then marked* stet *perhaps by WBY VR*

372 dreamers; *VQ, VR*

374 Teigue *circled ink VR* nothing, *VQ, VR*

375 Unless we are sure, prolonged *VN, VP, so VQ, VR but no comma*

376 *no comma VQ, VR*

377 now; *VK*

Is but to reason with himself. Let us away,
And find if there is one believer left.
WISE MAN. **Yes, yes. Find me but one that still believes**
The things that we were told when we were children.
3rd PUPIL. **Our Master'll mock and maul him.**
4th PUPIL **From the first**
I knew he'd have us find some disputant.
(THEY go)
WISE MAN. **I have no reason left, all dark, all dark.**
(PUPILS return laughing. They push
(forward 4th PUPIL)
1st PUPIL. **Here, Master, is the very man you want.**
He said, when we were studying the book,
That maybe after all the monks were right,
And you mistaken, and if we but gave him time,
He'd prove that it was so.
4th PUPIL. **I never said it.**
WISE MAN. **Dear Friend, dear Friend, do you believe in God ?**
4th PUPIL. **Master, they have invented this to mock me.**
WISE MAN. **You are afraid of me.**
4th PUPtL. **They know well, Master.**
That all I said was but to make them argue.
They've pushed me in to make a mock of me,
Because they knew I could take either side,
And beat them at it.
WISE MAN. **If you believe in God,**

381–382 *cut out and replaced with ink insert:*
Wise man
Yes, yes. Find me but one that still can say:
credo in patrem et filium et spiritus sanctum. [*Alan Porter had written* spiritum sanctum] *VQ, rev adopted VR but* Credo . . . spiritum

384 He'll mock . . . first I knew *VN, VP, VQ, VR*

385 He wanted somebody to argue with. (They *VN, VP, VQ, VR*

386 left. All . . . dark! *VQ, VR* Pupils *circled, ink note in margin* caps as on p. 25 *VR*

391 so, *VK*

392 friend, . . . friend, *VN, VP, VQ*

394 Master, *VK, VN, VP, VQ, VR Mask text presumably a misprint*

397 *no comma VN, VP, VQ, VR*

398 If you believe in God, *del VQ and rev in pencil at foot of page with arrow inserting text as follows at l. 398:*
If you still can say the creed
~~& keep~~ With but a grain, a mustard seed of faith *all del. Second rev in ink at top of page, also with arrow inserting text at l. 398, reads:* If you can say the creed ~~with~~
with but a grain, a muster *(del to* mustard*)* grain of faith

398–399 If you can say the creed
With but a grain, a mustard-grain of faith, *hyphen inserted in ink VR*

You are my soul's one friend. (PUPILS laugh)
Mistress or wife,
Can give us but our good or evil luck,
Amid the howling world, but you shall give
Eternity...and those sweet throated things
That drift above the moon. (PUPILS are silent)
2nd PUPIL. **How strange he is.**
WISE MAN. **The angel that stood there upon that spot,**
Said that my soul was lost unless I found, ...
Before the sands in the hour-glass had run out ...
One that believed.
4th PUPIL. **Cease mocking at me, Master.**
I am so certain that there is no God,
I'll curse him if you will, and after curse
The soul that has been made after his image ...
If but their lies were true. Will that convince you
That I have set my heart on what you teach ?
WISE MAN. **The giddy glass is emptier every moment,**
And you stand there, debating, laughing and wrangling.
Out of my sight ! Out of my sight, I say.
(HE drives them out)
I'll call my wife, for what can women do,
That carry us in the darkness of their bodies,
But mock the reason that lets nothing grow
Unless it grow in light. Bridget, Bridget,

---

399 *no comma VN, VP, VQ, VR*

400 *no comma VN, VP, VQ, VR*

402 Eternity, and . . . sweet-throated *VN, VP, VQ, VR*

403 pupils look at one another and are silent) *VN, VP* The pupils look . . . silent. *VQ, so VR but* The *del ink* he is.] *period del ink to exclamation VR*

404 spot, *ink note in margin reads* del? *VR, accepted WBY*

405 found, *VN, VP* found *VQ, VR*

406 Hour-glass . . . out, *VN, VP* *line omitted VQ, VR*

407 believed. *del and rev in ink to* had faith. *VQ* had faith. *VR* Master, *VP, VQ, VR*

408 For I am certain . . . God *VN, VP, VQ, VR*

409–412 Nor immortality, and they that said it
Made a fantastic tale from a starved dream
To plague our hearts. Will that content you master? *VN, VP, so VQ, VR but* you, Master? immortality *pencil note in margin* cap? *del ink WBY VR*

410 breathed out of his nostrils — *del and rev in ink to* made after his image *VK*

411 their] these *del in ink to* their *VK* were] are *del in ink to* were *VK*

415 (He drives them out) *del in ink to* (They go out) *VK* [He *VQ, VR*

419 light. *period rev in ink to* ? *VR* Bridget, Bridget. *VN, VP, VQ* Bridget. *period rev in ink to* ! *VR, accepted WBY*

419/420 A woman never ceases to believe. *VK, VN, VP, so VQ but* ceases to believe *del and rev in ink to* gives up all her faith *VR adopts revs to VQ but* faith,

Say what we will ... Bridget, come quickly, Bridget.
(BRIDGET comes in wearing her apron.
Her sleeves turned up from her
floury arms)
Wife, what do you believe in ? Tell the truth,
And not...as is the habit with you all ...
Something you think will please me. Do you pray
Sometimes when you're alone in the house, do you pray ?
BRIDGET. **Prayers ... no, you taught me to leave them off long ago.**
At first I was sorry, but I am glad now, for I am sleepy
in the evenings.
WISE MAN. **Do you believe in God ?**
BRIDGET. **Oh, a good wife only believes in what her husband tells her.**
WISE MAN. **But sometimes, when the children are asleep,**
And I am in the school, do you not think
About the Martyrs and the saints and angels,
And all the things that you believed in once ?
BRIDGET. **I think about nothing ... sometimes I wonder if the linen**
is bleaching white, or I go out to see if the crows are
picking up the chickens' food.
WISE MAN. **My God ... my God ! I will go out myself.**
My pupils said that they would find a man
That had the old belief...they may have found him.
Therefore I will go out ... but if I go
The glass will let the sands run out unseen.
I cannot go...I cannot leave the glass.
Go call my pupils..I can explain all now,
Only when all our hold on life is shaken,
Only in spiritual terror can the Truth
Come through the broken mind...as the pease burst

---

420 will. Bridget, . . . her arms which are covered with flour. *VQ , so VR but* arms, *comma inserted in ink*
421 Tell me the *VN, VP, VQ*
423 pray? *VQ, VR*
429 Oh, *rev to* O, *VR*
430 asleep *VN, VP, VQ, VR*
432 About *typed (ribbon) VK* martyrs *VR* the angels *VQ* the angels, *VN, VP, VR*
434 nothing — sometimes *rev in ink to* nothing. Sometimes *VR, accepted WBY*
436 chickens' *apostrophe inserted in ink VK* chicken's *VN, VP, VQ*
437 God, — my *VN, VP, VQ, VR*
439 Whose faith I never shook — they *VQ, VR*
440 I go, *VQ, VR*
443 now, *comma del to period VR*
444 is troubled, *VQ, VR*

Out of a broken pease-cod.
(He clutches BRIDGET as she is going)
Say to them,
That nature would lack all in her most need,
Could not the soul find truth as in a flash,
Upon the battle field or in the midst
Of overwhelming waves, and say to them ...
But no, they would but answer as I bid.

BRIDGET. You want somebody to get up an argument with.

WISE MAN. Look out and see if there is anyone
There in the street...I cannot leave the glass,
For somebody might shake it, and the sand
If it were shaken might run down on the instant.

BRIDGET. I don't understand a word you are saying. There's a crowd of people talking to your pupils.

WISE MAN. Go out and find if they have found a man
Who did not understand me when I taught,
Or did not listen.

BRIDGET. It is a hard thing to be married to a man of learning that must always be having arguments. Children, don't be meddling with the bread while I am out. (She goes out)

WISE MAN. Strange that I should be blind to the great secret,
And that so simple a man might write it out
Upon a blade of grass or bit of rush
With naught but berry juice, and laugh to himself
Writing it out, because it was so simple.
(ENTER FOOL and BRIDGET)

FOOL. Give me something ; give me a penny to buy bacon in the shops and nuts in the market, and strong drink for the time when the sun is weak.

BRIDGET. I have no pennies. (to WISE MAN) Your pupils cannot

---

447 them, *comma del VR, accepted WBY*

448 Nature *VQ, VR*

450 battle-field, *VN, VP, VQ, VR*

454 any one *VQ, VR*

464–465 Children . . . am out. *del in ink VK, omitted VQ, VR*

465–466 out.) *VN*

468–470 grass with the juice of a berry;
And laugh and cry, because *VQ, so VR but semicolon rev in ink to comma, accepted WBY*

470/471 FOOL and *del and* followed by the Fool *inserted in ink after* BRIDGET *VN* (Enter Bridget followed by the Fool. *VP, VQ, VR*

474 [To *VQ, so VR but* MAN.]

find anybody to argue with you. There's nobody in the whole country with belief enough for a lover's oath. Can't you be quiet now, and not always wanting to have arguments. It must be terrible to have a mind like that.

WISE MAN. Then I am lost indeed.

BRIDGET. Leave me alone now, I have to make the bread for you and the children. (SHE goes into kitchen)

WISE MAN. Children, children !

BRIDGET. Your father wants you, run to him.

(CHILDREN run in)

WISE MAN. Come to me, children. Do not be afraid.
I want to know if you believe in Heaven,
God or the soul ... no, do not tell me yet,
You need not be afraid I shall be angry,
Say what you please ... so that it is your thought ...
I wanted you to know before you spoke,
That I shall not be angry,

FIRST CHILD. We have not forgotten, Father.

SECOND CHILD. Oh, no, Father

BOTH CHILDREN. (as if repeating a lesson) There is nothing we cannot see, nothing we cannot touch.

FIRST CHILD. Foolish people used to say that there was, but you have taught us better.

WISE MAN. Go to your mother, go ...yet do not go
For she can teach you nothing. If I am dumb
You shall be lost among the woods of nothing,
And I because the sands are running out

---

476 belief *del in ink to* religion *VQ, rev adopted VR*

478 *period rev in ink to question mark VR*

482 the children *del in pencil (not WBY) to* your child *VK* The Fool follows her. *inserted in ink after* kitchen. *VR*

485 children *del in ink (not WBY) to* Winnie *VK*

487 yet; *VQ, VR*

488 *comma rev in ink to semicolon (WBY) VR*

490 spoke, *comma del VR*

491 angry. *VK, VN, VQ, VR*

492 We *del and rev in ink to* I *VK*

493 father. Oh [*del to* O] no, father. *VR* Oh no, Father. *VQ*

493–497 *del VK*

494 (As *VQ*

498 not go. *VQ, VR*

499 What can she say? If I am dumb you are lost; *VQ, so VR but* I *omitted then inserted in margin, accepted WBY*

500 I will have drowned you in the lake of spaces *after which* L / S / ~~Lake of Spaces~~ *inserted in VN omitted VQ, VR* I will have drowned you in the Lake of Spaces *VP*

501 I, because . . . out, *commas inserted in ink VN* I, because . . . out, *VP* And yet, because . . . out, *VQ, VR*

Have but a moment to show it all in. Children
The sap would die out of the blades of grass
Had they a doubt. They understand it all,
Being the fingers of God's certainty,
Yet can but make their sign into the air.
But could they find their tongues .... they'd show it all
But what am I to say that am but one,
When they are millions and they will not speak.
(CHILDREN have run out)
But they are gone ; what made them run away ?
(The FOOL comes in with a dandelion)
Look at me, tell me if my face is changed,
Is there a notch of the fiend's nail upon it
Already ? Is it terrible to sight ?
Because the moment's near. (Going to glass)
I dare not look,
I dare not know the moment when they come
To carry me away. (covers glass) Will there be a foot fall
Or will there be a sort of tearing sound,
Or else a cracking, as though an iron claw
Had gripped the threshold stone.
(FOOL has begun to blow the dandelion)
What are you doing ?
FOOL. **Wait a minute ... four ... five ... six ...**
WISE MAN. **What are you doing that for ?**
FOOL. **I am blowing the dandelion to find out what hour it is.**
WISE MAN. **You have heard everything, and that is why**
You'd find what hour it is ... you'd find that out,
That you may look upon a fleet of devils
Dragging my soul away. You shall not stop,
I will have no one here when they come in,

---

502 I have *VQ, VR* Children, *VN, VP, VQ, VR*
506 air; *VQ, VR*
507 tongues they'd *VQ, VR* all; *VQ, VR*
509 speak — *VQ* speak? — *question mark inserted in ink VR*
510 they are *del in ink (not WBY) to* she is *VK* them *del in ink (not WBY) to* her *VK*
512 fiend's *ink note in margin* F as on p. 80 *VR*
513 sight *VR*
514 near? *VR*
515 come. *VQ, VR*
516 No, no, I dare not. (Covers glass.) Will *VQ, VR* footfall *VN, VP* footfall, *VQ, VR*
517 tearing] rending *VQ,VR*
519 stone? *VN, VP, VQ* threshold- stone? *hyphen inserted in ink (WBY) VR* The *inserted in ink (WBY?) before* FOOL *VR*
524 out, *comma del VR, accepted WBY*

I will have no one sitting there ... no one ...
And yet .... and yet .... there is something strange about you.
Are you the one I seek ? Do you believe
In God and the soul, in the undying stuff
That all things have been made of from the first ?

FOOL. **So you ask me now. I thought when you were asking your pupils, " will he ask, Teigue the Fool. Yes, he will, he will, no, he will not...yes he will. " But Teigue will say nothing. Teigue will say nothing.**

WISE MAN. **Tell me quickly.**

FOOL. **I said, " Teigue knows everything, not even the green-eyed cats and the hares that milk the cows have Teigue's wisdom " but, Teigue will not speak, he says nothing.**

WISE MAN. **Speak, speak, for underneath the cover there**
The sand is running from the upper glass,
And when the last grain's through, I shall be lost
Unless I have lit upon unshaken faith
Somewhere in somebody.

FOOL. **I will not speak. I will not tell you what is in my mind. I will not tell you what is in my bag. You might steal away my thoughts. I met a bodach on the road yesterday, and he said, " Teigue, tell me how many pennies are in your bag ; I will wager three pennies that there are not twenty pennies in your bag ; let me put in my hand and count them. " But I gripped the bag the tighter and when I**

---

528 no one! — *exclamation mark inserted in ink VR, accepted WBY*

529 you *VK, VN* you, *VP* *ribbon copy from this line to end VK*

530 Are you the one I seek? Do you believe *del and rev in ink to* I half remember something. What is it. *VP, rev adopted VQ, VR, but* it? believe, *VK*

531 God, *VK* In God and the soul, in the undying stuff *del and rev in ink to* Do you believe in God & in the soul *VP, rev adopted but* and *and* soul? *VQ, VR*

532 *del in ink VP, omitted VQ, VR*

534 'Will he ask Teigue . . . Fool? *VQ, VR*

535 will; *VQ, VR* yes, *VK, VQ, VR*

534, 536, 538–540 Teigue *circled and marked* stet *in ink VR*

538 Teigue, *VK, so VR but circled and marked* stet *in ink VR*

540 But *VK* wisdom'; but Teigue *VQ, VR*

541 there, *VK*

543 lost. *VQ, VR*

544–545 *omitted VQ, VR*

548 *pencil note in right margin reads:* ? not bocach = fool VPl ii 376 *del ink WBY VR*

549 'Teigue, *circled VR*

552 tighter, and *VQ, VR*

go to sleep at night, I hide the bag where nobody knows.
WISE MAN. **There's but one pinch of sand,..and I am lost**
If you are not he I seek.
FOOL. **O, what a lot the Fool knows, but he says nothing.**
WISE MAN. **(seizing him) I kneel to you ... you are the man I have**
sought. You alone can save me.
FOOL. **No, no, what should poor Teigue know, Teigue that is out**
in all weathers, Teigue that sleeps in the fishers' loft, poor
Teigue the Fool. (HE breaks away and goes out)
WISE MAN. **The last hope is gone.**
And now that it's too late I see it all,
We perish into God and sink away
Into reality ... the rest's a dream.
FOOL. **(coming back on tip-toe and peering under**
cover of Hour-glass and singing in a low voice)

---

553 knows. *period inserted in ink VN* *no comma VQ, VR*
554 sand, and *VN, VP, VQ, VR* *no comma VK*
556 Oh, *VK* Oh, *rev to* O *VR, accepted WBY*
558 sought.] sought *VK, VN, VP*
557–561 *del in ink and rev to:*
Wise man.
Yes I remember now. You spoke of angels
You said but now that you had seen an angel
You are the one I seek and I am saved
Fool
On no. How could poor Teigue see angels. Oh Teigue tells
one tale here another there & everybody gives him pennies
If Teigue had not his tales he would starve. *VP*
557–561 WISE MAN
Yes, I remember now. You spoke of angels.
You said but now that you had seen an angel.
You are the one I seek, and I am saved.
FOOL
Oh no. How could poor Teigue
see angels? Oh, Teigue tells one tale
here, another there, and everybody
gives him pennies. If Teigue had not
his tales he would starve. [He breaks *VQ, so VR but* Teigue *circled each time,* Oh *del in ink to* O *both times*
559 Teigue, know, *VK*
561 (he *VK*
562 gone, *VK, VN, VP, VQ, VR*
563 all, *comma rev in ink to colon VR, accepted WBY*
565 (The Fool comes back) *added in ink after* dream. *other directions omitted VN* dream. (The Fool comes back.) *other directions omitted VP, VQ, VR* hour-glass . . . voice: — *VK*

" I hear the wind a-blow,
And the grass a-grow
And all that I know, I know, "
WISE MAN. I know what fixed the station
Of star and cloud.
And knowing all, I cry,
That what so God has willed,
On the instant he fulfilled,
Though that be my damnation.
The stream of the world has changed its course
And with the stream my thoughts have run,
Into some cloudy thunderous spring
That is its mountain source.
Aye, to some frenzy of the mind,
For all we have done's undone
Our speculation wind. (He dies)
FOOL. Wise man .... Wise man, wake up and I will tell you
everything for a penny. It is I, poor Teigue the Fool

566–569 There was one there — there by the threshold stone,
waiting there and said, 'go in Teigue, and tell him
everything that he asks you. He will give you a
penny if you tell him ' *quote inserted in ink*
WISE MAN I know enough, that know God's will prevails
FOOL Waiting till the moment had come — That is what
the one out there was saying, but I might tell you
what you asked. That is what he was saying.
WISE MAN Be silent. May God's will prevail on the instant. *period rev in ink to comma*
Although His will be my eternal pain. *period inserted in ink*
~~It will be my delight.~~ I have no question:
It is enough, I know what fixed the station *VN, so VQ, VR but* waiting there; and he said, 'Go in, . . . tell him.' . . . prevails. . . . instant, . . . pain. *both* stone, *and* It will be my delight. *omitted and* Teigue *circled; VP adopts revs to VN but* him. prevails. *and* enongh *apparently printed in error for* enough

566 a blow, *VK*

567 a grow, *VK*

568 know." *VK*

571 knowing all,] knowing, all *VR* cry,] cry *VQ, VR*

572 what so] *WBY turns into one word (ink) VR* willed *VQ, VR*

573 he] be *VK, VN, VP, VQ, VR Mask text presumably a misprint*

575 The world has changed *VK* course, *VK, VQ, VR*

576 And every stream has run, *VK* run *VN, VP, VQ, VR*

577 spring, *VK*

578 Even to its own mountain source. *VK* source — *VN, VP, VQ, VR*

580 that *inserted in ink before* we *VN* For all that we *VP, VQ, VR* undone, *comma inserted in ink VN* undone, *VP, VQ, VR*

581 speculation] speculative *VK* but as the *inserted in ink before* wind. *VN* speculation but as the wind. *VP, VQ, VR*

583 Teigue *circled VR* Fool. *VP, VQ, VR* Fool, *VK, VN*

that you were looking for. I am the man you were to find before the sand ran out...the man who believes in God. Why don't you wake up and say, " There is a penny for you, Teigue. " No, no, you will say nothing. You and I, we are the two fools, we know everything, but we will not speak.

ANGEL ENTERS holding a casket

O, look what has come from his mouth ! O, look what has come from his hands...the white butterfly. He is dead and I have taken his soul in my hands ; but I know why you open the lid of that golden box. I must give it to you. There then, (HE put butterfly in casket) He has gone through his pains, and you will open the lid in the Garden of Paradise. (HE closes curtain) He is gone, he is gone, he is gone, but come in everybody in the world and look at me.

" I hear the wind a-blow
I hear the grass a-grow,
And all that I know, I know. "

But I will not speak, I will run away. (HE goes out)

THE END.

---

584 that you were looking for. *del VN*
584–586 that . . . God *omitted VP, VQ, VR* I am . . . God *omitted VN*
586 up, and say *VK, VN, VP, VQ, VR*
587 Teigue," *VK* Teigue'? *VQ, so VR but* Teigue *circled*
589/590 golden casket) VK (Angel . . . casket) *VN, VP* casket. *VQ, VR*
590 Oh, *rev in ink to* O *both times VR*
591 his mouth — the *VN, VP, VQ, VR* butterfly! *VQ, VR*
592 dead, and *VQ, VR*
594 (he put *VK* (he puts *VN, VP, VQ, VR* then [. . . casket], *VR* he has *VP, VQ, VR*
596 (he *VK* curtain and remains outside it) *VN, VP, so VQ, VR but* it.)
597 in, . . . world, *commas inserted in ink VR*
598 me: — *VK*
599 a blow, *VK, VN, VP, VQ* a-blow *hyphen inserted in ink VR*
599, 601 *VR omits quotes*
600 a grow, *VK, VN, VP, VQ* a-grow *hyphen inserted in ink VR*
603 The End *inserted in ink VN, VR (by WBY) omitted VP, VQ*

MS. VO

Transcriptions, with facing photographs

[illegible] Page 7 2 etc

(1

. . . . . . from the fire

You told me something, while we were close
An hour ago — I cannot remember what.

Fool

So you ask me now . . . . . .

. . . . nothing

(leave out next line speeches & then
go on as before down to 'not he I seek)

If you are not he I seek — now I remember
You said that you had seen an angel & it may be
Have heard voices, the very gate of heaven
And looked on God

Fool

O what? What the fool knows he says
nothing, not even the green eyed cats
& the hares that milk the cows have
Tongues wisdom but Tongues are say
nothing.

[MS. VO, 1]

Insert at Page 72 etc (1

......from the first
You told me something while we were alone
An hour ago — I cannot remember what.

Fool

So you ask me now..........
.................nothing
(Leave out next two speeches & then
Go on as before down to 'not he I seek)
If you are not he I seek — Now I remember
You said that you had seen an angel & it may be
Have peered beyond the very gate of heaven
And looked on God

Fool

O what a lot the fool knows but he says
nothing, not even the green eyed cats
& the hares that milk the cows have
Teigues wisdom but Teigue will ~~say~~ say
nothing.

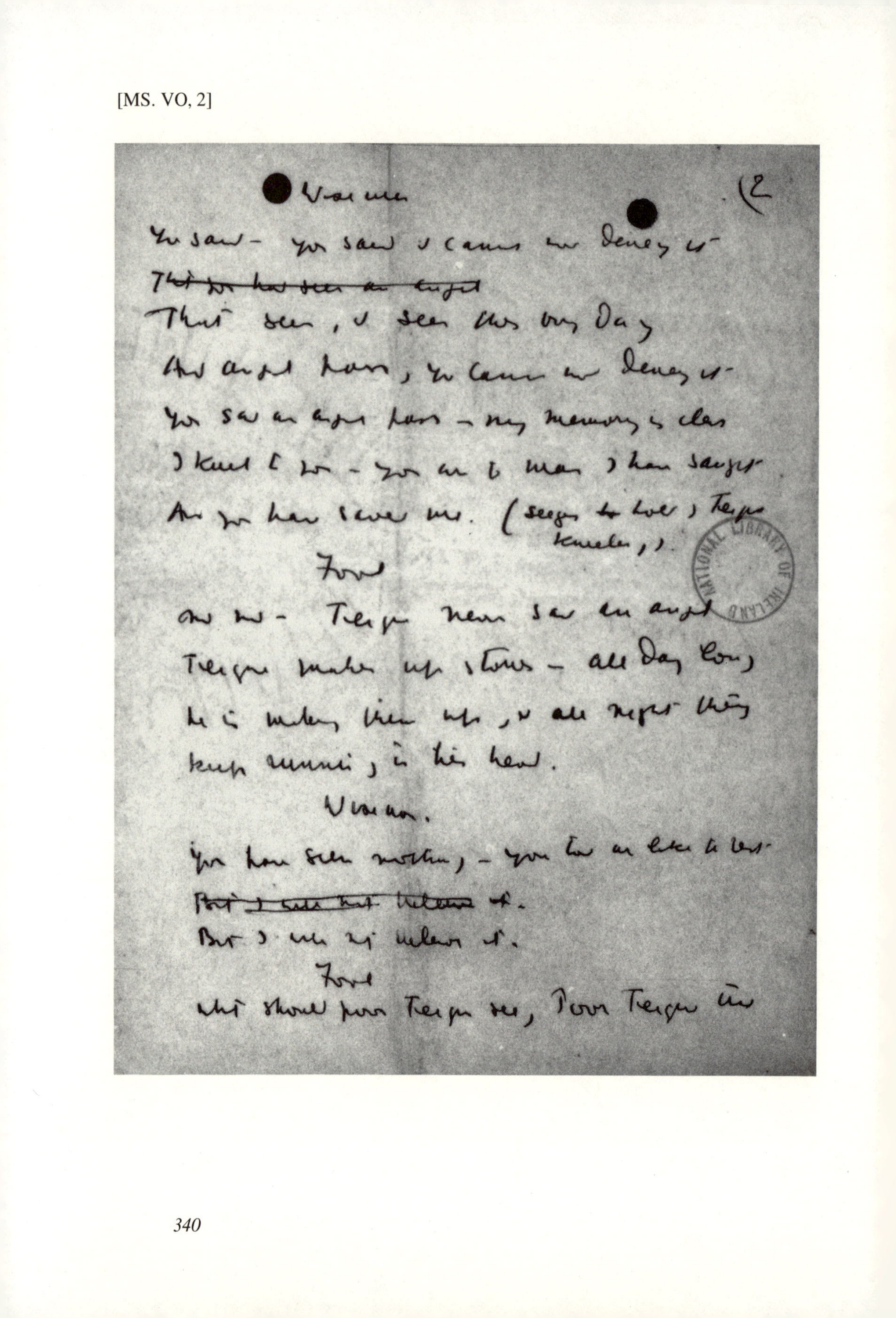

[MS. VO, 2]

[MS. VO, 2]

Wise man (2

You said — you said & cannot now deney it
~~That you had seen an angel~~
That seen, & seen this very day
And angel pass, you cannot now deney it
You saw an angel pass — my memory is clear
I kneel to you — you are the man I have saught
And you have saved me. (seizes ~~h~~ hold of Teigue
kneeling)

Fool

No no — Teigue never saw an angel
Teigue makes up stories — all day long
he is making them up, & all night they
keep running in his head.

Wise man.

You have seen nothing — you too are like the rest
~~But I will not believe it.~~
But I will not believe it.

Fool

What should poor Teigue see, Poor Teigue that

[MS. VO, 3]

why it all is his head is — [illegible] knows that
Poor, poor Teigue the Fool, I saw an angel
to day' says Teigue 'Then ~~grandson~~ says
grandson says Teigue 'There's a penny'
says you 'Some pennies' says you —
wouldn't I starve if I wasn't a fool —
(He runs out)

I alone have seen
~~I have so~~ He has seen nothing, —
~~As the lost [illegible] goes.~~
And now that it is too late I know it all
We perish into God & sink away
Into reality — the rest, a dream

(The Fool comes back)

The Fool

There was one there — there by the threshold stone
waiting there, & said 'go in Teigue — Do not
be afraid of him — Tell him that you know all
see.'

Wiseman.

~~Be silent, [illegible]~~
Be silent — if your tale is true or false
It is a dream, for all but God's a dream

[MS. VO, 3]

(3

Why its all in his head it is — every body knows that
Poor, poor Teigue the fool, ‘I saw an angel
to day’ says Teigue ‘There [?~~grandson~~] son
grandson says Teigue ‘Theres a penny’
says you ‘four pennies says you —
wouldnt I starve if I wasnt a fool.
(He runs out)

I alone have seen
~~I have se~~ He has seen nothing —
~~And the last hopes gone.~~
And now that it s too late I know it all
We perish into God & sink away
Into reality — the rest s a dream

(The fool comes back)

The Fool

There was one there — there by the threshold stone
Writing there & said ‘go in Teigue. Do not
be afraid of him — Tell him what you know and
see.~~’~~ ’

Wise man.

~~Be silent, whether~~
Be silent — if your tale is true or false
It is a dream, for all but Gods a dream

15 Quotation mark canceled then reinserted.

[MS. VO, 4]

Fool 4

Go to Teigue & tell him everything that he asked you 'this is what ~~[illegible]~~ the one who is out there said ~~the angel said~~' He will give you a penny if you tell him'

Wise man.

I know enough that ~~know~~ know gods will prevail

Etc. Etc

or page 75.

Take out casket & read 'I know why you hold out your hands' & 'you will open your hands in the garden of Paradise'

(To consider question whether it is worth keeping, casket & gen change of position)

[MS. VO, 4]

4

Fool
'Go in Teigue & tell him everything that he
the one who is out there said
asks you 'that is what ~~I was told~~ ~~the angel~~
~~said~~ 'He will give ~~a~~ you a penny if you
tell him'

Wise man.
I know enough that ~~knows~~ know Gods will prevails
etc. etc

on page 75.
take out casket & read 'know why you
hold out your hands' & 'you will open
your hands in the Garden of Paradise'

(To consider question whether it is
worth keeping casket to give change of
picture)

Appendixes

APPENDIX I

"The Priest's Soul" from Lady Wilde's *Ancient Legends, Mystic Charms, and Superstitions of Ireland*, vol.I (London: Ward and Downey, 1887), pp. 60–67.

An ethical purpose is not often to be detected in the Irish legends; but the following tale combines an inner meaning with the incidents in a profound and remarkable manner. The idea that underlies the story is very subtle and tragic; Calderon or Goethe might have founded a drama on it; and Browning's genius would find a fitting subject in this contrast between the pride of the audacious, self-reliant sceptic in the hour of his triumph and the moral agony that precedes his punishment and death.

In former days there were great schools in Ireland where every sort of learning was taught to the people, and even the poorest had more knowledge at that time than many a gentleman has now. But as to the priests, their learning was above all, so that the fame of Ireland went over the whole world, and many kings from foreign lands used to send their sons all the way to Ireland to be brought up in the Irish schools.

Now, at this time there was a little boy learning at one of them who was a wonder to every one for his cleverness. His parents were only labouring people, and of course very poor; but young as he was, and poor as he was, no king's or lord's son could come up to him in learning. Even the masters were put to shame; for when they were trying to teach him he would tell them something they never heard of before, and show them their ignorance. One of his great triumphs was in argument; and he would go on till he proved to you that black was white, and then when you gave in, for no one could beat him in talk, he would turn round and show you that white was black, or may be that there was no colour at all in the world. When he grew up his poor father and mother were so proud of him that they resolved to make him a priest, which they did at last, though they nearly starved themselves to get the money. Well, such another learned man was not in Ireland, and he was as great in argument as ever, so that no one could stand before him. Even the Bishops tried to talk to him, but he showed them at once they knew nothing at all.

Now, there were no schoolmasters in those times but it was the priests taught the people; and as this man was the cleverest in Ireland all the foreign kings sent their sons to him as long as he had house-room to give them. So he grew very proud, and began to forget how low he had been, and worst of all, even to forget God, who had made him what he was. And the pride of arguing got hold of him, so that from one thing to another he went on to prove that there was no Purgatory, and then no Hell, and then no Heaven, and then no God; and at last that men had no souls, but were no more than a dog or a cow, and when they died there was an end of them. "Who ever saw a soul?" he would say. "If you can show me one, I will believe." No one could make any answer to this; and at last they all came to believe that as there was no other world, every one might do what they liked in this; the priest setting the example, for he took a beautiful young girl to wife. But as no priest or bishop in the whole land could be got to marry them, he was obliged to read the service over for himself. It was a great scandal, yet no one dared to say a word, for all the kings' sons were on his side, and would have slaughtered any one who tried to prevent his wicked goings-on. Poor boys! they all believed in him, and thought every word he said was the truth. In this way his notions began to spread about, and the whole world was going to the bad, when one night an angel came down from Heaven, and told the priest he had but twenty-four hours to live. He began to tremble, and asked for a little more time.

But the angel was stiff, and told him that could not be.

"What do you want time for, you sinner?" he asked.

"Oh, sir, have pity on my poor soul!" urged the priest.

"Oh, ho! You have a soul, then," said the angel. "Pray, how did you find that out?"

"It has been fluttering in me ever since you appeared," answered the priest. "What a fool I was not to think of it before."

"A fool, indeed," said the angel. "What good was all your learning, when it could not tell you that you had a soul?"

"Ah, my lord," said the priest, "if I am to die, tell me how soon I may be in Heaven?"

"Never," replied the angel. "You denied there was a Heaven."

"Then, my lord, may I go to Purgatory?"

"You denied Purgatory also; you must go straight to Hell," said the angel.

"But, my lord, I denied Hell also," answered the priest, "so you can't send me there either."

The angel was a little puzzled.

"Well," said he, "I'll tell you what I can do for you. You may either live now on earth for a hundred years enjoying every pleasure, and then be cast into Hell for ever; or you may die in twenty-four hours in the most horrible torments, and pass through Purgatory, there to remain till the Day of Judgment, if only you can find some one person that believes, and through his belief mercy will be vouchsafed to you and your soul will be saved."

The priest did not take five minutes to make up his mind.

"I will have death in the twenty-four hours," he said, "so that my soul may be saved at last."

On this the angel gave him directions as to what he was to do, and left him.

Then, immediately, the priest entered the large room where all his scholars and the kings' sons were seated, and called out to them —

"Now, tell me the truth, and let none fear to contradict me. Tell me what is your belief. Have men souls?"

"Master," they answered, "once we believed that men had souls; but, thanks to your teaching, we believe so no longer. There is no Hell, and no Heaven, and no God. This is our belief, for it is thus you taught us."

Then the priest grew pale with fear, and cried out — "Listen! I taught you a lie. There is a God, and man has an immortal soul. I believe now all I denied before."

But the shouts of laughter that rose up drowned the priest's voice, for they thought he was only trying them for argument.

"Prove it, master," they cried, "prove it. Who has ever seen God? Who has ever seen the soul?"

And the room was stirred with their laughter.

The priest stood up to answer them, but no word could he utter; all his eloquence, all his powers of argument had gone from him, and he could do nothing but wring his hands and cry out —

"There is a God! there is a God! Lord, have mercy on my soul!"

And they all began to mock him, and repeat his own words that he had taught them —

"Show him to us; show us your God."

And he fled from them groaning with agony, for he saw that none believed, and how then could his soul be saved?

But he thought next of his wife.

"She will believe," he said to himself. "Women never give up God."

And he went to her; but she told him that she believed only what he taught her, and that a good wife should believe in her husband first, and before and above all things in heaven or earth.

Then despair came on him, and he rushed from the house and began to ask every one he met if they believed. But the same answer came from one and all — "We believe only what you have taught us," for his doctrines had spread far and wide through the county.

Then he grew half mad with fear, for the hours were passing. And he flung himself down on the ground in a lonesome spot, and wept and groaned in terror, for the time was coming fast when he must die.

Just then a little child came by.

"God save you kindly," said the child to him.

The priest started up.

"Child, do you belive in God?" he asked.

"I have come from a far country to learn about Him," said the child.

"Will your honour direct me to the best school that they have in these parts?"

"The best school and the best teacher is close by," said the priest, and he named himself.

"Oh, not to that man," answered the child, "for I am told he denies God, and Heaven, and Hell, and even that man has a soul, because we can't see it; but I would soon put him down."

The priest looked at him earnestly. "How?" he inquired.

Why," said the child, "I would ask him if he believed he had life to show me his life."

"But he could not do that, my child," said the priest. "Life cannot be seen; we have it, but it is invisible."

"Then if we have life, though we cannot see it, we may also have a soul, though it is invisible," answered the child.

When the priest heard him speak these words he fell down on his knees before him, weeping for joy, for now he knew his soul was safe; he had met at last one that believed. And he told the child his whole story: all his wickedness, and pride, and blasphemy against the great God; and how the angel had come to him and told him of the only way in which he could be saved, through the faith and prayers of some one that believed.

"Now, then," he said to the child, "take this penknife and strike it into my breast, and go on stabbing the flesh until you see the paleness of death on my face. Then watch — for a living thing will soar up from my body as I die, and you will then know that my soul has ascended to the presence of God. And when you see this thing, make haste and run to my school and call on all my scholars to come and see that the soul of their master has left the body, and that all he taught them was a lie, for that there is a God who punishes sin, and a Heaven and a Hell, and that man has an immortal soul, destined for eternal happiness or misery."

"I will pray," said the child, "to have courage to do this work."

And he kneeled down and prayed. Then when he rose up he took the penknife and struck it into the priest's heart, and struck and struck again till all the flesh was lacerated; but still the priest lived though the agony was horrible, for he could not die until the twenty-four hours had expired. At last the agony seemed to cease, and the stillness of death settled on his face. Then the child, who was watching, saw a beautiful living creature, with four snow-white wings, mount from the dead man's body into the air and go fluttering round his head.

So he ran to bring the scholars; and when they saw it they all knew it was the soul of their master, and they watched with wonder and awe until it passed from sight into the clouds.

And this was the first butterfly that was ever seen in Ireland; and now all men know that the butterflies are the souls of the dead waiting for the moment when they may enter Purgatory, and so pass through torture to purification and peace.

But the schools of Ireland were quite deserted after that time, for people said, What is the use of going so far to learn when the wisest man in all Ireland did not know if he had a soul till he was near losing it; and was only saved at last through the simple belief of a little child?

The allusion in this clever tale to the ancient Irish schools is based on historical fact. From the seventh to the tenth century Ireland was the centre of learning. The great Alfred of England was a student at one of the famous Irish seminaries, along with other royal and noble youths, and there formed a life-long friendship with the learned Adamnanl who often afterwards was a welcome guest at the Court of King Alfred. Other eminent Irishmen are known to history as the teachers and evangelizers of Europe. Alcuin, the Irish monk, became the friend and secretary of Charlemagne, and founded, at Aix-la-Chapelle, the first Grammar School in the imperial dominions. And the celebrated Clemens and Albinus, two Irishmen of distinguished ability and learning, aided the emperor not only in educating the people, but also to found a school for the nobles within his own palace.

APPENDIX II

[MS. PKa]

~~As~~ I was going the road one day
                & the yellow beer)
(O the brown ~~etc~~
I met with a man that was no right man
(O my dear, O my dear)

Give me your wife said he
(O - - - - - - - -)
Till the sun goes down by the hour of the clock
(O

Good bye, good bye my husband
(O
For a year & a day by the clock of the sun

APPENDIX III

[MS. P–VQb, 1]

(4) THE HOUR GLASS (in prose) 6

The
**The Hour-Glass was first played^in Molesworth Hall, Dublin
on March 14. 1903 with the following cast; — Wise Man, Mr T.
Dudley Digges; His Wife, Miss M. T. Quinn; the Fool, Mr F. J. Fay;
Pupils, Messrs P.J. Kelly, P. Coburn, C. C. Caufield. It has since
become a regular part of the repertoire of the Abbey Company,~~a~~
and has of recent years been played before screens designed by
Mr Gordon Craig, scene and costume being copied as far as possible
from the designs by Mr Craig in my "Plays for an Irish Theatre"
(1911) and from sketches sent me at the time. The early version
of the Play, which was only too effective, converting a Music-
-hall singer and sending him to Mass for six weeks, made me ashamed
but I did not know till very lately how to remedy it. I had made
my Wise Man humble himself to the Fool and receive salvation as**
a
~~the~~ reward, but now I have given it a new end which is closer to
own
**my thought as well as more effective theatrically. The Fool
too^, when it is now played at the Abbey Theatre, wears a Mask
designed by Mr Gordon Craig which makes him seem less a human
being than a principle of the mind.**

**One sometimes has need of a few words for the Pupils
to sing at their first or second entrance, and I have put into
English rhyme three of the many verses of a Gaelic Ballad.**

**I was going the road one day
(O the brown and the yellow beer')
And I met with a man that was no right man
(O my dear, O my dear)**

[MS. P–VQb, 2]

7

**"Give me your wife" said he,
(O the brown and the yellow beer)
Till the sun goes down and an hour of the clock
(O my dear, O my dear)**

**Goodbye, goodbye, my husband
(O the brown and the yellow beer)
For a year and a day by the clock of the sun
(O my dear, O my dear)**

1907–1922

"The" inserted in l. 1, the semi-colon in l. 3, the parens in l. 9, the commas in l. 10, and the revision in l. 14 are all in black ink.

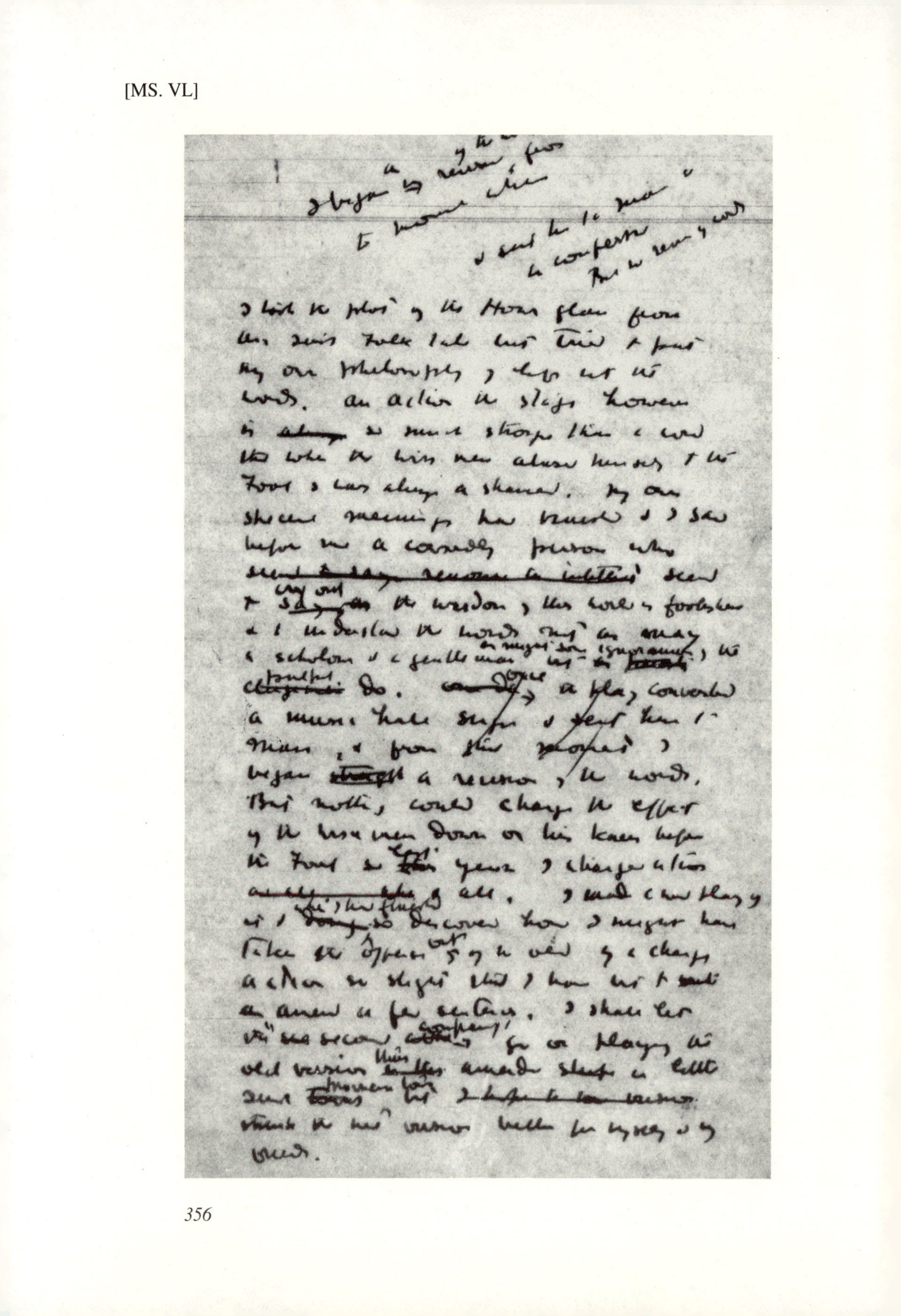

[MS. VL]

[MS. VL]

a of the words
I began ~~my~~ revision ^ from
the moment when
I sent him to mass &
to confession
But no revision of words

I took the plot of the Hour Glass from
an Irish Folk Tale but tried to put
my own philosophy of life into the
words. An action the stage however
is always so much stronger than a word
that when the wise man abused himself to the
Fool I was always ashamed. My own
[?special] meanings had vanished & I saw
before me a cowardly person who
~~seemed to say renounce the intellect~~ seemed
cry out
to ~~say~~ ~~as~~ the wisdom of this world is foolishness
& to understand the words not as may
as might some ignoramus of the
a scholar & a gentleman but ~~as~~ ~~priests~~
pulpit Once
~~clergymen~~ do. ~~One da~~ the play converted
a music hall singer & sent him to
mass, & from that moment I
began ~~straight~~ a revision of the words.
But nothing could change the effect
of the Wise man down on his knees before
last
the Fool so ~~this~~ year I changed action
and all [?] & all. I made a new play of
when I had finished
it & ~~doing~~ ^ so discovered how I might have
out
taken the offence of the old by a change

1–5 probably written after cancellation of ll. 19–22 “Once . . . words”.
9 “on” omitted after “action”?
28 “in” omitted after “change”?

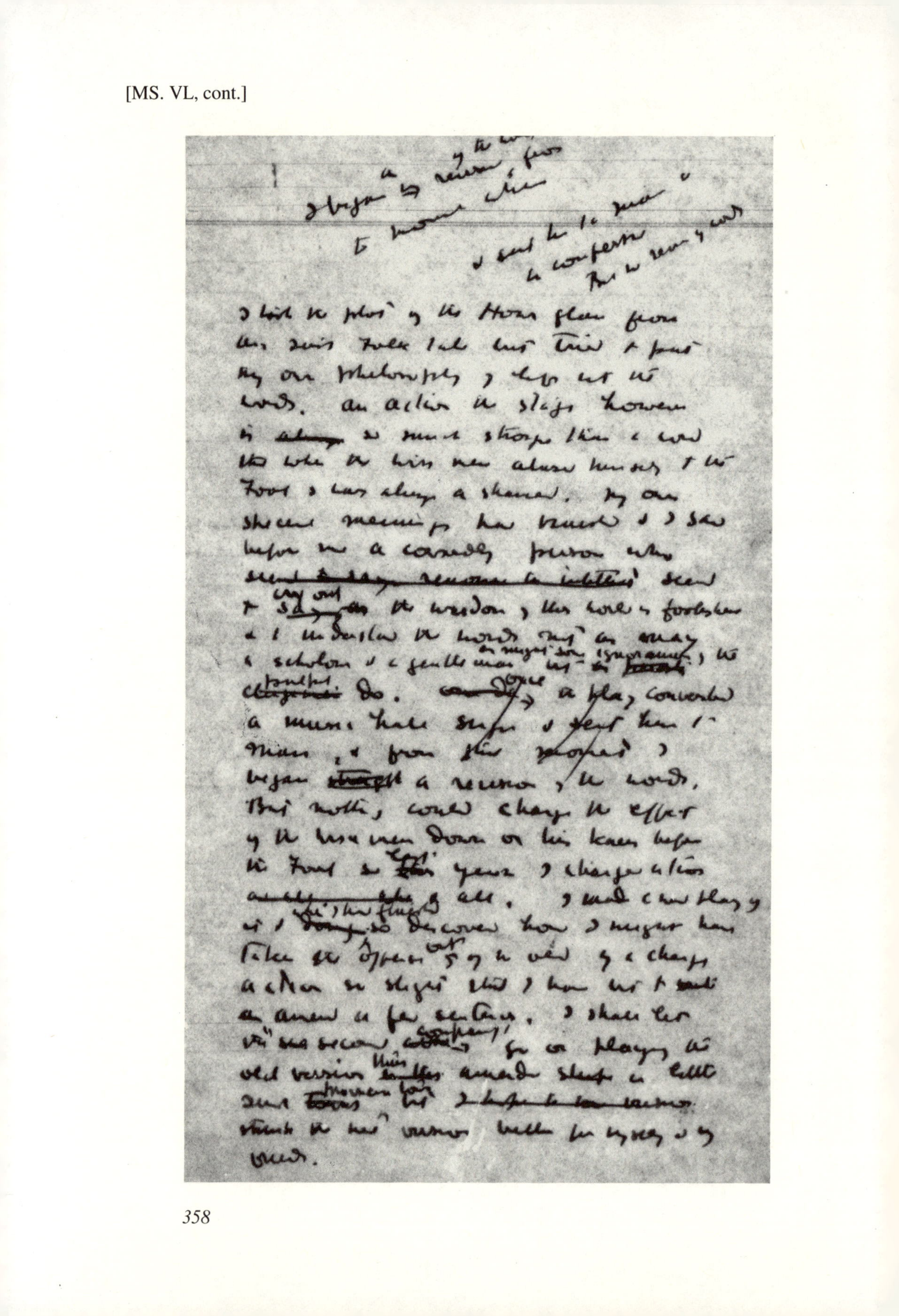

[MS. VL, cont.]

[MS. VL, cont.]

29 action so slight that I have but to ~~write~~

30 ~~a~~ amend a few sentences. I shall let

company

31 the ~~sce~~ second ~~Abbey~~ go on playing the

thus

32 old version ~~as thus~~ amended [~~?~~] in little

[?provincial] towns

33 Irish ~~towns~~ but ~~I hope the new version~~

34 I think the new version best for myself & my

35 friends.

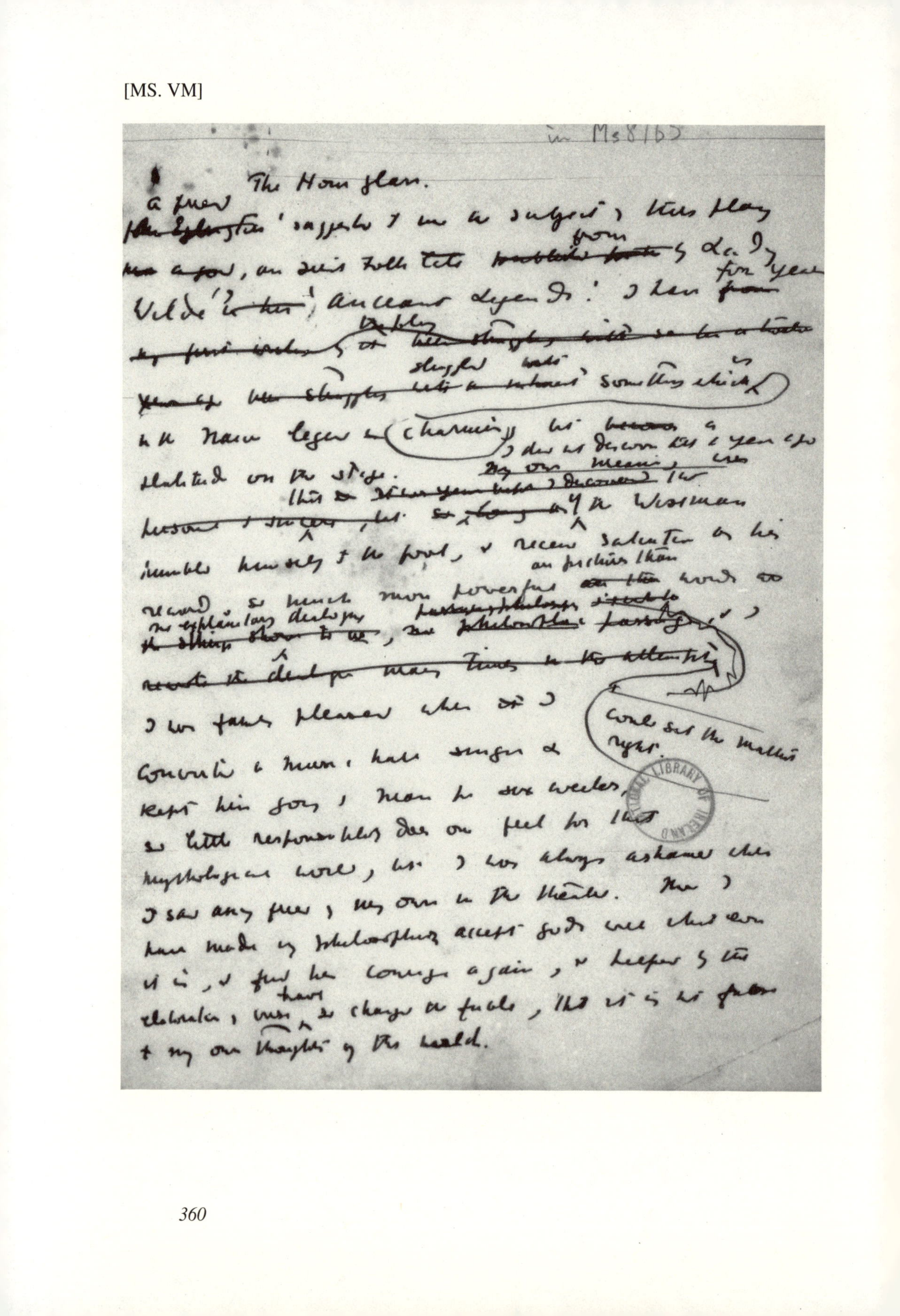

[MS. VM]

The Hour Glass.

[MS. VM]

The Hour Glass.

A friend
1 ~~John Eglington~~ suggested to me the subject of this play
from
2 from a good, an Irish Folk tale ~~published for the~~ by Lady
's for years
3 Wilde ~~in her~~ 'Ancient Legends'. I have ~~from~~
~~the play~~
4 ~~my first writing of it been struggling with so ten or twelve~~
struggled with is
5 ~~years ago been struggling with an inherent~~ something which
6 in the naive legend ~~is~~ charming but ~~becomes~~ a
I did not discover till a year ago
7 platitude on the stage. ~~My own meaning was~~
that ~~so~~ ~~It was years before I discovered~~ that
if
8 ~~personal & sincere, but so long as~~ the Wise man
9 humbled himself ^ to the fo^ol, & re^ceived salvation as his
are pictures than
10 reward, so much more powerful ~~are than~~ words ~~are~~
no explanatory dialogue ~~passage of philosophy~~ I'd write to
11 ~~the things shown to us~~, ~~no philosophic passage~~, & I
^ ^
could set the matter right.
12 ~~rewrote the dialogue many times in the attempt~~.
13 I was fairly pleased when ~~it~~ I
14 converted a music hall singer &
15 kept him going to mass for six weeks.
16 so little responsibility does one feel for that
17 mythological world, but I was always ashamed when
18 I saw any friend of my own in the theatre. Now I
19 have made my philosopher accept Gods will whatever
20 it is, & find his courage again, & helped by the
have
21 elaboration of verse ^ so changed the fable, that it is not false
22 to my own thoughts of the world.

5, 6 Clue line places "charming" after "which is".

[MS. VQb, 17]

11) THE HOUR GLASS; (in verse)

17

First performed at the Abbey Theatre Dublin with the following cast.

(will add cast in proof.)

Since then I have changed it a good deal, and got Mr Alan Porter to put into mediaeval latin certain passages, as I found that in performance certain verbal repeptitions which did not get on the nerves in the prose version, did so when all the first half of the play was in verse. We lis- -ten more intently to verse than to prose, and therefore not- -ice verbal repetition more quickly. Nothing said in latin, necessary to the understanding of the play, cannot be inferred from who speaks and who is spoken to.

1922.